C++ Programmer's Notebook

An Illustrated Quick Reference

Jim Keogh

To join a Prentice Hall PTR Internet mailing list, point to
http://www.prenhall.com/mail_lists/

ISBN 0-13-525940-1

9 780135 259405   90000

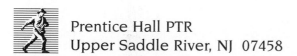

Prentice Hall PTR
Upper Saddle River, NJ 07458

Library of Congress Cataloging-in-Publication Date

Keogh, James Edward, 1948–
    C++ programmer's notebook : an illustrated quick reference / by
Jim Keogh.
      p.   cm.
    Includes index.
    ISBN 0-13-525940-1
    1. C++ (Computer program language)   I. Title
    QA76.73.C153K46   1997   97-17902
    005.13'3—dc21   CIP

Editorial/Production Supervision: Nick Radhuber
Acquisitions Editor: Greg Doench
Editorial Assistant: Mary Tracy
Marketing Manager: Stephen Solomon
Buyer: Alexis Heydt
Cover Design: Wee Design
Cover Design Direction: Jerry Votta
Interior Design: Meg Van Arsdale
Art Director: Gail Cocker-Bogusz

© 1998 Prentice Hall PTR
Prentice-Hall, Inc.
A Simon & Schuster Company
Upper Saddle River, NJ 07458

The publisher offers discounts on this book when ordered in bulk quantities. For more information, contact: Phone: 800-382-3419; FAX: 201-236-714; E-mail (Internet): corpsales@prenhall.com

    or write:

Corporate Sales Department,
Prentice Hall PTR
One Lake Street
Upper Saddle River, NJ 07458

Printed in the United States of America

10 9 8 7 6 5 4 3 2 1

ISBN 0-13-525940-1

Prentice-Hall International (UK) Limited, London
Prentice-Hall of Australia Pty. Limited, Sydney
Prentice-Hall Canada Inc., Toronto
Prentice-Hall Hispanoamericana, S.A., Mexico
Prentice-Hall of India Private Limited, New Delhi
Prentice-Hall of Japan, Inc., Tokyo
Simon & Schuster Asia Pte. Ltd., Singapore
Editora Prentice-Hall do Brasil, Ltda., Rio de Janeiro

This book is dedicated to Little Grandma,
who was taken from us suddenly,
but who will live in our hearts and memories forever.
—Anne, Sandra, Joanne, and Jim

Contents

Chapter Two

Working with Operators and Expressions   31

Chapter Three

Working with Arrays and Strings   59

Chapter Four

Working with Structures   105

Chapter Five

Working with Functions 139

Chapter Six

Working with Program Control 169

Chapter Seven

Working with Objects and Classes 195

Chapter Eight

Working with Overloading 211

Chapter Nine

Working with Inheritance   227

Chapter Ten

Working with Pointers   239

Chapter Eleven

Working with Virtual Functions   261

Chapter Twelve

Working with Keyboard Input—Screen Output   277

Chapter Thirteen

Working with Files and Streams   317

Chapter Fourteen

Working with Memory Management — 373

Chapter Fifteen

Working with Storing and Searching Data — 389

Chapter Sixteen

Working with Data Structures — 401

Chapter Seventeen

Working with Templates 429

Programmer's Checklist 437

Index 451

Preface

Software developers strive to build complex computer applications quickly, accurately, and at a reasonable expense. The methodology that is used by many developers is modular programming. This is a technique where the developer divides the application into logical components, each of which can be built independently and reused in other applications.

These modules are referred to as *subroutines*, *procedures*, or *functions*, depending on which computer language is used. In the C++ programming language as well as in C, these modules are called functions.

Regardless of the name, however, modules are limited. The modular programming approach to software design, at times, makes modeling into computer code a real life problem and a difficult task.

A real life problem involves real objects. For example, tracking college registration requires that a registration form be used. This registration form is an object. In fact, the form is actually composed of many objects, such as places to enter data and text that provides instructions to the applicant.

A real object has both data and procedures associated with an object. For example, a single copy (called an *instance*) of the registration has the student's name, course information, and other data that is directly related to only that copy of the form. Also associated with the form are the steps that are required to enter data onto the form and to process that copy of the form.

Traditional modularity does not lend itself to using an object-oriented design approach when translating a real life problem into a computer application. *Object-oriented design* requires software developers to visualize a real life object as an object and not as a set of procedures. For example, a college registration form is a physical object that is composed of other objects, such as a place to enter data and labels that provide directions for completing the form.

The C programming language provided flexibility for developers. They could write low-level applications, such as an operating system using C. C was also a language that could be used to create a simple business application. However, C could not properly handle an object-oriented design specification of an application.

In the early 1980s at Bell Laboratories, the birthplace of the C programming language, Bjarne Stroustrup created an enhancement of C called C++. Stroustrup set out to give the C language the capability of using code to better represent a real life object. He transformed the C programming language from a procedural language into an *object-oriented language*. C++ is a superset of C. That is, C++ has all the capabilities as C plus more features.

A Touch of Class

A real life object has both data and procedures associated with the object. This association is represented in C++ code through the use of a *class*. A class defines a real life object as having a set of data (called *data members*) and procedures (called *function members*).

A copy of the class is created by the software developer by using the name of the class to declare an instance of the class. The instance is given a unique name. This technique is illustrated later in this book. The instance of the class has its own copy of data and functions.

Stroustrup also gave C++ the capability to share classes (called *inheritance*). This enables software developers to use other classes (called *base classes*) to build new classes (called *derived classes*).

Return to the example of the registration form. The form is a new object that is composed of data (called an *edit object*) and text (called *label objects*). An edit object relates the data and the function members to accept, edit, and validate the data. A label object can store text used in the label and has function members that handle fonts, and other characteristics that can be used for the label.

Therefore, when the software developer needs to build a form, such as the student registration form, the developer can create instances of the edit and label objects. All of the text editing capabilities (i.e., insertion and deletion of characters) are inherited.

The Picture Book Approach

C++, as any computer language, is complex and has many rules that must be obeyed. Learning those rules can be time-consuming, especially for readers who already know how to program in a language other than C++. Those readers want to jump into the language and begin writing simple code almost immediately.

Many programmers who learn C++ as their second language have their own philosophy about learning the language. "Show me sample code and I'll figure out the rest," is a statement that summarizes their approach. And that's what I do in this book.

The picture book concept places the focus of the book on a picture of the code. Around this picture are callouts that describe each keyword and statement. The rules are presented in tables that are positioned near the picture. Furthermore, there is a picture for each variation of the topic that is discussed in the chapter.

A reader who wants to jump into C++ can study the picture, then copy the code into a compiler and make the executable program without having to sift through pages of text. The rules can be referenced later, when the reader needs to expand this use of the routine.

This approach is not intended to circumvent a thorough presentation of the C++ language. In fact, this book presents C++ in its completion. Instead, the picture-book approach presents material in the way programmers want to learn a new computer language.

Navigating This Book

I organized this book into traditional chapters. Each chapter covers a topic of C++ in a logical progression. So, if you are not familiar with the basics of C++, then begin with the first chapter and continue through each chapter in progression. At the end of the last chapter you will have a good foundation in C++.

However, these chapters can be used also for quick reference. Jump to the chapter that discusses the topic that you want to review. The topic within the chapter is presented in its entirety with a focus on examples of code.

Each chapter is further divided into two-page spreads. That is, careful attention is given to the relationship between the left and right pages. The left page contains text that describes the topic that is illustrated on the right page. The right page focuses on C++ code that contains callouts describing each facet of the code example.

The most efficient way to use a two-page spread is to first study the example on the right page. If you understand the function of each statement in the example, then you can continue and write your own program. However, if a statement or keyword is confusing, then read the callout that describes the item. Still confused? Read the text on the left page.

Careful attention is given to clarity of the code example, the right page. You will notice that the syntax of the C++ code is shown in color. Parts of the statements that are not colored are pieces that the programmer creates.

For example, the statement *char code*; declares a character variable. char and the semicolon (;) are colored. They are part of the syntax of C++. The word code, however, is the name of a variable that can be any name that complies with the rules of C++. This style is similar to the concept used with Integrated Development Environments (IDE) such as used in Borland C++ and Microsoft Visual C++.

All code in this book can be found at the following FTP site: /ftp/pub/ptr/professional_computer_science.w.-022/keogh/c++_notebook.

Working with Variables

- Naming Variables
- Using Variables
- Integer Variables
- Character Variables
- Escape Sequences
- Floating Point Variables
- Inside Exponential Notation
- Data Type Conversion
- Assigning Values to Variables
- Local Variables
- Global Variables
- Local Variables vs Global Variables
- Storage Class Specifiers
- Static
- Register
- Auto
- Storage Specific Rules

Naming Variables

C++ programs frequently manipulate information that is stored in the computerís memory. This information, called *data*, is placed in a memory location that is identified internally by the operating system as a specific *address of memory*. Although C++ enables programmers to access the data by referring to the memory address, a more common method is to use a symbol or alias to represent an address. This symbol is called a *variable*.

Each variable that is used by a C++ program must be declared within a program statement. A *variable declaration statement* requires that the *data type* of the variable be specified followed by the symbol that is to be used to represent that location of memory. This symbol is commonly referred to as the *variable name*. A *semicolon* is used to end the statement. This is illustrated in the examples on the opposite page and below.

```
int emp_number;
```

A declaration of a variable tells the compiler to reserve space in memory for a value that is the size of the data type. In the examples on the opposite page, the compiler will set aside memory to hold integers. C++ is capable of using several data types which are discussed in this chapter.

Any character, upper case or lower case, can be used to name a variable. Numbers can also be used in the variable name, however, the first character of the name must be a non-number character. The name cannot include spaces and keywords of the C++ language. A *keyword* is a word that has a special meaning to the compiler. Only the first 32 characters of the variable name will be used by the compiler as the symbol for the memory location.

C++ is a *case sensitive* language. This means that an upper case A is considered a different character than a lower case a. So the variable names First_Name and first_name refer to two different memory locations.

A variable is a symbolic name that is used to identify a value. When a value is assigned to a variable, the value is stored in a specific location in the computer's memory.

Naming Variables

The int keyword is used to declare an integer variable.

Any combination of upper and lower case letters and digits from 0 to 9 can be used in the name of a variable.

The first character must be a character or an underscore.

Only the first 32 characters of the variable name are recognized as the name.

6 different integers are named.

Illegal variable names will cause a compiler error.

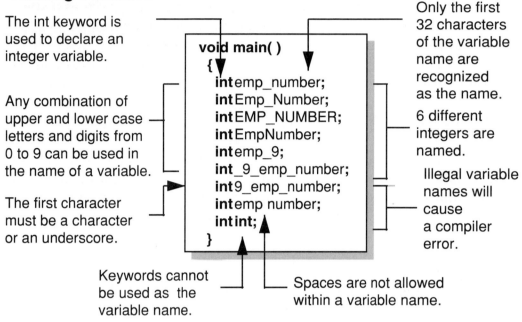

```
void main( )
{
    int emp_number;
    int Emp_Number;
    int EMP_NUMBER;
    int EmpNumber;
    int emp_9;
    int _9_emp_number;
    int 9_emp_number;
    int emp number;
    int int;
}
```

Keywords cannot be used as the variable name.

Spaces are not allowed within a variable name.

Terms You Should Know ...

○ ○	int	An int is the keyword used to declare an integer variable that holds integer number. These are numbers that have no fractional part.

Using Variables

When a variable is declared in a program statement, the compiler is told to reserve a specific amount of computer memory. The declaration statement does not place any data into that memory. Data is stored in a particular memory location by a program statement that contains an *assignment expression*.

An *expression* combines operators and operands to define a computation. *Operators* in C++ include +, -, *, and /, among others. Each operator will be discussed in the next chapter. An *operand* is a variable or constant value that is manipulated by an operator. In the example illustrated below, the variable pay and the constant value 10 are operands that are manipulated by the addition operator, a plus sign. A *constant value* is a literal number or character.

pay + 10

An *assignment expression* is used in a program statement to place a value into a memory location. This expression requires three elements: the name of the variable that represents the memory location, the assignment operator, and the data that will be placed into memory. Sample statements are shown on the opposite page and below.

salary = 1000;

Here, the value 1000, a constant value, is stored into the memory location that is represented by the variable name salary. The equal sign (=) is the assignment operator that transfers the data. Data can be transferred between memory locations using the same statement except the constant value (1000) is replaced by the variable name that represents the second memory location. The results of an expression can also be placed into memory, as is illustrated in the last line of the program on the opposite page and below.

total_compensation = salary + bonus;

Three integer variables are declared using variable names that identify the data that will be assigned to the variable.

The declaration of a variable must terminate with a semi-colon to form a statement.

Space is reserved in memory when a variable is declared.

Values are assigned to a variable by using the variable name, the assignment operator and the value.

Variable names are used to represent data in an expression.

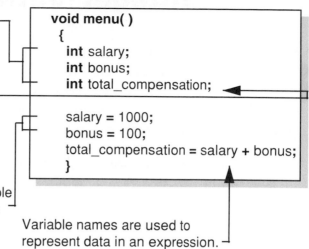

```
void menu( )
{
    int salary;
    int bonus;
    int total_compensation;

    salary = 1000;
    bonus = 100;
    total_compensation = salary + bonus;
}
```

In Memory

salary bonus total_compensation

| 1000 | 100 | 1100 | | | | | | | | | | | | | | | | | |

Terms You Should Know ...

| ○ | Expression | An expression is the arrangement of operands and operators to define a computation. |
| ○ | Statement | A statement tells the computer to do something and is terminated with a semicolon. |

Integer Variables

The *int* keyword is used to specify the integer data type. When an int is used in a declaration statement, the compiler reserves space in memory large enough to hold an integer. Memory space is defined in *bytes of memory*. An integer on many computers requires two bytes of memory. The actually number of bytes is computer-dependent.

An integer data type can hold values that are whole numbers. Fractional numbers cannot be stored in a memory location that is designated for an integer. This limitation will be overcome using a different data type as is explained later in this chapter. In the following example, only the whole number (4) is stored in memory. The fraction (.5) is discarded.

salary = 4.5;

The size of the number that can be stored in an integer location is another limiting factor. Only values from -32,768 through 32,767 can be assigned to an integer variable. A different data type must be used for larger numbers. One of these data types is called a long.

A *long* data *type* instructs the compiler to reserve additional space in memory so a much larger number than an int data type can be stored in memory. On personal computers, four bytes are reserved for a long date type. A long data type can hold integer values within the range of -2,147,483,648 through 2,147,483,648 on a personal computer. The size of an int is system-dependent No fractional values are allowed. A long is declared using the statements show on the opposite page and below.

long big_number;

On some computers, small integer values can be stored using the short data type. A *short* data type is the same as an int data type on a personal computer. The technique for declaring short is shown on the opposite page.

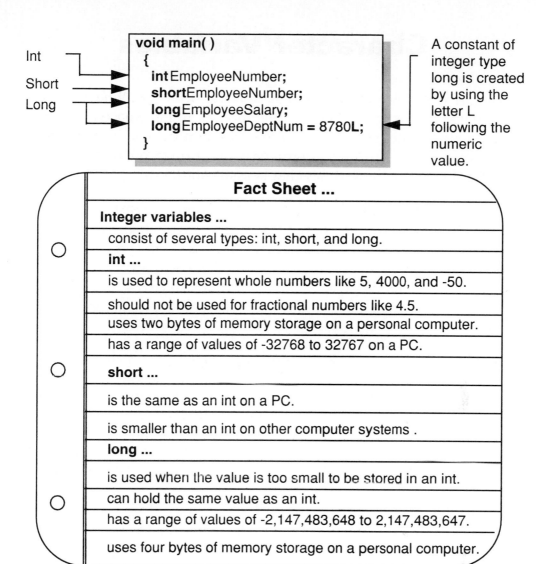

Int

Short

Long

```
void main( )
  {
    int EmployeeNumber;
    short EmployeeNumber;
    long EmployeeSalary;
    long EmployeeDeptNum = 8780L;
  }
```

A constant of integer type long is created by using the letter L following the numeric value.

Fact Sheet ...

Integer variables ...

consist of several types: int, short, and long.

int ...

is used to represent whole numbers like 5, 4000, and -50.

should not be used for fractional numbers like 4.5.

uses two bytes of memory storage on a personal computer.

has a range of values of -32768 to 32767 on a PC.

short ...

is the same as an int on a PC.

is smaller than an int on other computer systems .

long ...

is used when the value is too small to be stored in an int.

can hold the same value as an int.

has a range of values of -2,147,483,648 to 2,147,483,647.

uses four bytes of memory storage on a personal computer.

Character Variables

A *character* is an element of a word. However, to a computer (with few exceptions) a character is an interpretation of an integer value. A computer can recognize a value, such as 65, as a number or as a symbol for a character, such as 'A'. Which interpretation is given to the value depends on the data type of the variable that is assigned the value.

A *char* data type instructs the compiler to reserve space in memory to hold an integer value that will be interpreted as a character. On most computers, a byte is reserved for each character data type. The declaration of a character data type is similar to the declaration of an integer data type except the keyword char is used in place of the int keyword in the statement. This is illustrated in examples below and on the opposite page.

char EmployeeCode;

Values of a character data type can range from 0 through 127. This range is expanded on a personal computer to include 0 through 255. The additional values are used to represent graphic characters and characters used for foreign languages.

The compiler is able to relate the integer values of a character data type to the character that is displayed on the screen by using the ASCII *code*. The ASCII code is a standard which assigns each character to a value within the range of a character data type.

A value can be assigned to a character data type by using the assignment expression. This is illustrated on the opposite page and below. The character can be represented by either using the ASCII integer value for the character or by placing the literal character within single quotation marks.

EmployeeCode = 'A';

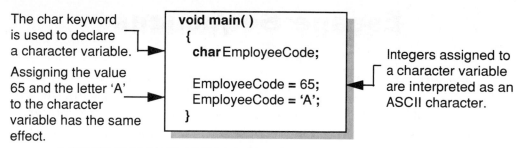

The char keyword is used to declare a character variable.

Assigning the value 65 and the letter 'A' to the character variable has the same effect.

```
void main( )
  {
    char EmployeeCode;

    EmployeeCode = 65;
    EmployeeCode = 'A';
  }
```

Integers assigned to a character variable are interpreted as an ASCII character.

Fact Sheet ...

Character variables ...

- are really another type of integer variable.
- are used to store ASCII characters.
- are assigned integer values associated with ASCII characters.
- can range from 0 to 127.
- can range from 0 to 255 on a personal computer to accommodate graphics characters and characters that are used with foreign languages.
- are translated by the compiler into ASCII values and stored in the program as the ASCII value.
- use one byte of memory storage on a personal computer.

Terms You Should Know ...

	ASCII	The American Standard Code for Information Interchange. The code contains decimal values for letters, numbers, punctuation and special control characters.

Escape Sequences

C++ can use special characters called *escape sequences* to perform unique functions, such as ejecting a page from the printer or relocating the cursor, among other routines. Examples of escape sequences are contained on the opposite page. Notice that the \f escape sequence is used to instruct the compiler to issue a formfeed, which ejects a page.

The *backslash character* (\) has a special meaning in C++. This character instructs the compiler to ignore the normal meaning of the next character. In the previous example, the character f is used following the backslash. The character f is really an interpretation of its corresponding integer value. Normally, the character f is created when its corresponding integer value is contained in a character data type or in a character constant. A *character constant* is the literal character without the character being assigned to a variable. In the previous example, the character f is a character constant.

However, the backslash characters tells the compiler to ignore this normal interpretation and consider the character a symbol for an escape sequence. In this example, the character f is a symbol for a formfeed. The backslash is also known as the *escape character*.

Escape sequences are typically used with formatted data, such as strings of characters that are used for reports. Typically, the \t (tab) escape sequence is used to align characters in columns. Likewise, the \n (newline) escape sequence signifies that the following text will appear on a new line of the report.

The backslash character can also be used with a string of characters to include a double quotation mark with in the string. A string of characters is represented by double quotations ("ABC"). Normally, a double quotation character cannot be a character within the string ("A"BC") unless the double quotation is preceded by a backslash ("A\"BC"). This is a useful trick to remember whenever there is a need to change the normal meaning of a character in C++.

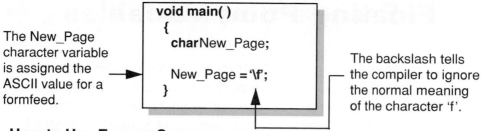

The New_Page character variable is assigned the ASCII value for a formfeed.

```
void main( )
{
  charNew_Page;

  New_Page = '\f';
}
```

The backslash tells the compiler to ignore the normal meaning of the character 'f'.

How to Use Escape Sequences

\b	Causes the cursor to move back one space (backspace).
\f	Forces a page to be ejected from the printer (formfeed).
\n	Moves the cursor to the beginning of the next line (newline).
\r	Creates the effect of pressing the return key on the keyboard (carriage return).
\t	Inserts a tab character (tab).

Tricks of the Trade

The backslash comes in handy when you want to include a quotation mark within a string of characters. Like this: "Anne said, "Hello." "You'd have to write it "Anne said, \"Hello\"."

Terms You Should Know ...

○ ○	Escape Sequence	The backslash character (\ ) is used to tell the compiler to escape from the normal meaning of the next character.

Floating Point Variables

A *integer* data type can be used to store a whole number. However, the range of the integer (and long) data type is limiting for some C++ applications. Furthermore, many applications require the use of whole and fractional values, which cannot be accommodated with an integer data type.

In such situations, a *floating point* data type can be used to store very large or very small (fractional) values. A floating point data type is declared using the *float* keyword. This technique is illustrated on the opposite page and below. Here, the variable EmployeeSalary is declared as a float data type.

loat EmployeeSalary;

When the compiler reads the keyword float, the compiler reserves space in memory large enough to hold a float value. On a personal computer, four bytes are reserved for a float. Other kinds of computers might use a different number of bytes to store a float. Values that can be stored in a float range from 1.7E-38 through 3.4E38. The E signifies exponential value to the right of the E.

Two other data types can be used for extremely large or small values. These are double and long double. The *double* data type is declared by using the keyword double in place of the keyword float in the statement. Eight bytes of memory are used for a double on a personal computer and the range of values that can be stored in a double is from 1.7E-308 through 1.7E308.

The *long double* data type extends this range to 3.4E-4932 through 1.1E4932. A long double data type is declared by using the keyword *long* in place of the float in the previous example. Ten bytes of memory are used to store a long double data type.

The float keyword is used to declare a float variable.

The long double keywords are used to declare a long double variable.

```
void main( )
{
    float EmployeeSalary;
    double EmployeeBonus;
    long double TotalCompensation;
}
```

The double keyword is used to declare a double variable.

Fact Sheet ...	
⃝	**Floating point variables ...**
	are used for numbers that have fractions.
	consist of several types: float, double and long double.
	float ...
⃝	can range from 3.4E-38 to 3.4E38.
	uses four bytes of memory storage on a personal computer.
	double ...
	can range from 1.7E-308 to 1.7E308.
	uses eight bytes of memory storage on a personal computer.
⃝	**long double ...**
	can range from 3.4E-4932 to 1.1E4932.
	uses 10 bytes of memory storage on a personal computer.

Terms You Should Know ...

⃝ ⃝	Floating Point	Numbers are represented in two parts: digits and a fraction. This allows the decimal point to be moved around freely so that extremely large and small numbers can be represented.

Inside Exponential Notations

Reading the number 123456E3 is not as clear as reading 1234.56. Yet both represent the same value. The letter E is the exponential representation of a value. The number following the E is the exponent. This is a way to represent the value 1.23456×10^3. The exponent indicates the position of the decimal point within the non-exponent value.

For example, 123456E3 has a positive number exponent. That is, the value 3 is not a negative number. The sign of the exponent is critical to the positioning of the decimal point. If the exponent is a positive number, then the decimal point is somewhere to the right of the second digit in the value (remember 123456E3 is really 1.23456X103). The number is large. In the previous example, the decimal point is some place to the right of the digit 2. In comparison, a negative exponent value means that the decimal place is somewhere to the left of the second digit. The value is small.

The exponent value indicates the number of decimal places. In the previous example, the exponent 3 indicates that the decimal point is three digits to the right of the second digit. This is 1234.56.

Signed and Unsigned Variables

All numeric data types in C++ store signed numbers by default. That is, negative values are acceptable within the permissible range of the particular data type. However, the sign of a value consumes memory. C++ enables a programmer to recoup this memory when no negative values will be assigned to a numeric data type by using the unsigned qualifier. Examples of using both the signed and unsigned qualifiers are shown on the opposite page.

The *signed qualifier* is not necessary since all numeric data types are signed by default. However, using the *unsigned qualifier* doubles the size of the value that can be stored in a specified numeric data type.

Inside Exponential Notations

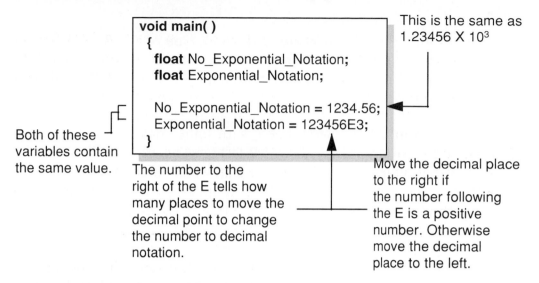

```
void main( )
  {
    float No_Exponential_Notation;
    float Exponential_Notation;

    No_Exponential_Notation = 1234.56;
    Exponential_Notation = 123456E3;
  }
```

This is the same as 1.23456×10^3

Both of these variables contain the same value.

The number to the right of the E tells how many places to move the decimal point to change the number to decimal notation.

Move the decimal place to the right if the number following the E is a positive number. Otherwise move the decimal place to the left.

Signed and Unsigned Variables

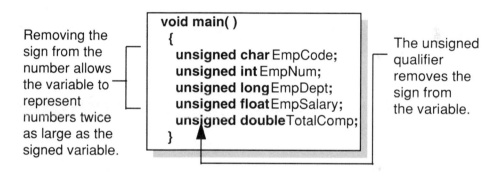

```
void main( )
  {
    unsigned char EmpCode;
    unsigned int EmpNum;
    unsigned long EmpDept;
    unsigned float EmpSalary;
    unsigned double TotalComp;
  }
```

Removing the sign from the number allows the variable to represent numbers twice as large as the signed variable.

The unsigned qualifier removes the sign from the variable.

Data Type Conversion

C++ programmers must be aware of the data type of a variable whenever the variable is used in an expression. This is critical since conflicting data types can be used for data manipulation but may produce unexpected results.

There are two methods used to deal with unlike data types. These are *automatic data type conversion* and *manual data type conversion*. Automatic data type conversion takes place by the compiler when different data types are detected in the same expression. The compiler copies the value in the lower data type to a temporary variable that is of the higher data type, then the expression is evaluated using the temporary variable.

The first example on the opposite page adds the value of bonus to the value of salary then assigns the sum to the total compensation variable. Notice that salary is an integer data type and bonus is a float data type. When this statement is executed the compiler creates a temporary variable of float data type and copies the value of salary into that variable before the expression is evaluated.

A data type can be temporarily changed manually by using manual data type conversion. This technique is also called casting and requires the programmer to specify the temporary data type within parenthesis to the left of the original variable. Casting is illustrated in the second example on the opposite page and below. Here, the data type of salary is temporarily changed to (float).

total_compensation = (float) salary + bonus;

Casting does not change the original data type. The compiler copies the value of the original data type to a temporary variable of the cast data type before evaluating the expression.

Data Type Conversion

Expressions that involve different data types will not cause a compiler error. A data type can be converted from one type to another automatically by the compiler or manually within the program.

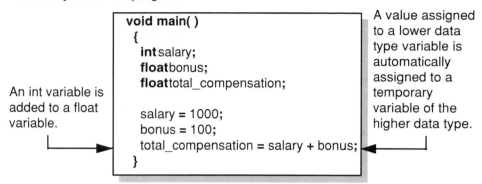

An int variable is added to a float variable.

```
void main( )
{
    int salary;
    float bonus;
    float total_compensation;

    salary = 1000;
    bonus = 100;
    total_compensation = salary + bonus;
}
```

A value assigned to a lower data type variable is automatically assigned to a temporary variable of the higher data type.

Casting, Manual Data Type Conversion

The data type of the salary variable is temporarily changed by specifying the new data type within parentheses to the left of the salary variable.

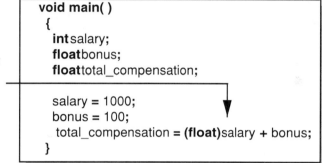

```
void main( )
{
    int salary;
    float bonus;
    float total_compensation;

    salary = 1000;
    bonus = 100;
    total_compensation = (float)salary + bonus;
}
```

Terms You Should Know ...

○	Data Type	The type of a variable (i.e. int, long, float) is called the variable's data type.

Assigning Values to Variables

There are several methods that can be used to assign a value to a variable. The most common method is to use the *assignment operator* (=). This technique is illustrated on the opposite page and below. Here, the value 100 is placed in memory at the address that is represented by the symbol bonus, which is a variable. The variable must be declared prior to assigning a value to the variable.

bonus = 100;

Another technique is to assign a value to a variable in the same statement that declares the variable. An example of this is shown on the opposite page and below. This method is an excellent way to initialize a variable. *Initialization* is the term used for assigning a default value to a variable.

float salary = 10000;

A statement can be constructed to assign the results of an expression to a variable. This is shown below. The value of the bonus variable is added to the value of the salary variable, then the sum is assigned to TotalCompensation.

TotalCompensation = salary + bonus;

The assignment operator is also used to place the value of a character into a character variable. This is illustrated below. Notice that the character must be enclosed within single quotation marks. If the single quotation marks are omitted, then the compiler will assume that the character is a symbol for another variable and try to copy the value of that variable.

char EmpCode = 'A';

Values can be assigned to a variable when the variable is declared.

The const qualifier is used to tell the compiler that the value assigned to the variable will not change. It will remain constant. Constants should be in all upper case as a reminder that the variable is a constant.

More than one variable of the same type can be declared in the same statement.

A variable can be declared anywhere in the program.

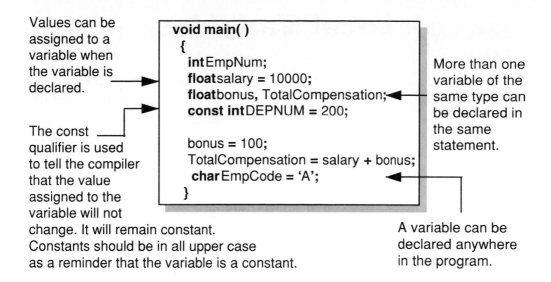

```
void main( )
  {
    int EmpNum;
    float salary = 10000;
    float bonus, TotalCompensation;
    const int DEPNUM = 200;

    bonus = 100;
    TotalCompensation = salary + bonus;
     char EmpCode = 'A';
  }
```

Helpful Tips ...
The fastest operation is performed using the int data type.
The slowest operation is performed using the float data type.
The float data type creates a large code size.
Always use the smallest data type possible.
Data types that are too small can cause strange errors in the program.
The actual memory storage used by a variable is determined by the word size of the computer and its operating system.

Local Variables

A memory location is reserved for data when a variable is declared. This space remains reserved until the variable is discarded by the program. Programmers must be concerned about designing software that properly manages memory. For example, a large program would soon use up available memory if all the variables remained available for the entire life of the program.

A simple technique for temporarily reserving space for a variable is to declare the variable as a local variable. *Local variables* are declared within a code block. A code block begins with an open French brace ({) and ends with a closed French brace (}). The top example on the opposite page illustrates the declaration of local variables salary and total_comp. Statements contained within a code block are treated as one statement.

Only statements that are placed within the code block can use a local variable that is declared within the same code block. Therefore, statements within the main( ) function cannot use the local variables salary and total_comp. Space reserved for local variables is freed when the program reaches the end of the code block. That is, when the program in the previous example returns to the main( ) function after executing the last statement in the add_bonus( ) function, local variables salary and total_comp no longer exits.

Global Variables

In contrast to local variables, a programmer can declare a variable as global by declaring the variable outside any function within the program. This is illustrated with the bonus variable shown in the second example on the opposite page. Memory used for *global variables* remain in use for the entire length of the program. Also, global variables can be used by any statement in the program, including statements that are contained within any code block.

Local Variables

Variables that are defined within a code block are recognized only within the code block. These variables are called local variables.

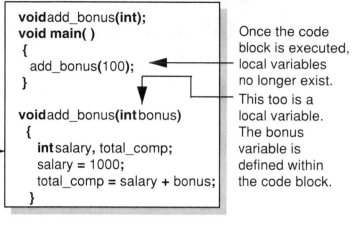

```
void add_bonus(int);
void main( )
{
   add_bonus(100);
}

void add_bonus(int bonus)
{
   int salary, total_comp;
   salary = 1000;
   total_comp = salary + bonus;
}
```

Once the code block is executed, local variables no longer exist. This too is a local variable. The bonus variable is defined within the code block.

Global Variables

Variables that are defined outside a code block are recognized by all code blocks in the program. These variables are called global variables.

```
void add_bonus( );
int bonus;
void main( )
{
   bonus = 100;
   add_bonus();
}

void add_bonus( )
{
   int salary, total_comp;
   total_comp = salary + bonus;
}
```

Global variables can be used by any code block in the program without first having to declare the variable.

Working with Variables

Local Variables vs Global Variables

The question that every programmer must answer is whether to declare a variable as local or global. There is no easy answer to this question, however, there are several factors that influence the programmer's choice. Here is one of them. Will the value that is assigned to the variable need to be accessed by several code blocks within the program?

If the answer is yes, then consider declaring the variable as a global variable so long as not too many variables within the program fall into this category. Keep in mind that every computer has a limited amount of memory. Global variables are placed in fixed memory and remain there until the program is terminated.

Although the answer to this question is yes, a programmer can still use a local variable and pass the value of that variable to functions that need to use the value. For example, a local variable in a function can pass the value of one of its local variables to another function. This value is then assigned to a local variable within the second function. When each function terminates, memory used by the local variable within the function is freed. A complete discussion about functions and passing a variable to a function is contained in Chapter Four.

If the answer is no, then declare the variable as a local variable. A word of caution! Always initialize a local variable when the variable is declared. The compiler will not assign an initial value to a local variable. This means that unexpected results will occur if an uninitialized local variable is used by the program.

On the other hand, all global variables are automatically initialized by some compilers when the variable is declared. Therefore, a programmer does not have to assign an initial value to a global variable. Global variables can be used immediately without the fear of unexpected results.

Fact Sheet ...

Local Variables ...

occupy memory temporarily for the life of the code block.

can be passed as arguments to other functions.

can only be used and changed by the code block within which the variable is defined.

Global Variables ...

are stored in a fixed region of memory.

are used when the same data is used by many code blocks.

take up memory for the life of the program and could increase the memory requirements for the program.

cause code blocks that use the variable to rely on data that is defined and changeable from outside the code block.

Tricks of the Trade

A common bug is trying to use an uninitialized variable. This is where a variable is declared but not assigned a value and a statement uses the variable. Local variables are not automatically initialized. Global variables are always automatically initialized by the compiler.

Terms You Should Know ...

Fixed Memory	When a program is linked, a specific place in memory called an address is reserved for each global variable that is declared in the program. This address can't be used for any other variable.

Storage Specifiers

The C++ compiler reserves memory according to source code files. A *source code file* is the file that contains the uncompiled program statements that compose the program. Simple programs use one source code file so that all the variables are declared within the same source code file. There is no confusion for the compiler.

In more complex programs, more than one source code file is used. Each of these source code files is compiled into an object file separately then linked into an executable program. Therefore, the compiler is unaware of variables that are declared in source code files other than the one being compiled. This is not confusing so long as a reference is not made to variables contained in other source files.

For example, in source code file one the variable bonus is declared as a global variable. Remember, global variables are accessible to every code block—even those code blocks that are defined in other source code files. Source code file two uses the variable bonus in an expression. However, an error message is displayed when the second source code file is compiled. The compiler is confused and reports that the variable bonus is undefined.

The confusion stems from the fact that the compiler does not know that the variable bonus is declared in the first source code file. This confusion is clarified by using the storage specifier extern. The *extern storage specifier* is placed outside code blocks in all source code files that reference a variable declared in another source code file. This is illustrated on the opposite page and below.

extern int bonus;

The extern storage specifier informs the compiler that the specified variable is declared in another source code file. The extern storage specifier statement must contain the declaration of the variable.

Storage Specifiers

There are four types of Storage Class Specifiers. These are extern, static, register, and auto.

extern

The extern specifier tells the compiler that this variable is already declared as a global variable in another source code file of the program.

```
void add_bonus( );

extern int bonus;

void main( )
{
    bonus = 100;
    add_bonus();
}

void add_bonus( )
  {
     int salary, total_comp;
     total_comp = salary + bonus;
  }
```

A program might have more than one file that contains source code. Each of these files is compiled independently of the other. If the extern specifier isn't used, the compiler will try to create a duplicate variable.

Terms You Should Know ...

	extern	The extern storage specifier tells the compiler that the variable that follows is declared as a global variable elsewhere. The compiler will not reserve memory for the variable.

Static

Local variables are commonly declared within a code block. Values that are assigned to local variables are lost when control of the program leaves the code block. Therefore, the next time the code block is called, local variables within the code blocks must be re-declared and values re-assigned to the variables.

In most situations, the re-declaration and re-assignment of values is an acceptable technique. However, there are occasions when the application requires that a local variable maintain its value between function calls. That is, the value of the variable is not lost when control leaves the code block.

This is possible by using the static storage specifier. The *static storage specifier* instructs the compiler not to destroy the value of the local variable and to retain the value the next time the code block is called. This is illustrated in the top example on the opposite page. The variable bonus is declared as a static integer and assigned the value of 100. Each time the add_bonus( ) function is called, the value of bonus is 100.

Register

Manipulation of data occurs in the central processing unit (CPU) of the computer. Typically, the program moves data to and from memory locations into the CPU. When data enters the CPU the data is stored in the CPU memory, which is called a *register*.

The movement of data between the CPU and memory is a time-consuming process. One method of reducing data transfer is to store frequently used data in the register of the CPU. This is accomplished by using the register storage specifier, as illustrated in the bottom example on the opposite page. The *register storage specifier* asks the compiler to use the CPU register. The compiler has the option to ignore the programmer's request.

Static

The static specifier tells the compiler to retain the variable after the function has finished executing. Normally, all variables within a function are destroyed.

```
void add_bonus( );
void main( )
{
  add_bonus();
}

void add_bonus( )
{
  static int bonus;
  int salary, total_comp;
  bonus = 100;
  salary = 1000;
  total_comp = salary + bonus;
}
```

A variable that is specified as static holds its value similar to a global variable except that only the code block that declares the static variable can use it.

Register

The central processing unit of the computer has its own memory called a register.

```
void main( )
{
  register int bonus;
  int salary, total_comp;
  salary = 1000;
  bonus = 100;
}
```

The register specifier asks the compiler to place the variable that follows in the register rather than in Random Access Memory.

Terms You Should Know ...

	static	The static storage specifier when used with a local variable, tells the compiler to retain the variable and its value after the code block is destroyed. When used with a global variable, the variable is known only to the file where the variable is declared.
	register	The register storage specifier asks the compiler to use the register in the central processing unit when possible. There is no guarantee that the register will be used.

auto

A programmer can explicitly specify that a variable must be destroyed when a code block is finally executed by using the *auto storage specifier*. The auto storage specifier is illustrated on the opposite page. All of the variables in this example will be destroyed when code block of the add_bonus( ) function finishes execution.

However, C++ compilers treat all local variables as auto by default. Therefore, the use of the auto storage specifier in a C++ program is optional. Programmers continue to use the auto storage specifier to clarify the scope of local variables. The *scope of a variable* refers to the life of the variable and the availability of the variable to other components of the program.

Storage Specifier Rules

There are a few basic guidelines that must be followed when using storage specifiers in a program. Any time a variable is referenced in a different source code file, the extern storage specifier must be used in the variable declaration statement in subsequent source code files. Otherwise, if extern is omitted, a linker error will occur.

When there is a need to retain the value of a local variable between function calls, the variable must be declared using the static storage specifier. Failure to use this declaration will cause the value to be lost between function calls.

The register storage specifier minimizes data transfer between the CPU and memory. However, this specifier only requests the compiler to use the register. The compiler makes the final determination. Only variables that are an integer or character data type can be declared as a register. Global variables cannot be declared using the register storage specifier.

auto

The auto specifier tells the compiler that the variable that follows is local to the code block and must be destroyed when the code block finishes execution.

```
void add_bonus( );
void main( )
{
  add_bonus();
}

void add_bonus( )
{
    auto int bonus;
    auto int salary, total_comp;
    bonus = 100;
    salary = 1000;
    total_comp = salary + bonus;
}
```

All variables declared in a code block are local and auto by default. Therefore, the use of the auto specifier is optional.

Fact Sheet ...
extern
If the specifier extern isn't used, the source code file will compile. However, the linker will display an error message stating that an attempt was made to declare a duplicate variable.
static
A static variable is used to maintain the value that is assigned to the variable during multiple calls of a function.
register
A register variable must be either an int or char data type.
Global variables cannot be a register variable. Global variables are placed in a fixed location in memory. The CPU register is temporary memory storage.

Chapter Two

Working with Operators and Expressions

- Expressions
- Arithmetic Operators
- The +=, -=, *=, /= Operators
- The % Operators
- The ++, -- Operators
- Relational Operators
- The <=, ==, != Operators
- Logical Operators
- Bitwise Operators
- Bitwise AND
- Bitwise OR
- Bitwise XOR (exclusive OR)
- Bitwise NOT
- The Shift Left Operator
- The Shift Right Operator
- The ? Operator
- The & and * Pointer Operators
- A Brief Look at Pointers
- The Precedence Table
- Working with Expressions

Expressions

In the previous chapter, statements are used to instruct the compiler to do something. A *statement* contains keywords and symbols that are recognized by the compiler and end with a semicolon. Statements almost always contain mathematical or logical expressions.

An *expression* uses *operators* and *operands* to instruct the compiler to perform computation. A typical expression is illustrated in the example on the opposite page and shown below. Here, the assignment operator and the addition operator are used to sum the operands salary and bonus, the result of which is stored in total_comp. Within this statement, salary, bonus, and total_comp are considered variables and within the expression; they are operands.

total_comp = salary + bonus;

A *mathematical expression* is one which uses *arithmetic operators* to perform mathematical operations on the operands. In comparison, a *logical expression* uses logical operators and *relational operators* to evaluate the relationship between operands. All the operators that are available in C++ are discussed in this chapter.

When the computer performs mathematical or logical operations in an expression, the computer *evaluates* the expression. All expressions result in a specific value. This is obvious in the mathematical expression shown above. However, less obvious is the logical expression that is illustrated within the if statement on the opposite page.

The if statement contains a logical expression that determines if the value of bonus is greater than the value zero. This expression can evaluate to either a true or false. In C++ a *true* is represented by any non-zero value. A *false* is symbolized with a zero value. Therefore, this expression evaluates to a true, or a non-zero value.

An expression is an organization of variables and operators that specify a computation. When the expression ends with a semicolon, it becomes a statement that tells the computer to perform the computation.

Expressions are composed of two basic elements: operands and operators.

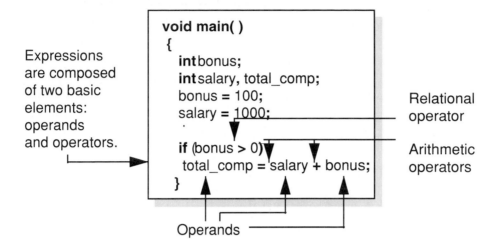

void main( )
{
    int bonus;
    int salary, total_comp;
    bonus = 100;
    salary = 1000;

    if (bonus > 0)
        total_comp = salary + bonus;
}

Relational operator

Arithmetic operators

Operands

Terms You Should Know ...

○	Arithmetic Operator	An arithmetic operator tells the compiler to perform a mathematical manipulation.
	Logical Operator	A logical operator tells the compiler to perform a logical manipulation.
○	Logical Manipulation	A logical manipulation results in a true or false. Zero represents a false and a non-zero value represents a true result.

Arithmetic Operators

C++ offers a broad complement of arithmetic operators that are presented in the table on the opposite page. The first few of the operators are familiar since they are used in nearly every computer programming language. These are the addition operator (+), the *subtraction operator* (-), the *multiplication operator* (*), and the *division operator* (/).

Besides these fundamental arithmetic operators, C++ offers eight more. For example, a group of arithmetic operators is used to combine two operations into one. These are the *addition assignment operator* (+=), the *subtraction assignment operator* (-=), the *multiplication assignment operator* (*=), and the *division assignment operator* (/=).

These multi-function operators are discussed elsewhere in this chapter. However, the example below illustrates the typical functionality of one of these operators. Here, f and c are integer variables. The addition assignment operator instructs the compiler to add the value of c to itself then assigns the results to f.

$$f +=c;$$

Rounding out the available arithmetic operators are the modulus division operator (%), the decremental operator (--) and the incremental operator (++). These are also discussed in detail later in this chapter, however, an example of each will add clarity.

The *modulus division operator* assigns to a variable the fractional part of the remainder of dividing two numbers. The *decremental operator* reduces the value of a variable by one and assigns the new value to the same variable. The *incremental operator* is similar to the decremental operator except the value of the variable is incremented by one. The results are assigned to the same variable.

Operator	Mathematical Manipulation
-	Subtraction or unary minus
+	Addition
*	Multiplication
/	Division
+=	Addition Assignment
-=	Subtraction Assignment
*=	Multiplication Assignment
/=	Division Assignment
%	Modulus Division
%=	Modulus Division Assignment
--	Decrement
++	Increment

The +, -, *, / Operators

Add 5 to the value of variable a then assign the results to the variable e.

Subtract 10 from variable b then assign the results to variable f.

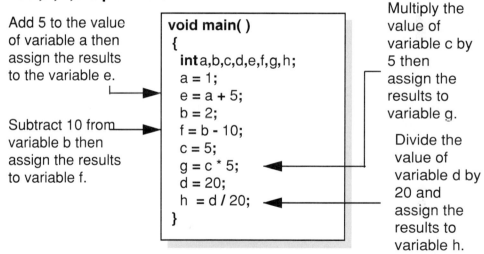

```
void main( )
{
  int a,b,c,d,e,f,g,h;
  a = 1;
  e = a + 5;
  b = 2;
  f = b - 10;
  c = 5;
  g = c * 5;
  d = 20;
  h = d / 20;
}
```

Multiply the value of variable c by 5 then assign the results to variable g.

Divide the value of variable d by 20 and assign the results to variable h.

The +=, -=, *=, /= Operators

C++ makes available operators that perform multiple functions with a single statement. This category of arithmetic operators contains the *addition assignment operator (+=)*, the *subtraction assignment operator (-=)*, the *multiplication assignment operator (*=)*, *modulus division assignment operator (%=)*, and the *division assignment operator (/=)*. All of these operators are illustrated in the top example on the opposite page.

The addition assignment operator instructs the compiler to add the value of the variable to itself then assign the results to another variable. In the example at the top of the opposite page, variable a is assigned the value 1. In the next statement, the addition assignment operator is used to add the contents of variable a to itself (1 + 1), then assign the results to variable e. Therefore, the value of variable e is 2.

The subtraction assignment operator has a similar function. Here, the value of b is 2. The subtraction assignment operator is then used to subtract the value of b from itself (2 - 2), the assign the result to variable f. The value of variable f is 0.

The multiplication assignment operator on the opposite page multiplies the value of variable c, which is 5, by itself (5 * 5). Next, the value of variable g is changed to the product of variable c times itself. Variable g is equal to the value 25.

The division assignment operator is used to divide the value of variable d by itself (20 / 20). The results of this manipulation (1) is assigned to the variable h.

The % Operator

C++ contains an arithmetic operator that returns the fractional portion of the results of division. This is the modulus division operator (%), which is shown in the bottom example on the next page. Here, the value of variable a (15) is divided by the value of variable b (4) which results in the value 3.75. The modulus division operator returns 3.

The +=, -=, *=, /= Operators

Add the value of variable e to variable a then assign the results to the variable e.

Subtract the value of variable b from itself then assign the results to the variable f.

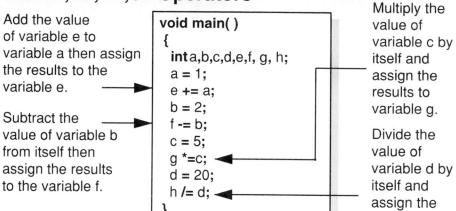

```
void main( )
{
    int a,b,c,d,e,f, g, h;
    a = 1;
    e += a;
    b = 2;
    f -= b;
    c = 5;
    g *=c;
    d = 20;
    h /= d;
}
```

Multiply the value of variable c by itself and assign the results to variable g.

Divide the value of variable d by itself and assign the results to variable h.

The % Operator

The variable c is assigned the remainder results of the modulus division. The value of variable c is 3.

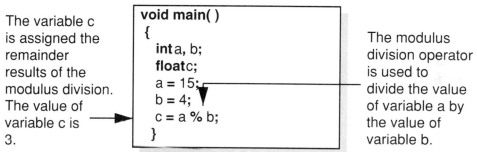

```
void main( )
{
    int a, b;
    float c;
    a = 15;
    b = 4;
    c = a % b;
}
```

The modulus division operator is used to divide the value of variable a by the value of variable b.

Terms You Should Know ...

○	Unary Minus	The unary minus operator switches the sign of the operand. This is the same effect as multiplying the single operand by -1.
○	Modulus Division	A modulus division results is the remainder of an integer division. Modulus division cannot be used on float and double data types.

The ++, -- Operators

The value of a variable can be increased or decreased by 1 through the use of the *incremental operator* (++) and the *decremental operator* (--). The simplest form of both of these operators is illustrated in the top example on the opposite page. A more advanced use of these operators is shown in the bottom example.

The incremental operator is used to increase the value of variable c by 1. This results in variable c, which has an original value of 1, having a final value of 2. The incremental operator has the effect of an expression that uses the addition operator and the assignment operator to increase the value of a variable by 1.

Next is the decremental operator, which decreases the value of variable d by 1. The initial value of variable d is 2. Once the decremental operator executes, the value becomes 1. The same result is achieved by using the subtraction operator and the assignment operator to lower the value of a variable by 1.

The position of the incremental and decrement operator plays an important role in how the compiler manipulates the data. In the bottom example on the opposite page, both operators are shown positioned before and after the variable. The first statement that uses the incremental operator places that operator to the left of the variable. This is shown below.

$$e = ++a;$$

The initial value of variable a is 5. When the incremental operator (or decremental operator) appears before the variable in an expression, the value of the variable is incremented by one (or decremented by one) before the assignment operator is executed. Therefore, variable e has a value of 6. However, if the incremental operator (or decremental operator) appears after the variable (e = a++), the assignment operator is executed first, then the incremental operator. The initial value of variable a is 5. This value is incremented by 1 after the value 5 is assigned to variable e.

The incremental operator adds one to the operand.

The decremental operator subtracts one from the operand.

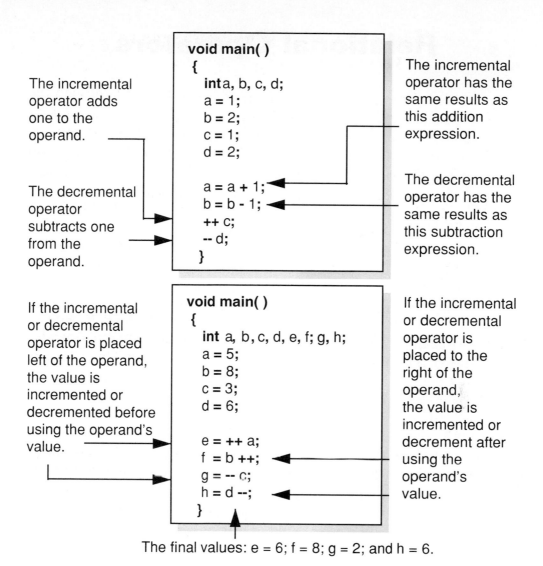

```
void main( )
{
    int a, b, c, d;
    a = 1;
    b = 2;
    c = 1;
    d = 2;

    a = a + 1;
    b = b - 1;
    ++ c;
    -- d;
}
```

The incremental operator has the same results as this addition expression.

The decremental operator has the same results as this subtraction expression.

If the incremental or decremental operator is placed left of the operand, the value is incremented or decremented before using the operand's value.

```
void main( )
{
    int a, b, c, d, e, f; g, h;
    a = 5;
    b = 8;
    c = 3;
    d = 6;

    e = ++ a;
    f = b ++;
    g = -- c;
    h = d --;
}
```

If the incremental or decremental operator is placed to the right of the operand, the value is incremented or decrement after using the operand's value.

The final values: e = 6; f = 8; g = 2; and h = 6.

Relational Operators

Relational operators are used to compare two expressions or two values. The result of this comparison is either true or false. A *true* is represented by any non-zero value. A *false* is represented by a zero. There are six relational operators in C++. These are the *greater than operator* (>), the *greater than or equal operator* (>=), the *less than operator* (<), the *less than or equal operator* (<=), the *equal operator* (==), and the *not equal operator* (!=).

Frequently, these operators are used to evaluate expressions used in an if statement. Three of these operators are illustrated in the examples on the opposite page. The first example uses the greater than operator to determine if the value on the left side of the operator is greater than the value on the right side of the operator.

In the next example, the greater than or equal operator is used to decide if the value of a is greater than or equal to the value 15. If so, the expression evaluates to a non-zero value (1) the less than operator is used to test whether or not the value of a is less than the value 15.

Most of the relational operators that are listed in the table on the opposite page are familiar since they are used in other computer languages. However, the equal operator can be confusing. The equal operator, sometimes called the *equivalent operator*, is symbolized as a double equal sign (==). This is different than other computer languages where the assignment operator (=) is also used as the symbol for the equal operator.

Another symbol that might be confusing is the not equal operator (!=). In C++, the exclamation mark reverses the operation that appears to the right of the exclamation mark. Therefore, the exclamation mark is also called the *not operator*. Other computer languages use the greater than and less than operators (<>) to symbolize not equals.

Operator	Relational Operation
>	Greater than
>=	Greater than or equal
<	Less than
<=	Less than or equal
==	Equal
!=	Not equal

If a is greater than 15...

If a is greater than or equal to 15 ...

If a is less than 15 ...

```
void main( )
{
   int a, b;

   a = 15;
   if (a > 15)
      b = 3;
}
```

```
void main( )
{
   int a, b;

   a = 15;
   if (a >= 15)
      b = 3;
}
```

```
void main( )
{
   int a, b;

   a = 15;
   if (a < 15)
      b = 3;
}
```

Terms You Should Know ...

Relational Operator	Relational operators evaluate the relationship one operand has to another operand. The result of this evaluation is either false or true. A false is represented by a zero and a true is represented by a non-zero value.

The <=, ==, != Operators

Examples at the top of the opposite page contain three relational operators. These were introduced earlier in this chapter. The first example illustrates the less than or equal operator. This operator is used to determine if the value of variable a is less than or equivalent to the value 15. If so, a non-zero value is returned otherwise a zero is returned.

The next example shows the equal operator (==) which compares the value of variable a with the value 15. If they are the same value, then this expression is true, a non-zero value. If the values are not equivalent, a false or a zero is returned. The final example uses the not operator (!=) to test two values. A true is returned if the value of variable a is not equal to the value 15.

Logical Operators

A *logical operator* is used to relate two relational expressions. A *relational expression* is one in which a relational operator is used. The table on the opposite page contains the logical operators that are available in C++. They are the AND (&&) operator, the OR operator (||), and the NOT (!) operator.

The AND (&&) logical operator is used to join two relational expressions. This is illustrated in the first example at the bottom of the opposite page. Both relational expressions must be true for the logical order to return a true. That is, variable a must be less than 15 and variable b must be less than 15.

The OR (||) logical operator returns a true if either of the two relational expressions is true. In the second example, the OR operator returns a true if either variable a is less than 15 or variable b is less than 15. The NOT(!) logical operator evaluates to true only if the first relational expression is true and the second relational expression is false. In the last example, the NOT operator returns a true if variable a is less than 15 and variable b is not less than 15.

```
void main( )
{
  int a, b;

  a = 15;
  if (a <= 15)
    b = 3;
}
```

```
void main( )
{
  int a, b;

  a = 15;
  if (a == 15)
    b = 3;
}
```

```
void main( )
{
  int a, b;

  a = 15;
  if (a != 15)
    b = 3;
}
```

	Operator	Logical Operation
○	&&	AND
○	||	OR
	!	NOT

If a is less than 15 and
b is less than 15 ...

If a is less than 15 or
b is less than 15 ...

If a is less than 15 and
not b is less than 15 ...

```
void main( )
{
  int a, b, c;
  a = 14;
  b = 15;
  if ((a < 15) && (b< 15))
    c = 3;
}
```

```
void main( )
{
  int a, b, c;
  a = 14;
  b = 15;
  if ((a < 15) II (b< 15))
    c = 3;
}
```

```
void main( )
{
  int a, b, c;
  a = 14;
  b = 15;
  if ((a < 15) ! (b< 15))
    c = 3;
}
```

Bitwise Operators

Typical applications require manipulation of bytes of information such as an integer, float, and characters. A *byte* is composed of eight pieces, each called a *bit*. A bit can have a value of *zero* or *one*. The combination of these values in a collection of eight bits (a byte) is used to represent numbers and characters (ASCII values).

C++ provides six operators that enable a programmer to manipulate bits. These operators are referred to as *bitwise operators*. The table on the opposite page contains bitwise operators. These are the AND *operator* (&), the OR *operator* (|), the *exclusive* OR *operator* (^), the NOT *operator* (~) which is also called the *one's complement operator*, the *shift right operator* (>>), and the *shift left operator* (<<).

Bitwise AND

The AND(&) *bitwise operator* compares every bit of each operand. If the bit in the same position of each operand is one, the resulting bit is one. However, if either bit is zero, then the resulting bit is set to zero. The example on the opposite page illustrates this technique.

The first operand used in this bitwise expression is 11010111. These numbers are meaningful only if they are converted to an ASCII value which is 'W.' The second operand is 01111111, which is the binary equivalent to the decimal number 127. The objective in this example is to change the value of the first bit in the first operand from 1 to 0.

The AND (&) bitwise operator compares each bit in 11010111 and in 01111111. By following the rules, only the first bit is changed. The values of the other bits in the first operand remain unchanged. In this example, the first bit is used as a parity bit in data communications. Parity was originally activated but is deactivated by using the AND bitwise operator.

Operator	Bitwise Operation
&	AND
|	OR
^	Exclusive OR (XOR)
~	One's complement (NOT)
>>	Shift right
<<	Shift left

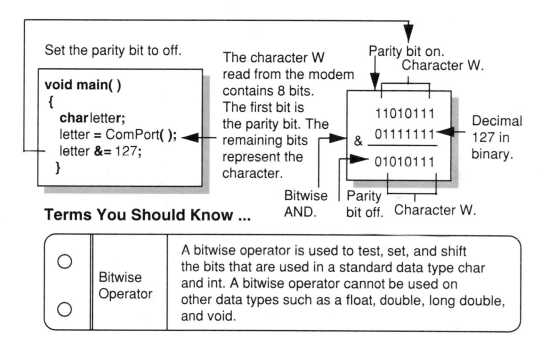

Set the parity bit to off.

```
void main( )
{
    char letter;
    letter = ComPort( );
    letter &= 127;
}
```

The character W read from the modem contains 8 bits. The first bit is the parity bit. The remaining bits represent the character.

Parity bit on.
Character W.

```
      11010111
&     01111111
      ──────────
      01010111
```

Decimal 127 in binary.

Bitwise AND.   Parity bit off.   Character W.

Terms You Should Know ...

○ ○	Bitwise Operator	A bitwise operator is used to test, set, and shift the bits that are used in a standard data type char and int. A bitwise operator cannot be used on other data types such as a float, double, long double, and void.

Bitwise OR

The *bitwise* OR(|) *operator* is also referred to as the *inclusive* OR *operator*. This means that either bit that is being compared can meet the rule for the resulting bit value to become the binary value one.

The inclusive OR (|) operator functions similarly to the AND (&) bitwise operator in that a comparison is made between bits of two operands. However, if either bit in the comparison is one, then the resulting bit is set to one, otherwise the resulting bit is set to zero.

In the top example on the opposite page, the OR(|) operator is used to change the value of the first bit from zero to 1. This is reversed from the operation that is performed on the preceding page. Notice that the binary representation of the decimal number 128 is compared with bits that represent the character W.

Bitwise XOR
(exclusive OR)

Another type of OR operator is the *exclusive* OR *operator* (^) also referred to as the XOR *operator*. The exclusive OR operator is different than the inclusive OR (|) operator in that the bit of each operand must meet the rule for the resulting bit value to be set to binary value one.

The exclusive OR(^) operator compares the bits of each operand then creates a resulting bit value. If the bit in one operand is a 0 and the bit in the other operand is 1, then the resulting bit is set to 1, otherwise the resulting bit is set to 0.

Notice that the bit value of both operands must have a specific value for the bit to be set to one. In the inclusive OR (|) operations, either bit could have a specific value.

In the bottom example, the binary representation of the decimal numbers 123 and 122 are used to illustrate the use of the exclusive OR operations.

Bitwise OR

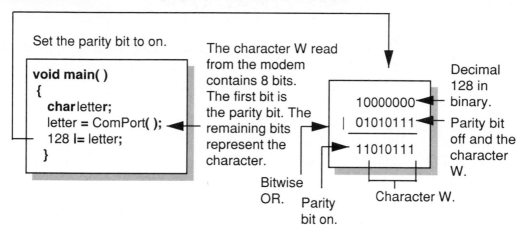

Set the parity bit to on.

```
void main( )
{
    char letter;
    letter = ComPort( );
    128 |= letter;
}
```

The character W read from the modem contains 8 bits. The first bit is the parity bit. The remaining bits represent the character.

Bitwise OR.

Parity bit on.

```
10000000
| 01010111
  11010111
```

Character W.

Decimal 128 in binary.

Parity bit off and the character W.

Bitwise XOR (exclusive OR)

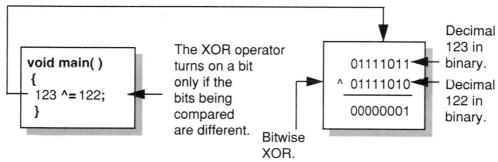

```
void main( )
{
    123 ^= 122;
}
```

The XOR operator turns on a bit only if the bits being compared are different.

Bitwise XOR.

```
  01111011
^ 01111010
  00000001
```

Decimal 123 in binary.

Decimal 122 in binary.

Bitwise NOT

The bitwise NOT *operator* (~) also called the *one's complement operator* is used to reverse the bit setting of the operand. If the bit value is zero, then the resulting bit value is one. Likewise, a bit value of one will result in a bit value setting of zero.

At the top of the opposite page the bitwise NOT(~) operator is used to reverse the bit settings of the binary representation of the decimal number 122.

The Shift Left Operator

Unlike the previous bitwise operators that are discussed in this chapter, the shift operators do not compare bit values. Instead, this operator moves bits one bit to the left or right.

The *shift left operator* (<<) sets the current bit to the value of the bit to the right. That is, if the current bit has a value of 1 and the bit to the right has a value of zero, then the shift left operator sets the current bit to the value of zero.

This technique is illustrated in the center example on the opposite page. Here, the binary representation of the decimal number 122 is changed by the shift left operator.

When values of the bits are moved to the left, the right most bit appears to lose its value. However, the bitwise shift left operator sets the right most bit in the resulting bit to a zero. The left most bit is destroyed by moving out of range.

The Shift Right Operator

The bitwise *shift right operator* (>>) performs a similar operation as the shift left operator except that the value of the bits are shifted to the right. The value of the left most bit is set to zero.

Bitwise NOT (one's complement

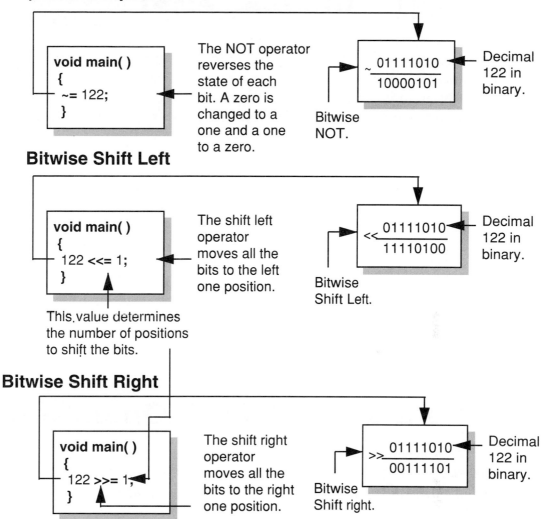

The NOT operator reverses the state of each bit. A zero is changed to a one and a one to a zero.

```
void main( )
{
   ~= 122;
}
```

Bitwise NOT.

```
~ 01111010
  10000101
```

Decimal 122 in binary.

Bitwise Shift Left

The shift left operator moves all the bits to the left one position.

```
void main( )
{
   122 <<= 1;
}
```

This value determines the number of positions to shift the bits.

Bitwise Shift Left.

```
<< 01111010
   11110100
```

Decimal 122 in binary.

Bitwise Shift Right

The shift right operator moves all the bits to the right one position.

```
void main( )
{
   122 >>= 1;
}
```

Bitwise Shift right.

```
>> 01111010
   00111101
```

Decimal 122 in binary.

The ? Operator
(if...the...else)

It is hard to conceive that a question mark is an operator in C++ but it is. The question mark is called the *ternary operator* and performs the functionality of an inline if statement. An example of the ternary operator is shown in the top example in the opposite page and below.

$$b = a > 15 ? 3 : 0;$$

The ternary operator evaluates the expression that appears to the left of the operator. In this example, the expression of a > 15 is evaluated first. This expression will either be true or false.

If the expression is true, then the value or expression that appears between the ternary operator and the colon is assigned to the variable b. The value or expression to the right of the colon is assigned to b if the expression is false.

In this example, the value of a is 15. Therefore, the expression evaluates to a false and the value zero is assigned to the variable b.

The & and * Pointer Operators

A pointer is a variable that contains the address of another variable. The concept of pointers is covered in Chapter 10 in this book. However, there are two operators that are used with pointers that are discussed in this chapter.

Every variable that is used in a C++ program has an address in memory and, if assigned a value, has a value stored at that memory address. The & operator is used to reference the address of a variable. This technique is illustrated in the example at the bottom of the page.

The * *operator* is used to declare a pointer. This operator is also used to reference the value at the address pointed to by the pointer.

The ? Operator
(if...the...else)

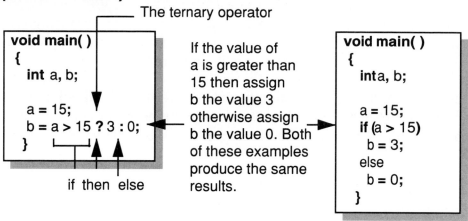

The ternary operator

```
void main( )
{
    int a, b;

    a = 15;
    b = a > 15 ? 3 : 0;
}
    if then else
```

If the value of a is greater than 15 then assign b the value 3 otherwise assign b the value 0. Both of these examples produce the same results.

```
void main( )
{
    int a, b;

    a = 15;
    if (a > 15)
        b = 3;
    else
        b = 0;
}
```

The & and * Pointer Operator

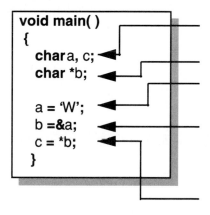

```
void main( )
{
    char a, c;
    char *b;

    a = 'W';
    b = &a;
    c = *b;
}
```

Two character variables are declared and one variable is declared as a pointer to a character variable.

The letter 'W' is stored in character variable a.

The & operator is used to assign the memory address of variable a to the character pointer variable b.

The * operator is used to assign the value that is contained at the address stored in variable b to variable c.

A Brief Look at Pointers

The use of pointer operators in a C++ program can be confusing. The example on the opposite page will clarify the use of pointers. A more complete discussion about pointers is presented in Chapter 10.

The diagram on the opposite page depicts the values contained in memory when the program example is executed. The program declares three variables. Variable a and c are character variables and variable b is a pointer variable.

In the first assignment statement, the character W is assigned to variable a. Although the character W is used in the diagram, the binary representation of the ASCII value of W is actually placed in memory.

Next, the & pointer operator is used to assign the address of variable a to pointer variable b. The address of variable a is 123456 which becomes the value of the pointer variable b.

Finally, the * pointer operator is used to assign the value pointed to by the pointer to the variable c. The actions of this statement are a little complicated. Let's examine each step of this process closely.

Variable b contains the address of variable a (123456). At the address of variable a (123456) is the value W. When the variable b is referenced, the compiler refers to the address 123456.

However, when the * pointer operator precedes variable b, the compiler references the value at the address contained in variable b. That is, the value at the address 123456 is the character W.

Therefore, the character W is assigned to the variable c in the last statement of the program.

In Memory

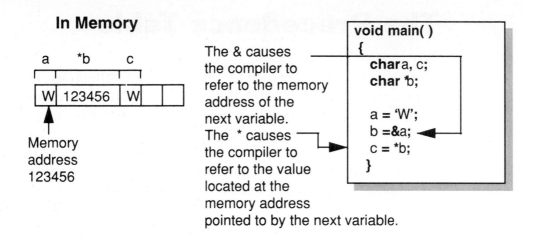

a   *b   c

| W | 123456 | W | |

Memory
address
123456

The & causes the compiler to refer to the memory address of the next variable.

The * causes the compiler to refer to the value located at the memory address pointed to by the next variable.

```
void main( )
{
    char a, c;
    char *b;

    a = 'W';
    b = &a;
    c = *b;
}
```

Terms You Should Know ...

○	Memory Address	Every location in the computer's memory is assigned a memory address. This is very similar to an address of a house in a town.
○	Pointer Operator	A pointer operator is used to reference a value by the memory address where the value is stored in memory.

Note:

A complete discussion about pointers is contained later in Chapter 10.

The Precedence Table

Simple expressions are used throughout this chapter to illustrate the proper use of operators. However, more complex expressions are necessary in a typical C++ application. These complex expressions combine many operators in a single statement of C++ code.

The order in which these operators are executed determines the value of a complex expression. For example, does the following expression evaluate to 15 or 35?

5*2 +5;

The proper answer is determined only if it is known if the multiplication or the addition operation is performed first. A compiler has the same conflict when executing this statement.

However, the compiler resolves this conflict by referencing the rules that are specified in the *precedence table*. A copy of the precedence table is shown in the opposite page.

Each operator in C++ is assigned a precedence rank. When the compiler is asked to evaluate a complex expression, the compiler refers to the precedence rank of each operator that is used in the expression to determine the order of operation.

Notice that the multiplication operator has a higher order of precedence than the addition operator. Therefore, the correct answer to the previous example is 15. The compiler multiplies 5 by 2 then adds 5 to the product.

Portions of an expression that are contained within parentheses are performed first regardless of the precedence rank. Therefore, 5*(2+5) will result in the value 35.

Precedence Rank	Operator
1	( ) [ ] -> .
2	! ~ ++ -- - (type cast) * &
3	* / %
4	+ -
5	>> <<
6	< <= > >=
7	== !=
8	&
9	^
10	|
11	&&
12	||
13	?
14	= += -= *= /=
15	%=

Terms You Should Know ...

Precedence	Expressions can contain more than one operator. The compiler executes each operator in the order in which the operator appears in the precedence table. The operation with the highest rank (lowest number) is performed first. For example, multiplication (3) is performed before addition (4). Operations with the same ranking are performed left to right within the expression.

Working with Expressions

Avoid conflicts within complex expressions by using parentheses to identify subexpressions. This technique is illustrated in the right most example on the opposite page.

The use of parentheses to clarify the order of operations in an expression has a dual purpose. First, this technique properly instructs the compiler to evaluate the expression in a particular sequence regardless of the precedence ranking of the operators.

The use of parentheses also makes the C++ code easier to read. Another programmer can quickly analyze the statement without having to consider the order of precedence. Most programmers do not have the precedence table committed to memory.

The last example on the opposite page illustrates the importance of using parentheses in a compound expression. First, parentheses are used to resolve a conflict arising from operators that have the same precedence rank. This is shown below.

$$d = a * [b + (c + 30)];$$

The expression contained within the inner most parentheses (called *nested expression*) is executed first. If the parentheses are not used in a complex expression, then the compiler evaluates left to right when operations of equal precedence ranks must be performed. That is, the operation on the left is performed first followed by the operation on the right within the expression.

When a complex statement contains multiple parentheses (not nested), the compiler follows the left to right rule. This is shown in the last statement in the bottom example on the opposite page. First, the compiler adds a and b, then b and c are added together. Finally, the sum of both additions is totaled.

```
void main( )
{
    int a, b, c, d;

    a = 5;
    b = 10;
    c = 3;

    d = a * b + c;
}
```

You can override the precedence of any operation by using the parentheses operator.

Subexpressions that are contained within the parentheses are performed first.

```
void main( )
{
    int a, b, c, d;

    a = 5;
    b = 10;
    c = 3;

    d = a * (b + c);
}
```

The value of the variable d in this expression is 53. The multiplication component of the expression is performed before the addition. Multiplication has a higher precedence rank than addition.

The value of variable d in this expression is 65. The addition component of the expression is performed before the multiplication.

A subexpression can be created within another subexpression by nesting parentheses. The innermost subexpression is resolved first.

```
void main( )
{
    int a, b, c, d;

    a = 5;
    b = 10;
    c = 3;

    d = a * [b + (c+30)];
    d = (a+b) + (b+c);
}
```

When subexpressions appear separately in the expression, the compiler resolves the subexpressions from left to right.

Chapter Three

Working with
Arrays and Strings

- Arrays and Strings
- Other Ways to Assign Values to an Array
- Loop
- Multidimensional Arrays
- Other Ways to Assign Values to a Multidimensional Array
- Loop
- Strings
- Copying a String to Another String strcpy
- Reading a String from the Keyboard gets()
- Another way to Read a String from the Keyboard scanf()
- Still Another Way to Read a String from the Keyboard with the Extraction Operator
- Comparing Two Strings strcmp()
- Displaying a String printf()
- Another Way to Display a String puts()
- Still Another Way to Display a String with The Insertion Operator
- Concatenating Strings strcat()
- Determining the Length of a String strlen()
- Determining the Length of a Substring strcspn()
- Another Way to Determine the Length of a Substring strspn()
- Concatenating a Substring strncat()
- Comparing Substrings strncmp()
- Locating a Character within a String
- Locating the First Occurrence of a Substring in a String strstr()
- Dividing a String into Several Substrings strtok()

Arrays and Strings

Information called *data* is stored in memory locations so that statements within a C++ program can manipulate the data. Data is stored into memory by declaring a variable. A variable declaration instructs the compiler to reserve space in memory in a size appropriate for the variable data type. Furthermore, this statement instructs the compiler to associate the address of that memory location with the name that is given to the variable. This technique is illustrated below and is used in previous chapters.

int num;

Data is usually related to other data within a program. For example, a student's grade for a course is a piece of data that is traditionally related to the grades of other students in the course. This relationship can be identified within the program by grouping grades under a single name. That is, instead of having a separate variable for each grade, all the grades for the course can be identified by specifying a single name.

A programmer can use an array. An *array* enables a collection of like data types to be referenced by a single name called the *array name*. Each member of the collection is called an *element of the array* or a *member of the array*. Elements of an array are identified by the name of the array followed by a unique *index number* contained in square brackets.

The method of declaring an array is similar to the declaration of a variable. An example is shown on the opposite page. The data type of the array is followed by the name of the array, then by the required total number of elements of the array. An array element is used similar to that of a variable. In the example on the opposite page, the assignment operator is used to store the value 23 to the first element of the EmpNum[0] array. The zero is the element's index number. Notice that the first element of an array begins with zero—not one.

An array is a type of variable that can group together values of the same data type. A string is an array of character data type values where the last value in the array is a null character '\0'.

Array

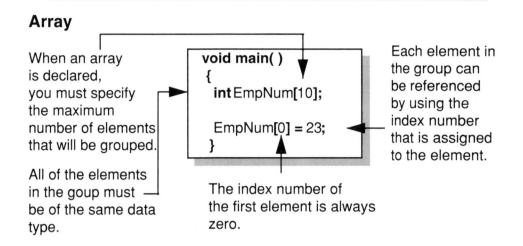

When an array is declared, you must specify the maximum number of elements that will be grouped.

All of the elements in the goup must be of the same data type.

```
void main( )
{
    int EmpNum[10];

    EmpNum[0] = 23;
}
```

Each element in the group can be referenced by using the index number that is assigned to the element.

The index number of the first element is always zero.

Terms You Should Know ...

○	Array Size	The maximum number of elements grouped by the array is called the array size.
○	Array Element	Each item that is grouped by the array is called an array element.

Other Ways to Assign Values to an Array

On the previous page, a value is assigned to an element of an array by specifying the index number of the element. This technique requires that the array be declared in a previous statement. However, values can be assigned to array elements when the array is declared. This is illustrated on the opposite page and below.

```
int DaysOfWeek[] = {1, 2, 3, 4, 5, 6, 7};
```

The DaysOfWeek is the name of the array. Notice that the square brackets that follow the array name are empty. In a declaration where no values are immediately assigned to array elements, the maximum number of array elements is specified with the square brackets. This is also called the *size of the array*.

However, the size of the array can also be set by assigning values when the array is declared. The value must appear within French braces and the values must be separated by commas. This technique is called *appending values to an array*. The size of the array is determined by the compiler when the statement is executed. The compiler counts the number of values then uses that number as the size of the array.

Loop

Assigning values to each element of a large array can involve numerous statements if the elements are not assigned an initialized value when the array is declared. An efficient way to assign values to array elements is by using a for loop. This is illustrated in the bottom example on the opposite page.

Here, the counter variable (I) is used as the index number for each element of the array in the assignment statement. The maximum value of the for loop counter is the same value as the size of the array.

Append

Values can be appended to an array when the array is declared.

The values must be contained within French braces.

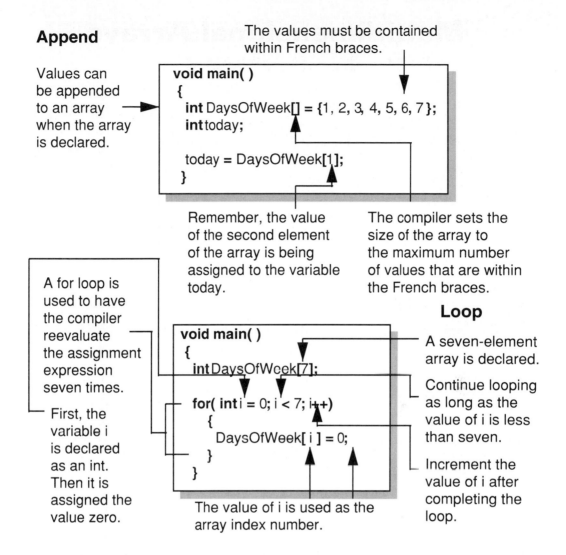

```
void main( )
{
  int DaysOfWeek[] = {1, 2, 3, 4, 5, 6, 7 };
  int today;

  today = DaysOfWeek[1];
}
```

Remember, the value of the second element of the array is being assigned to the variable today.

The compiler sets the size of the array to the maximum number of values that are within the French braces.

A for loop is used to have the compiler reevaluate the assignment expression seven times.

First, the variable i is declared as an int. Then it is assigned the value zero.

Loop

A seven-element array is declared.

```
void main( )
{
  int DaysOfWeek[7];

  for( int i = 0; i < 7; i++)
  {
    DaysOfWeek[ i ] = 0;
  }
}
```

Continue looping as long as the value of i is less than seven.

Increment the value of i after completing the loop.

The value of i is used as the array index number.

Multidimensional Arrays

The array that is declared in the previous example is called a *single dimensional array*. That is, there is a single set of elements which is represented by a single square bracket in the statement. A single dimensional array enables the programmer to relate the same kind of data, such as grades in a course.

However, grades by themselves are not sufficient information for a program. Grades are associated with students. This relationship can be represented in C++ by a *multidimensional array*. A multidimensional array contains two or more sets of data. Each set has its own square bracketed index.

A two-dimensional array is illustrated on the opposite page. The size of the first dimension is 10. This represents the number of students in the course. The size of the second dimension is two, one element to hold the student's number and the other to contain the grade.

The declaration statement for a multidimensional array is very similar to the statement that declares a single dimensional array. This technique is illustrated on the opposite page and below. Here, 10 sets of 2 are declared.

```
int students[10][2];
```

A specific element of the array is referenced by specifying the index numbers for the element. For example, assume that data must be assigned for the fifth student in the course. The following example references the student number and grade elements for the fifth student.

```
student[4][0] = 201;
```

```
student[4][1] = 85;
```

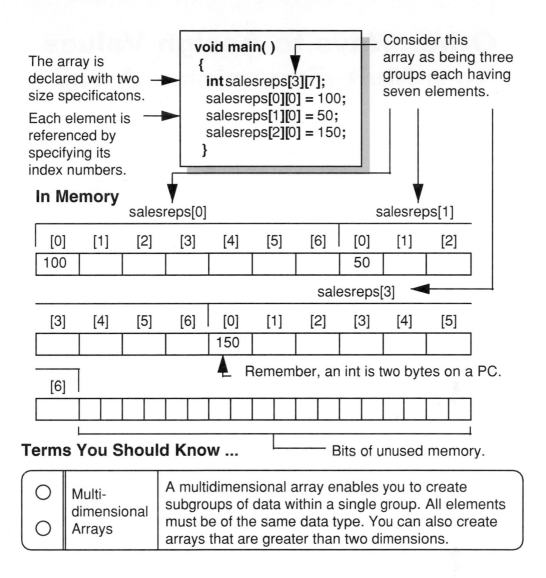

The array is declared with two size specificatons.

Each element is referenced by specifying its index numbers.

void main( )
{
  int salesreps[3][7];
  salesreps[0][0] = 100;
  salesreps[1][0] = 50;
  salesreps[2][0] = 150;
}

Consider this array as being three groups each having seven elements.

In Memory

salesreps[0]

[0]	[1]	[2]	[3]	[4]	[5]	[6]	[0]	[1]	[2]
100							50		

salesreps[1]

salesreps[3]

[3]	[4]	[5]	[6]	[0]	[1]	[2]	[3]	[4]	[5]
				150					

Remember, an int is two bytes on a PC.

[6]

Terms You Should Know ...

Bits of unused memory.

○ ○	Multi-dimensional Arrays	A multidimensional array enables you to create subgroups of data within a single group. All elements must be of the same data type. You can also create arrays that are greater than two dimensions.

Other Ways to Assign Values to a Multidimensional Array

Values can be assigned to a multidimensional array when the array is declared. This technique is illustrated in the top example on the opposite page and below. Notice that this declaration statement does not explicitly specify the size of the array. The square brackets for both dimensions are empty.

```
int students[][] = {{201,75}, {202,90}};
```

French braces are used to delimit each set of data. There are two inner French braces. Each set is used by the compiler to determine the size of the first dimension of the array, that is, the first square bracket. Therefore, the size of the first dimension is two.

The number of values within the inner French brace is used to determine the size of the second dimension of the array. In this example, the dimension of the second dimension is also two. Values within the inner French brace are then assigned to each element of the array.

The number of values within each of the inner French braces must be the same. In this example, each inner French brace contains two values (student number and grade). The compiler will report an error if the number of values are different in each inner French brace.

Loop

Nested for loops can be used to efficiently assign values to a multidimensional array. This is shown in the bottom example on the opposite page. Notice that two counter variables (i) (x) are used to represent the index number of the array. The i counter is for the outer for loop and the x counter for the inner for loop.

Append

The number of sets of French braces determines the size of the first dimension of the array.

Values can be appended to a multidimensional array by using French braces.

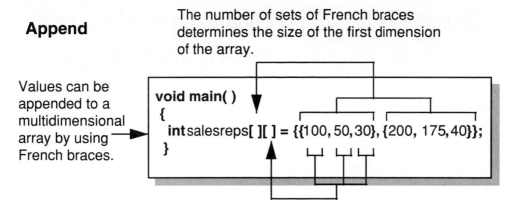

```
void main( )
{
    int salesreps[ ][ ] = {{100, 50, 30}, {200, 175, 40}};
}
```

The number of sets within the French braces determines the size of the second dimension of the array.

A nested for loop is used to assign zero as the value to each element in the array.

Loop

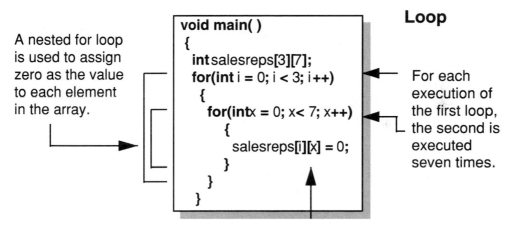

```
void main( )
{
    int salesreps[3][7];
    for(int i = 0; i < 3; i++)
    {
        for(int x = 0; x < 7; x++)
        {
            salesreps[i][x] = 0;
        }
    }
}
```

For each execution of the first loop, the second is executed seven times.

The variables i and x are used to reference each element of the multidimensional array.

Strings

Elements of an array can contain characters by using the char keyword to declare the array as a *character array*. This is illustrated on the opposite page. Each element of a character array can reference a single character that is represented by the ASCII value of that character. This example shows how to assign a character to an element of a character array. Notice that each character must be enclosed within a single quotation mark—not a double quotation mark.

Unlike other computer languages, a word that is assigned to a character array is treated as individual letters by C++. That is, the programmer treats BOB as the name Bob. However, C++ treats the same word as the characters B O B. The difference becomes apparent when the programmer needs to manipulate the word and not the individual characters.

For example, the strlen( ) function in C++ determines the length of a string of characters. This function answers the question, how many characters are there in this word? C++ does not recognize a word. However, certain functions in C++ recognize a string.

A *string* is a character array where the last character in the array is a null character ('\0'). Some functions, called *string functions*, can be told to treat an array of characters as a word by placing a null '\0' character as the last character in the array. Notice that a null character is placed in the fourth element of the character array name shown on the top example on the next page. (Remember, index values begin with zero, not one.).

The null character is a stop sign for string functions. For example, the strlen( ) function starts counting characters from the beginning of the character array and stops counting when the null character is encountered. If the null character is not placed in the character array, then any string function continues reading the contents of the next memory location until a null character is found. The function reads garbage and could hang the computer if a null character is not found near the character array in memory.

An array of characters is declared as having 20 elements.

Characters assigned to elements beyond the null character are not part of the string.

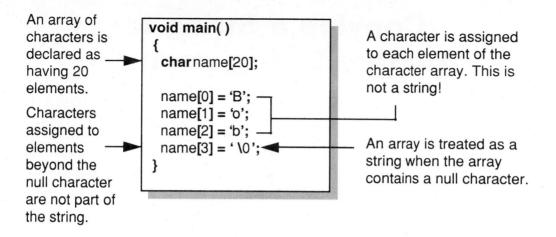

```
void main( )
{
    char name[20];

    name[0] = 'B';
    name[1] = 'o';
    name[2] = 'b';
    name[3] = ' \0';
}
```

A character is assigned to each element of the character array. This is not a string!

An array is treated as a string when the array contains a null character.

In Memory

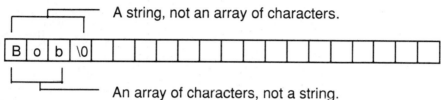

A string, not an array of characters.

| B | o | b | \0 | | | | | | | | | | | | | | | | |

An array of characters, not a string.

Terms You Should Know ...

○ ○	String	A string is a special kind of array where each element in the array is a char data type and is assigned a character value. The last character in the array must be a null character ('\0').

Copying a String to Another String strcpy( )

C++ can copy a value from a memory location to another memory location by using the assignment operator (=). For example, the following code segment copies the letter 'A' from the memory location represented by the variable let1 to the variable let2. However, a string cannot be copied in this manner.

$$let1 = 'A';$$
$$let2 = let1;$$

Instead of using the assignment operator, the programmer can use the strcpy( ) function or one of its variations to copy a string of characters from one memory location to another. The technique for using the strcpy( ) is illustrated in the example on the opposite page.

The strcpy( ) function requires two arguments. The first argument is the name of the array that will receive the string. The second argument is the string that will be copied to the array. In this example, the string "Bob" is copied to the array called name.

Notice that Bob is enclosed within double quotations. One or more characters enclosed in double quotations is treated as a string and is called a *literal constant*. That is, the value of the string "Bob" will not change during the life of the program.

After the strcpy( ) function successfully executes, memory referenced by the array name will appear to be similar to the memory diagram shown on the opposite page. Notice that the strcpy( ) function automatically placed a null character at the last character in the array. Caution! When declaring a character array, be sure to make the array large enough to hold the null character. That is, an array with the size of three can hold two characters and the null character.

The strcpy( ) function copies the contents of the string referenced in the second argument to the string referenced in the first argument. The previous value of the string referenced in the first argument is overwritten.

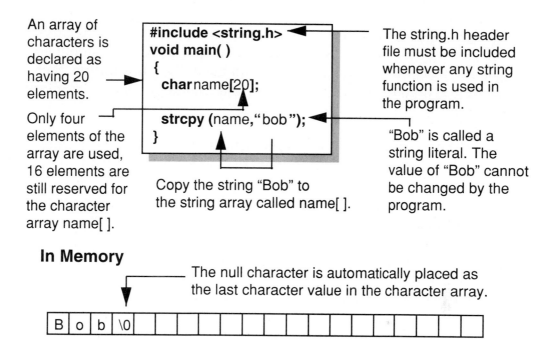

An array of characters is declared as having 20 elements.

Only four elements of the array are used, 16 elements are still reserved for the character array name[ ].

```
#include <string.h>
void main( )
{
    char name[20];

    strcpy (name,"bob");
}
```

The string.h header file must be included whenever any string function is used in the program.

"Bob" is called a string literal. The value of "Bob" cannot be changed by the program.

Copy the string "Bob" to the string array called name[ ].

In Memory

The null character is automatically placed as the last character value in the character array.

| B | o | b | \0 | | | | | | | | | | | | | | | | |

Reading a String from
the Keyboard gets( )

The C++ language provides various methods of reading a string from the keyboard. All the functions that are available in the C programming language to perform this task are also available in C++. In addition, there is a newer technique offered only in C++ that will be discussed later in the book.

The *gets*() is a function that will work with either C or C++. The purpose of the gets() function is to read a stream of characters from standard in and save them to memory. *Standard in* refers to the default input source for the computer and in many computers is established by assigning a value to an environment variable.

Standard in is the keyboard on most computers, although this source can be changed through the redirection process discussed in Chapter 12. For now, assume that standard in is the keyboard.

The gets( ) function requires a single argument, which is the name of the array that is to receive the characters. This is illustrated in the example on the opposite page. Notice that only the name of the array is used without any reference to an element. Remember, a reference to the name of the array is the same as referencing the address of the first element. Therefore, the gets( ) function is passed to the address of the first element of the array.

Characters are automatically stored in elements of the array sequentially. The gets() stops this process when a carriage return character is received from the keyboard. This occurs when the Enter key is pressed. The gets() function replaces the carriage return character with a null character that transforms the series of character in the array to a string.

Be sure that the array is large enough to hold all the characters that are entered at the keyboard!

The gets( ) function reads characters from the keyboard until the Enter key is pressed. Those characters are copied to the character array referenced in the argument passed to the gets( ) function. A null character is automatically added to the character array to create a string.

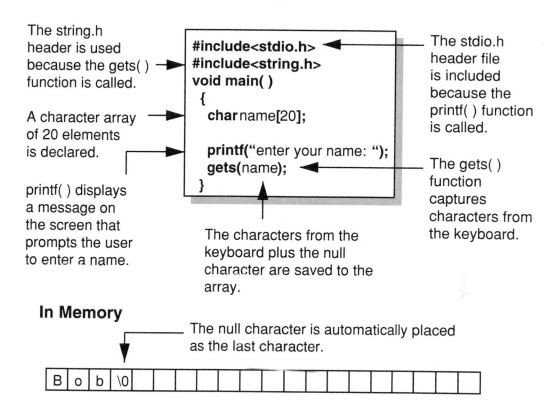

The string.h header is used because the gets( ) function is called.

A character array of 20 elements is declared.

printf( ) displays a message on the screen that prompts the user to enter a name.

```
#include<stdio.h>
#include<string.h>
void main( )
  {
    char name[20];

    printf("enter your name: ");
    gets(name);
  }
```

The stdio.h header file is included because the printf( ) function is called.

The gets( ) function captures characters from the keyboard.

The characters from the keyboard plus the null character are saved to the array.

In Memory

The null character is automatically placed as the last character.

| B | o | b | \0 | | | | | | | | | | | | | | | | |

Another Way to Read a String from the Keyboard
scanf( )

On the previous page the gets( ) function is used to read a string from the keyboard into an array. Only strings can be read using this function. The gets( ) function cannot read any other data type from the keyboard. For this purpose, use the scanf( ) function.

The scanf( ) function can read any data from the keyboard. This function requires two or more arguments. The first argument is a string that contains one or more *format specifiers*. A format specifier defines the data type of the data read from the keyboard. In the example on the opposite page, the %s format specifier signifies that data read from the keyboard is a string.

The next series of arguments are the locations in memory where the data is to be stored. Memory locations are referenced by specifying the name of the variable or array. There is an unlimited number of arguments that can be passed to the scanf( ) function. That is, this function can read more than one set of data from the keyboard at the same time.

Each format specifier within the first argument must have a corresponding type data argument. For example, the scanf( ) function cannot be called as shown below because the first argument informs that function that two strings are to be read from the keyboard and there is only one memory location specified.

scanf("%s %s", name);

There is a complete discussion on the techniques for using the scanf( ) function in Chapter 12. Refer to Chapter 12 before using this function in an application. A table of format specifiers is available in that chapter. The scanf( ) is also available in the C language.

The scanf( ) function is used to read characters from the keyboard and copy those characters to a previously defined character array. A null character is placed as the last character value in the character array to form a string. The scanf( ) function requires two arguments. The first argument contains the format specifier within quotations. The second argument contains the character array. The scanf( ) function takes more program memory and runs slower than the gets( ) function. This is because the scanf( ) function can read more than string values from the keyboard. A complete discussion about scanf( ) can be found in Chapter 12.

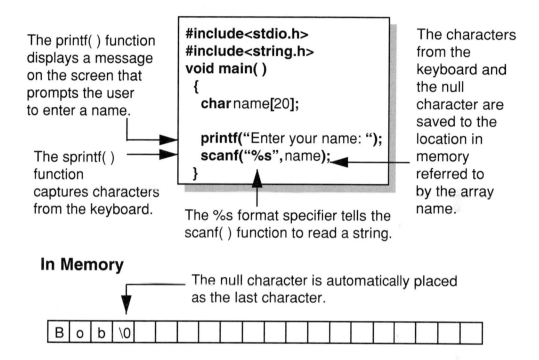

The printf( ) function displays a message on the screen that prompts the user to enter a name.

The sprintf( ) function captures characters from the keyboard.

```
#include<stdio.h>
#include<string.h>
void main( )
  {
    char name[20];

    printf("Enter your name: ");
    scanf("%s", name);
  }
```

The %s format specifier tells the scanf( ) function to read a string.

The characters from the keyboard and the null character are saved to the location in memory referred to by the array name.

In Memory

The null character is automatically placed as the last character.

B	o	b	\0																

Still Another Way to Read a String from the Keyboard with the Extraction Operator

A preferred method of reading a string or any data from the keyboard in C++ is by using the cin object with the extraction operator (>>). The *cin object* is an instance of the iostream class that reads data from the input stream, which in this case is the keyboard.

The *extraction operator* (>>) is then used to take the stream of data from the object on the left of the extraction operator and relay the data to the variable or array that is to the right of this operator. This is illustrated on the opposite page and in the statement below.

cin >> name;

In this example, the cout object followed by the insertion operator (<<) are used to display a message on the screen. (More about the cout object and the insertion operator in Chapter 12.) Next, the cin object and the extraction operator are used to read the response from the user and to place the data into the array name.

Notice that this procedure does not require the specification of the data type of the incoming data. The compiler knows the data type by referencing the data type of the variable used to store the data in memory.

Caution! Neither the cin operator nor the extraction operator determines if sufficient space in memory is allocated for the data. That is, 25 characters can be entered at the keyboard in the example shown on the opposite page. However, the program reserves space for only 20 characters. The statement that contains the insertion operator does not display any warning when reserved memory is exceeded. Review Chapter 7 and Chapter 12 for more information about objects and the extraction operator.

A preferred way to read a string from the keyboard in C++ is by using the extraction operator and the cin object. The extraction operator takes input from a data stream and places the data into memory.

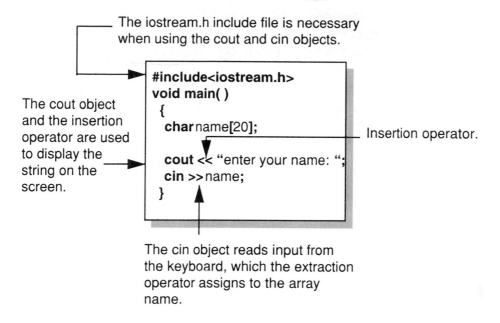

The iostream.h include file is necessary when using the cout and cin objects.

```
#include<iostream.h>
void main( )
  {
    char name[20];

    cout << "enter your name: ";
    cin >> name;
  }
```

The cout object and the insertion operator are used to display the string on the screen.

Insertion operator.

The cin object reads input from the keyboard, which the extraction operator assigns to the array name.

Terms You Should Know ...

○	<<	The insertion operator is used for data output.
○	>>	The extraction operator is used for data input.

Comparing Two Strings
strcmp( )

A string comparison is made by comparing each character of the two strings. This task is handled by the *strcmp*( ) function, which is available both in C and in C++. Behind the scenes, this function subtracts the binary representation of each character. If the results are zero, then the characters match, otherwise a mismatch occurs.

The strcmp( ) requires two arguments, which are the strings that are to be compared. After the comparison, the function returns to the calling statement a zero if there is a match or a non-zero number if there is not a match.

In the example on the opposite page, the strcmp( ) is called as part of the if statement. Here, the function is comparing the value of the array name to the string constant "Bob." After the comparison is made, the returning value is used as input to the if statement. That is, the return value from the strcmp( ) function is evaluated by the if statement.

However, there is a conflict between the strcmp( ) function and the if statement. A match returns a zero. An expression that is true in C++ evaluates to a non-zero value. In C++ a true expression is represented by a non-zero while a false statement is represented by a zero value.

Therefore, a match by the strcmp( ) is interpreted as a false by the if statement. See Chapter 6 for a full discussion about the if statement. This means that the printf( ) statement in the example will not be called. This condition can be remedied by using the NOT operator (!) preceding the strcmp( ) function call. The NOT operator reverses the logic of the expression that is being evaluated by the if statement. The zero value (returned by the strcmp() function) is treated as false. The NOT operator changes this to not false. A non-false value is, of course, true, which causes the if statement code block to execute.

The strcmp( ) function is used to determine if two strings are the same. This function determines if there is a match by subtracting the ASCII values of the string. The results are then returned to the calling program. A return value of zero means both strings are the same. A return value less than zero means the first argument's total ASCII value is less than that of the second argument. A return value of greater than zero means that the first argument's total ASCII value is more than that of the second argument.

The strcmp( ) function is used to compare the string that is assigned to the character array name with the string literal "Bob." →

```
#include<stdio.h>
#include<string.h>
void main( )
  {
    char name[80];

    printf("Enter your name: ");
    gets(name);
    if (!strcmp(name, "Bob"))
      printf("Hello, Bob");
  }
```

◄ The string "Hello, Bob" is displayed if the strcmp( ) function returns a zero that is reversed by the not operator. An if statement must evaluate to true (non-zero) to execute the if code block.

		First Argument			Second Argument		
○	Character	B	o	b	B	o	b
	ASCII Value	66	111	98	66	111	98

○ First Argument   66   111   98
Second Argument − 66 − 111 − 98
               0   0   0

Displaying a String
printf( )

There are several techniques that are used to display a string on the screen. Three of these are briefly discussed on the next several pages. A more thorough presentation of these techniques is contained in Chapter 12. The first method is to use the printf( ) function.

The printf() function requires at least one argument but it can receive any number of arguments. The first argument contains the string that is to be displayed on the screen. This argument can contain literal strings, such as the word, Hello, shown on the opposite page.

This string can also contain format specifiers, such as the %s format specifier in the example on the opposite page. A *format specifier* has two purposes. The first is to identify the data type of the data that will be displayed on the screen. In this example, the %s indicates that the data is a string. The second purpose is as a placeholder for the data. That is, the first character of the data will be printed within the string of the first argument at the location of the specifier.

The number of arguments that are passed to the printf( ) function is dependent on the number of data values that needs to be displayed. Each data value is passed as an argument to the function. These arguments must be separated by a comma and must have a corresponding format specifier in the string of the first argument.

The printf( ) function sends the string in the first argument to standard out. This is the display screen on most computers but can be redirected using an operating system command.

Make sure that the stdio.h include file is used in the program whenever the printf() function is called.

The printf( ) function is used to display values to the the standard out, which is usually the screen. This function requires one argument and can use more than one argument if data is to be displayed. The first argument contains the literal string that is to be displayed. The literal string also contains format specifiers as a placeholder for any data. A format specifier takes the position of the data within the literal string. Variables that represent the data become the remaining arguments to the function. The prinft( ) is discussed in detail in Chapter 12.

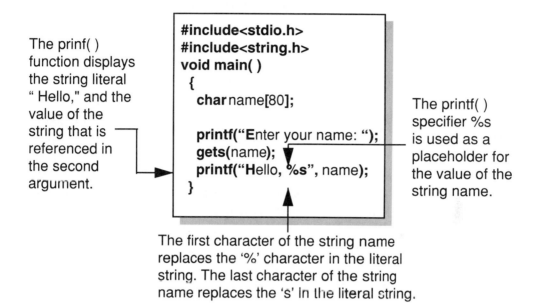

The prinf( ) function displays the string literal " Hello," and the value of the string that is referenced in the second argument.

```
#include<stdio.h>
#include<string.h>
void main( )
  {
    char name[80];

    printf("Enter your name: ");
    gets(name);
    printf("Hello, %s", name);
  }
```

The printf( ) specifier %s is used as a placeholder for the value of the string name.

The first character of the string name replaces the '%' character in the literal string. The last character of the string name replaces the 's' In the literal string.

Another Way to Display a String puts( )

The puts( ) function is also used to display a string to the screen. This function requires one argument, which is the name of the array that contains the string. Only the array name is required. The is no need to specify any elements of the array explicitly in the argument.

Remember, using the name of the array is a way to reference the address of the first element of the array. This is the starting point for the puts() function. This function evaluates the value of each element in the array. First, the function determines if the character is a null character. When a null character is recognized, the puts( ) function terminates and returns control back to the statement that called the function.

However, if the character is not a null character, then the puts( ) function displays the character to the standard output, which is typically the screen. The function loops through the array until the end of the string is reached.

Caution! Be sure that the array passed to the puts( ) function contains a null character. Remember, the puts( ) function requires a string—not simply an array of characters. The puts( ) continues to display values of consecutive memory location beginning with the first element of the array and ending with the null character. The function will not stop until a null character is found.

Another factor to keep in mind is that the puts( ) function displays only strings. Integer, floats, and other non-string data type cannot be processed by the puts( ) function. Instead, either the printf( ) function or the insertion operator can be used. The printf( ) function is discussed on the previous page and the insertion operator is briefly discussed in the next section. A more in-depth presentation of the insertion operator is given later in this book.

The puts( ) function displays the string referenced in the argument to the screen. This function takes up less program memory and runs faster than the printf( ) function. The puts( ) function can only display a string. The printf( ) function displays strings and variables of other data types.

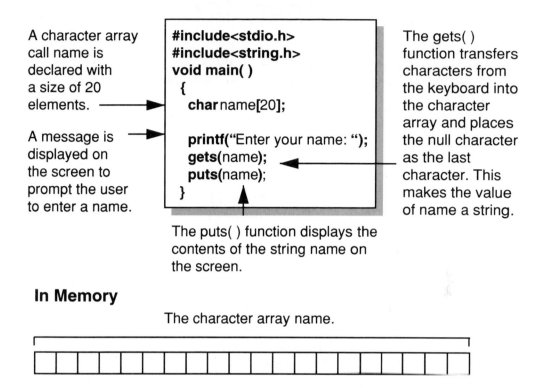

A character array call name is declared with a size of 20 elements. ——▶

```
#include<stdio.h>
#include<string.h>
void main( )
  {
    char name[20];

    printf("Enter your name: ");
    gets(name);
    puts(name);
  }
```

A message is displayed on the screen to prompt the user to enter a name. ——▶

The gets( ) function transfers characters from the keyboard into the character array and places the null character as the last character. This makes the value of name a string.

The puts( ) function displays the contents of the string name on the screen.

In Memory

The character array name.

Still Another Way to Display a String with the Insertion Operator

The insertion operator (<<) when coupled with the cout object will display a string on the screen. The cout object is an instance of the iostream class. This class contains data members and function members that manage the task of sending and receiving streams of data.

The insertion operator takes the object that appears to the right of the operator and transfers the stream to the object on the left side of the operator. That is, the string that is to be displayed is placed to the right of the insertion operator. When the statement is executed, the insertion operator sends this string to the cout object, which in turn displays the string on the screen.

In the example on the opposite page, a char array called name is declared. The strcpy( ) function initializes the array with string Bob. Remember, this function automatically places a null character as the last character in the array. Notice that the array size is large enough to hold the string including the null character. Beware that the strcpy( ) does not display a warning message if the array is too small for the string.

Next, the cout object and the insertion operator are used to display a string constant on the screen. The string constant is "Hello," and this value will not change during the life of the program.

The last statement of the program also uses the cout object and the insertion operator to display data to the screen. This time, however, the value of the array name is displayed on the screen.

The cout and the extraction operator can be used only in C++ programs. and can display any data type on the screen without having to use a format specifier.

A preferred way to display a string on the screen in C++ is by using the insertion operator and the cout object. The insertion operator takes output from a data stream and places the data on the screen.

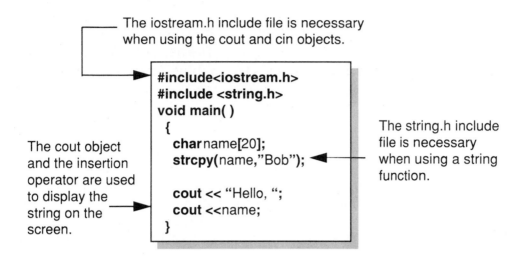

The iostream.h include file is necessary when using the cout and cin objects.

```
#include<iostream.h>
#include <string.h>
void main( )
  {
   char name[20];
   strcpy(name,"Bob");

   cout << "Hello, ";
   cout <<name;
  }
```

The string.h include file is necessary when using a string function.

The cout object and the insertion operator are used to display the string on the screen.

Terms You Should Know ...

○	<<	The insertion operator is used for data output.
○	>>	The extraction operator is used for data input.

Concatenating Strings
strcat( )

The technique for joining two strings together in C++ is different than the method used in other computer languages. The assignment operator (=) is commonly used in many languages to combine strings. However, this method will cause a compiler error in C++.

The easiest way to concatenate strings in C++ is to call the *strcat( )* function. This function requires two arguments. The first argument is the string that will receive characters that are in the second argument. Once this function has terminated, the first string will contain the second string. No changes are made to the second string.

Caution! The array used as the first argument of the strcat( ) function must be of a size to hold both strings. The strcat( ) function does not adjust the size of the array when the length of the resulting string extends beyond the size of the array. Failure to adjust the size of the array could result in a bug in the program that is very difficult to detect.

The technique for concatenating a string is illustrated in the example on the opposite page. Here the gets( ) function is used to read input from the keyboard, which is assigned to the array name.

Next, the string constant ",my name is Jim" is concatenated to the end of the array name. Finally, the new contents of the array name are displayed on the screen. Assuming that the user entered the name "Bob," this program will display "Bob, my name is Jim." on the screen.

This example includes two header files. The first is stdio.h, which contains the prototype for the gets( ) and printf( ) functions. The string.h header file contains the prototype for the strcat( ) function. The proper header file must be included in the program whenever the function is used in the source code.

The strcat( ) function concatenates the string referenced in the second argument to the end of the string referenced in the first argument. The first character in the string referenced in the second argument replaces the null character located at the end of the string referenced in the second argument.

The strcat( ) function is used to combine the value of the string name with the string literal ",my name is Jim."

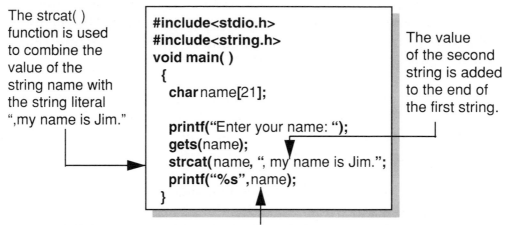

```
#include<stdio.h>
#include<string.h>
void main( )
  {
    char name[21];

    printf("Enter your name: ");
    gets(name);
    strcat(name, ", my name is Jim.";
    printf("%s",name);
  }
```

The value of the second string is added to the end of the first string.

If "Bob" was entered at the keyboard, the string "Bob, my name is Jim." is displayed on the screen.

In Memory

The value of the string name before strcat( ) is called.

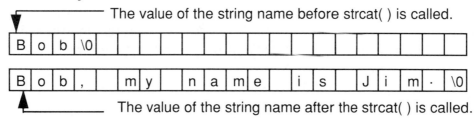

The value of the string name after the strcat( ) is called.

Determining the Length of a String strlen( )

The easiest way to determine the number of characters in a string is by calling the *strlen*( ) function, which is available in both C and C++. The strlen( ) function requires a single argument, which is the string that will be evaluated.

Only the name of the array that contains the string is passed to the strlen( ). This enables the function to reference the address of the first element of the array. Internally, the strlen( ) function evaluates each character in the array beginning with the first element.

The strlen( ) function moves throughout memory consecutively. This is possible because the declaration of an array reserves memory locations for the element consecutively. This is illustrated in the memory diagram located at the bottom of the opposite page.

If the value of an element is not a null character, then a counter internal to the strlen( ) function is incremented. However, if the character is a null character, then the strlen( ) function terminates by returning the value of the internal counter to the statement in the calling program.

Remember, the null character signals the end of the string. The return value is an integer that can be assigned to a variable by using the assignment operator. This technique is shown on the opposite page.

The value that is returned by this function does not include the null character. In the example, the string Bob is entered by the user. The memory diagram shows that four elements of the array are used although only the first three elements contain letters of the name. The return value of the strlen( ) function is three and not four as would be suspected when reviewing the memory diagram.

The strlen( ) function returns an integer value that represents the number of characters in the string that is referenced in the argument. The return value does not count the null character in the string.

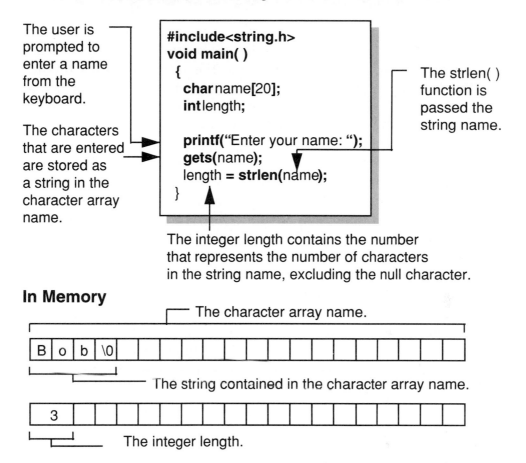

The user is prompted to enter a name from the keyboard.

The characters that are entered are stored as a string in the character array name.

```
#include<string.h>
void main( )
  {
    char name[20];
    int length;

    printf("Enter your name: ");
    gets(name);
    length = strlen(name);
  }
```

The strlen( ) function is passed the string name.

The integer length contains the number that represents the number of characters in the string name, excluding the null character.

In Memory

The character array name.

| B | o | b | \0 | | | | | | | | | | | | | | | | |

The string contained in the character array name.

| 3 | | | | | | | | | | | | | | | | | | | |

The integer length.

Determining the Length of a Substring strcspn( )

At times C++ programmers are required to locate the position of a substring from within a string of characters. The *strcspn*( ) makes this task easy. The strcspn( ) function requires two arguments, both of which are strings. The first argument contains the string that will be searched. The second argument is the string that is the search criteria. This function must also include the string.h header file in the source code.

The strcspn( ) function begins with the address of the first character of the string then proceeds to the next address and continues the evaluation until the null character is identified or until the search criteria is found.

For each character in the string, the stcspn( ) function compares that character to the search criteria. If they do not match, the internal counter is incremented and the function moves to the next address. If there is a match, then the function terminates by returning the value of the internal counter to the calling statement. The value that is returned corresponds to the position within the string immediately preceding the search criteria.

The return value can also be considered the size of the substring that ends with the search criteria. This technique is illustrated in the example on the opposite page. Here, the strcspn( ) function is told to return the size of the substring that ends with character "B." The value of the integer variable length is 11.

Notice how the data is depicted in memory. First, the program declares an integer variable called length. Space for an integer is then reserved in memory. Next, two strings are stored as constants in memory. Finally, the variable length is assigned the substring position by the strcspn( ) function. At this point, the compiler places the value 11 into the memory space that is reserved for the variable length.

The strcspn( ) function is used to determine the length of a substring of the string referenced in the first argument. The second argument contains a string that is used to determine the substring in the string referenced in the first argument. All characters up to, but not including, the first occurence of the value of the string referenced in the second argument are considered the substring of the string referenced in the first argument. The number of characters in the substring is returned as an integer.

The strcspn( ) function is told to find the number of characters in the substring that ends with the character "B."

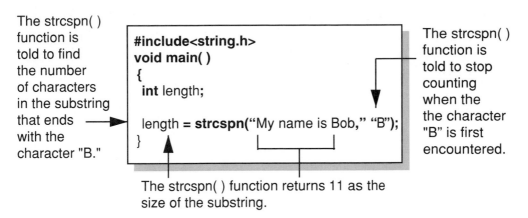

```
#include<string.h>
void main( )
{
 int length;

 length = strcspn("My name is Bob," "B");
}
```

The strcspn( ) function is told to stop counting when the the character "B" is first encountered.

The strcspn( ) function returns 11 as the size of the substring.

In Memory

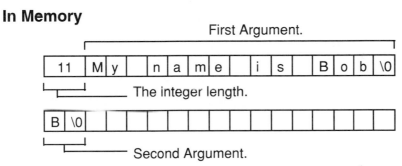

First Argument.

| 11 | M | y | | n | a | m | e | | i | s | | B | o | b | \0 |

The integer length.

| B | \0 | | | | | | | | | | | | | | | | | |

Second Argument.

Another Way to Determine the Length of a Substring strspn( )

In a typical C++ program, there is a need to copy a substring of an existing string. On the previous page, the *strcspn*( ) function is used to accomplish this task. However, this function accepted a single character search criteria. Once the criteria was found, the evaluation stopped.

The strspn( ) function operates similarly to the strcpn( ) function except that the search criteria is a series of characters rather than a single character. The return value of the strspn( ) is the last character in the search criteria.

On the opposite page there is an example that illustrates this technique. The strspn( ) function requires two arguments. The first argument is the string that will be searched. Although this example used a string constant, the strspn( ) function can also use the name of an array.

The second argument is the search string. The strspn( ) function begins matching each character of the search criteria against the characters contained in the first argument. The search ends when the last "b" in "Bob" is found. The value of the strspn( ) function's internal counter is then returned to the calling statement.

The memory diagram on the opposite page shows how memory is used by this program. First, space is reserved for the length variable. A value is not placed in this location until the return value from the stspn( ) function is assigned to the length variable.

Next, the string in the first argument of the strspn( ) function is placed into memory. This is followed by the string in the second argument. Notice that the null character is automatically stored as the final character in each of these arguments. This is because each argument is enclosed within double quotation marks.

The strspn( ) function returns the length of a substring of the string referenced in the first argument. The function stops counting the characters in the string referenced in the first argument when the characters stop matching the string referenced in the second argument. An integer is returned by the function.

The strspn( ) function is told to count the characters in "Bob Smith" as long as the characters match the string "Bob."

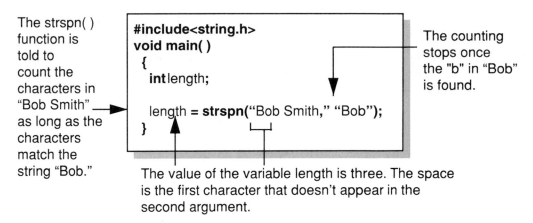

The counting stops once the "b" in "Bob" is found.

The value of the variable length is three. The space is the first character that doesn't appear in the second argument.

In Memory

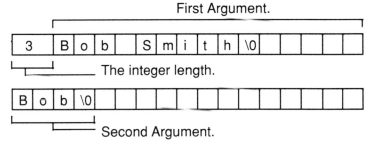

First Argument.

The integer length.

Second Argument.

Concatenating a Substring
strncat( )

A substring can be copied and placed at the end of another string by using the *strncat( )* function. This function requires three arguments. The first argument is the string that will receive the substring. The second argument is the string that contains the substring. The third argument is an integer that specifies the size of the substring.

In the example on the opposite page, the strncat( ) function is used to add the substring "Smith" to the string "Bob". In the first statement, the program reserves space to hold both the original string and the substring. This location is for the array name.

Next, the strcpy( ) function is called to copy the string "Bob," to the array name. Notice that the null character is automatically placed in the array.

The strncat( ) function is called. The array name is used as the first argument. This is really the pointer to the address of the first element in the array. The second argument is the string constant "Smith & Jones." This is the string that will be searched.

Starting with the first character of the second argument, the strncat( ) function begins copying the first five characters into the memory reserved for the array name. The first character that is copied, "S," replaces the null character in the array name. The remaining characters in the substring fill consecutive memory locations in the array name. The strncat( ) function automatically places a null character as the last character in the array name.

Notice that the last line in the memory diagram on the opposite page contains the final contents of the space reserved for array name. This line is actually the first line and not a new block of memory.

The strncat( ) function concatenates part of the string referenced in the second argument to the string referenced in the first argument. The integer value that is referenced in the third argument specifies the number of characters that are to be concatenated.

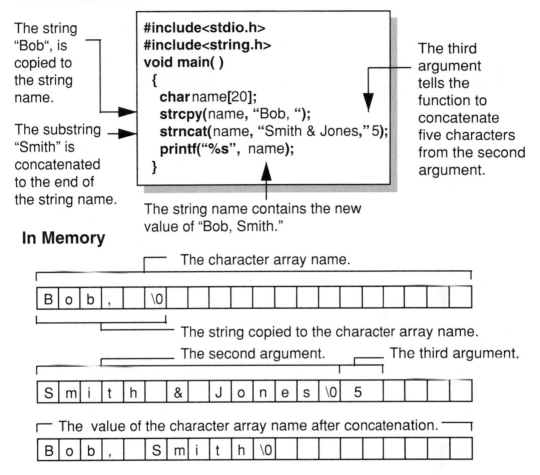

The string "Bob", is copied to the string name.

The substring "Smith" is concatenated to the end of the string name.

```
#include<stdio.h>
#include<string.h>
void main( )
  {
    char name[20];
    strcpy(name, "Bob, ");
    strncat(name, "Smith & Jones," 5);
    printf("%s", name);
  }
```

The third argument tells the function to concatenate five characters from the second argument.

The string name contains the new value of "Bob, Smith."

In Memory

The character array name.

| B | o | b | , | | \0 | | | | | | | | | | | | | | |

The string copied to the character array name.

The second argument.   The third argument.

| S | m | i | t | h | | & | | J | o | n | e | s | \0 | 5 | | | | |

The value of the character array name after concatenation.

| B | o | b | , | | | S | m | i | t | h | \0 | | | | | | | |

Comparing Substrings
strncmp( )

Two strings can be compared by using the *strncmp*( ) function. This function requires three arguments. The first argument is a string, as is the second argument. These are the strings that will be compared. The third argument is an integer that specifies the number of characters that are to be compared.

In the example on the opposite page, the strncmp( ) function is told to compare the first three characters of strings in the first and second argument.

The strncmp( ) function compares each character of the strings by subtracting the character's ASCII value. This is illustrated at the bottom of the opposite page. The function first totals the ASCII values of both strings before subtracting the sums. This is the value that is returned to the calling statement.

A return value of zero signifies that both strings match. However, a non-zero value indicates a mismatch. A word of caution. The return value of the strncmp( ) function must not be equated as a C++ true or false value. Actually, the return value is opposite of the true and false values.

A false value in C++ is a zero value and a true value is any non-zero value. When the strncmp( ) function is called, in effect, the statement asks if the two strings are equal. The response from the function should be a true or false. However, the return value is not a true or false value. Instead, the return value is the result of subtracting the ASCII values of both strings.

Hint! Since the return value of the strncmp( ) function is opposite of the values that represent true and false, the NOT (!) operator can be used to evaluate the results of the strncmp( ) as a true or false value.

The strncmp( ) function is used to determine if the first several characters of two strings match. There are three arguments required by this function. The first two arguments reference the strings that are to be compared. The third argument is an integer that contains the number of characters that are to be compared. A return value of zero means that there is a match. A return value of less than zero means that the specified characters of the first argument have a lower ASCII value than that of the first argument. A return value of more than zero means that the specified characters of the first argument have a higher ASCII value than that of the second argument.

The strncmp( ) function is used to determine if the first three characters in both the strings match.

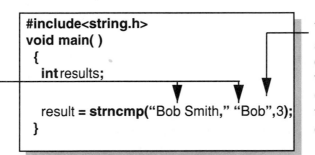

```
#include<string.h>
void main( )
{
    int results;

    result = strncmp("Bob Smith," "Bob",3);
}
```

The third argument determines the number of characters that will be compared.

		First Argument			Second Argument		
Character		B	o	b	B	o	b
ASCII Value		66 + 111 + 98 = 275			275 = 66 + 111 + 98		

275	String Entered from the Keyboard.
- 275	String Literal.
0	Returned Value.

Locating Character within a String strpbrk( )

The *strpbrk*() is used to locate a character within a string of characters. Two arguments are required by this function. The first argument is the string that will be searched. The second argument is the search criteria. When the search criteria is found, the function returns a pointer to the character within the string. A null pointer is returned if there is not a match.

In the example on the opposite page, the strpbrk( ) function is told to find the first occurrence of either "S" or "m" in the string "Bob Smith." The search begins with the left-most character and continues until either one of the search criteria is found or the null character is detected.

When the strpbrk( ) function terminates, a pointer is returned to the calling statement. In this example, the substring pointer is assigned the address containing the character "S" in the first argument. Notice that the character and the substring remain at their existing memory locations. The pointer enables the program to easily access the value within the string contained in the first argument.

For example, assume that the substring "Smith" needs to be used by another function. Instead of copying this substring to a new location in memory, the strpbrk( ) function can be used to identify the address where the substring resides in memory. Once this address is known, the address can be used as an argument to the other function.

Remember, a pointer is a reference to an address in memory. This is the same as if the name of a character array is used in an expression. Both reference the address of a character. As long as the array of characters pointed to by either the pointer or by the name of an array ends with a null character, both are acceptable arguments to functions that manipulate a string. This becomes obvious by looking at the memory diagram at the bottom of the opposite page.

The strpbrk( ) function returns a character pointer to the first character in the string referenced in the first argument that is contained in the string that is referenced in the second argument.

The first occurence of either character is "S."

The address that contains "S" is assigned to the character pointer Substring.

The strpbrk( ) function is told to find the first occurence of "S" or "m."

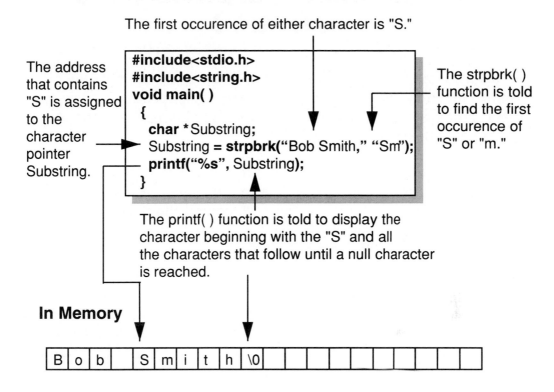

```
#include<stdio.h>
#include<string.h>
void main( )
  {
    char *Substring;
    Substring = strpbrk("Bob Smith," "Sm");
    printf("%s", Substring);
  }
```

The printf( ) function is told to display the character beginning with the "S" and all the characters that follow until a null character is reached.

In Memory

| B | o | b | | S | m | i | t | h | \0 | | | | | | | | | | | | |

Locating the First Occurrence of a Substring in a String strstr( )

A substring can be copied from a string by using the combination of the strstr( ) function and the *stcmp*( ). The strstr( ) function requires two arguments. The first argument is the string that is to be searched. The second argument is the search criteria.

The strstr( ) function returns a pointer to the first character in the string that matches the search criteria. The return value can then be used as input to the strcmp( ) function. This technique is illustrated below.

```
char lname[40], *sub;
sub = strstr("Bob Smith," "Smith");
strcmp(lname, sub);
```

In the example on the opposite page, the strstr( ) function is used to find the location of the substring "Smith" in the string "Bob Smith." The pointer to the first character in the substring, "S," is returned and assigned to the substring character pointer variable.

The printf( ) function then uses the substring pointer to display the substring "Smith" on the screen. Notice that in the example discussed on this page, the substring value is copied to another memory location. In the example on the opposite page, a copy of the substring is not made. Instead, the program points to the appropriate segment of the search string.

When possible avoid making unnecessary copies of data. Copying data to another location in memory is time-consuming and wastes resources. Use pointers instead.

The strstr( ) function returns a pointer to the portion of the string referened in the first argument that matches the string referenced in the second argument.
If the string referenced in the second argument isn't found in the string referenced in the first argument, then a null character is returned.

The character pointer Substring contains the address of the "S."

The strstr( ) function searches the string "Bob Smith" for the string "Smith."

The second argument contains the string that is to be found in the first argument.

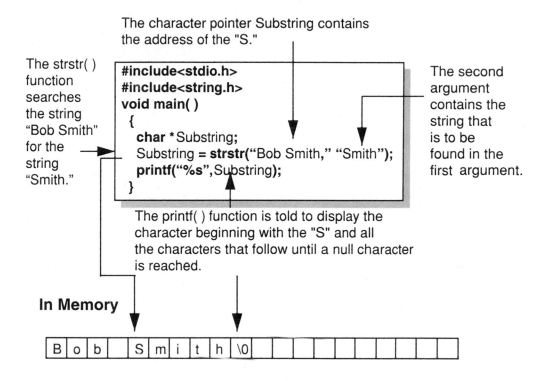

```
#include<stdio.h>
#include<string.h>
void main( )
  {
  char *Substring;
  Substring = strstr("Bob Smith," "Smith");
  printf("%s",Substring);
  }
```

The printf( ) function is told to display the character beginning with the "S" and all the characters that follow until a null character is reached.

In Memory

B	o	b		S	m	i	t	h	\0										

Dividing a String into Several Substrings strtok( )

A string can be divided into several substrings by using the *strtok*( ) function. Before this function can be used, each substring must be delimited by the same character, which is called the *token*. For example, a token can be a space. This means that each word that ends with a space will be considered a separate substring.

In the example on the opposite page, the string contains three words: Bob, Mary, and Joe. Each word ends with a space character. Therefore, the strtok( ) function can easily be used to copy each word to a separate variable or, as is the case in this example, display each word separately on the screen.

The strtok( ) function requires two arguments. The first argument is the string that will be searched. The second argument is the character that is to be used as the separator, or token, within the string.

When the strtok( ) function is called the first time, a pointer is returned to the calling statement that points to "B" in Bob. The next time that the strtok( ) function is called, the name of the string is replaced with a null character. This instructs the function to use the previous string and to find the next space character. On the second pass, Mary is located and displayed on the screen.

Any character can be used as a token as long as the characters appear at the end of each substring within the search string. For example, it is common to have a string that ends with a line feed character that represents a record of data. Within the line are substrings that are fields of the record.

Each field could be separated with a comma. This allows the strtok( ) function to be used to identify substrings (fields) by using the comma character as the token.

The strtok( ) function breaks a string into substrings by using special characters within the string to indicate where substrings begin. These special characters are called tokens. The first argument to the function contains the reference to the string. The second argument contains the character that is to be used as the token. On subsequent calls of the function, the first argument is replaced with a null.

The strtok( ) function is used to divide the string name into substrings.

```
#include<stdio.h>
#include<string.h>
void main( )
  {
    char *Substring, name[80];
    strcpy(name, "Bob Mary Joe");
    Substring = strtok(name, " ");
    printf("%s\n",Substring);
    Substring = strtok(NULL," ");
    printf("%s\n", Substring);
  }
```

The space character is used as the token that divides the string into three substrings.

First, "Bob" is assigned to the character pointer substring. Next, "Mary" is assigned to the character pointer substring.

The second time that the strtok( ) function is called, the null character replaces the string name.

In Memory

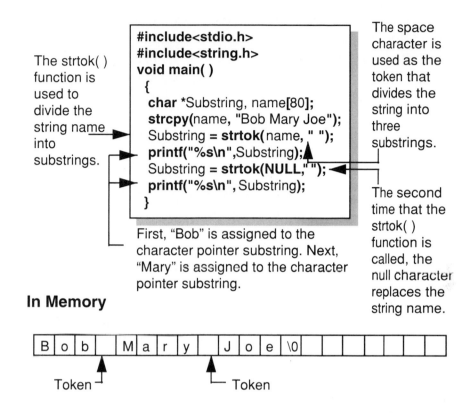

| B | o | b | | M | a | r | y | | J | o | e | \0 | | | | | | |

Token ⬆   ⬆ Token

Working with Structures

Structures

A typical C++ application uses an assortment of variables. These variables can be related by using a structure. A *structure* enables like and unlike data types to be grouped under one name.

A structure can be used to organize variables into a database record. Each data member of the structure represents a field of the record.

In the example on the opposite page, a structure called employee is defined. The structure definition begins with the keyword *struct* followed by the name of the structure.

French braces are used to group variables that are to become members of the function. Each statement that defines a structure member must end with a semicolon. The definition of the structure is completed by placing a semicolon at the end of the closed French brace.

The name of the structure—called the tag—is employee. Each variable that is associated with the structure is called a *member of the structure*. These are first_name, last_name, and employee_number; each is a member of the employee structure.

Notice that members of the structure are defined exactly as they are defined outside the structure. All the rules that apply to defining a variable also apply when defining a variable as a member of a structure.

There isn't any memory allocated when a structure is defined. Although variables are defined as members of the structure, these variables are not declared. Memory is allocated only when a structure is declared.

A structure is a collection of variables. Each variable in this collection can be of a different type. Structures are typically used to group a set of related variables such as a record for a database application.

Structure Definition

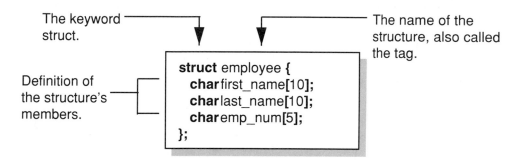

The keyword struct.

The name of the structure, also called the tag.

Definition of the structure's members.

```
struct employee {
    char first_name[10];
    char last_name[10];
    char emp_num[5];
};
```

Terms You Should Know ...

	Member	A data item that is contained within the structure.
	Tag	The name given to the structure. The tag is used to declare an instance of the structure.
	struct	The keyword that is used to direct the compiler to create a structure.

A Structure at Work

The *structure definition* is a template that can be used to replicate the structure in the program. A copy of a structure is called an *instance of the structure*. Each instance is given a unique name. Creating an instance of a structure is also called *declaring an instance* of the structure.

In the example on the opposite page, the structure is called employee and contains the employee's name and the employee's number. The name of the structure is used to declare an instance of the structure.

The declaration statement consists of two parts: the name of the structure followed by the name of the instance. The statement must end with a semicolon. The following example is a declaration of an instance of employee.

employee record;

Notice in this example that the name of the structure, employee, is followed by the name of the instance, record.

Once an instance of a structure is declared, memory is then set aside for members of the structure. Memory is allocated based upon the order in which members are placed in the structure's definition. This is illustrated in the memory diagram on the bottom of the opposite page.

Each member of the instance of the structure can be accessed by specifying the name of the instance then the name of the member separated by the *dot operator* as shown below. A member of an instance can be used in the program as if it were a variable.

record.emp_num.

Define the structure called employee outside the main( ) function. No memory is reserved when the structure is defined.

A single copy of the structure is declared and called record. Memory is now reserved.

The user is prompted to enter data, which is assigned to members of the structure.

Members of the structure are referenced by specifying the name of the instance of the structure followed by the dot operator then the name of the data member.

```
#include <iostream.h>
struct employee {
    char first_name[10];
    char last_name[10];
    int emp_num[5];
};
void main( )
{
    employee record;
    cout << "First  Name: ";
    cin >>  record.first_name;
    cout << "Last Name: ";
    cin >> record. last_name;
    cout << "Number: ";
    cin >> record.emp_num;
}
```

In Memory

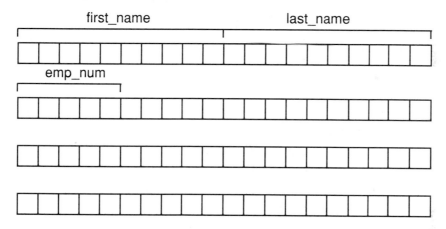

first_name   last_name

emp_num

Running the Sample Program

The program illustrated on the previous page is a typical application that uses a structure to organize data under one name. First, the program defines the structure called employee. This is a global definition since it is defined outside the main( ) function. Within the main( ) function, an instance of the employee structure is declared. This instance is called record.

The next statement displays a prompt on the screen. The prompt tells the user to enter the first name of the employee. There are three components to this statement.

First is the *cout object*, which is used to display text and data to the standard out, normally the screen. Then there is the *insertion operator* (<<). This operator takes data (a stream) referenced to the right of the insertion operator and places the data into the object to the left of the insertion operator. The final piece of the statement is the data that will be inserted into the cout object. When this statement is executed, the text "First Name:" will be displayed on the screen.

The next line in the program receives characters from the keyboard and assigns those characters to the structure member. This statement also consists of three parts.

The first is the *cin object*, which reads input from the standard in, normally the keyboard. Then there is the *extraction operator* (>>). The extraction operator removes characters from the cin object and places them into the structure member that appears to the right of the extraction operator. In this case, the structure member is record.first_name. This process continues until all the data is read into memory.

A more complete discussion about the insertion and extraction operators is presented in Chapter 12.

```
First Name: Mary
Last  Name: Jones
Number: 35
```

In Memory

| M | a | r | y | \0 | | | | | J | o | n | e | s | \0 | | | |

| 3 | 5 | | | | | | | | | | | | | | | | | | | | | | | |

| | | | | | | | | | | | | | | | | | | | | | | | | |

| | | | | | | | | | | | | | | | | | | | | | | | | |

Remember ...

	The size of a char is one byte.
	The cin >> sequence places a NULL ('\0') as the last character of the data entered from the keyboard (standard in), which converts the array of characters to a string.
	All data is saved in memory as a binary value, not the ASCII value, as illustrated above.

Another Way to Declare an Instance

An instance of a structure is declared by using the tag name of the structure followed by the instance name. This is illustrated on the previous page and below.

```
employee record;
```

Another way an instance of a structure is declared is when the structure is defined. This technique is illustrated in examples on the opposite page and below. Notice that the name of the instance is inserted between the closed French brace and the semicolon.

```
struct employee{
    char first_name[10];
    char last_name[10];
    int age;
} record;
```

An instance declared as part of the structure definition is used just like an instance that is declared by using the tag name of the structure. Members of the structure are accessed the same way regardless of how the instance is declared.

The scope of the instance depends on where the instance is declared. If the declaration occurs outside a code block, then the instance is global. If the declaration occurs inside a code block, then the instance is local.

The tag name of the structure is optional when an instance is declared as part of the structure definition.

An instance of a structure can be created as part of the structure's definition.

The structure remains defined outside of the the main( ) function.

However, declaration of record as an instance of the employee structure occurs as part of the definition of the structure.

```cpp
#include <iostream.h>
struct  employee {
   char  first_name[10];
   char  last_name[10];
   char  emp_num[5];
} record;
void main( )
  {
    cout << " First  Name: ";
    cin >> record.first_name;
    cout << " Last Name: ";
    cin >> record.last_name;
    cout << " Number: ";
    cin >> record.emp_num;
  }
```

```cpp
#include <iostream.h>
struct {
   char first_name[10];
   char last_name[10];
   char emp_num[5];
} record;
void main( )
  {
    cout << "First  Name: ";
    cin >> record.first_name;
    cout << "Last Name: ";
    cin >> record.last_name;
    cout << "Number: ";
    cin >> record.emp_num;
  }
```

Whenever an instance of a structure is declared as part of the structure's definition, the name of the structure becomes optional.

However, another instance of the structure cannot be declared within the body of the program unless the structure is named.

Assigning Values to Structure Members

Any member of a structure can be accessed by referencing the name of the instance of the structure followed by the dot operator then the name of the member of the structure. This technique is illustrated in the first example at the top of the next page. Here, record is declared as an instance of the structure employee.

In this example, string values are then assigned to the first_name, last_name by using the string copy function. A more complete discussion about strings and the string copy function is covered in Chapter 13.

Members of an instance are used the same way as any data of the same data type is used in a C++program.

Values can also be assigned to one or more members of an instance when the instance is declared. This technique is illustrated in the second example on the next page. Here, the equal operator is used to assign the values within the French braces to each member of the instance.

Values within the French braces must appear in the same order as the order in which the members appear in the structure. String values must be enclosed within double quotation marks. Character values must be enclosed within single quotation marks. Numeric data types must not be enclosed in quotation marks. Values must be separated by commas. Values must obey the rules for the data type of the structure member.

Some programmers use this technique to initialize members of an instance with default values. Those values can be overwritten later in the program if the need arises.

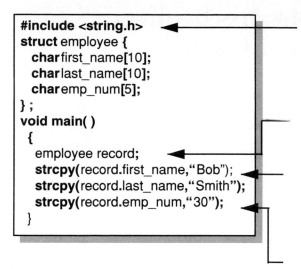

```
#include <string.h>
struct employee {
  char first_name[10];
  char last_name[10];
  char emp_num[5];
} ;
void main( )
  {
    employee record;
    strcpy(record.first_name,"Bob");
    strcpy(record.last_name,"Smith");
    strcpy(record.emp_num,"30");
  }
```

The string.h header file must be
included with this program since the
strcpy( ) function is used to assign
values to the first_name
and last_name members.

An instance of the structure
employee is declared as record.

The strcpy( ) function is used
to copy string values to the
first_name and last_name data
members of the record instance
of the employee structure.

The value 30 is assigned to the
emp_num member of the structure.

Values can also be assigned
to members of a structure
when the instance of the
structure is declared.

Notice that the order of the
values in the declaration
corresponds to the order
of the members within the
structure.

```
struct employee {
  char first_name[10];
  char last_name[10];
  char emp_num[5];
} ;

void main( )
  {
  employee record = {"Bob," "Smith," "30"}
  }
```

Multiple Instances

An advantage to using structure is that it can easily be replicated within a program by using a single statement. Remember that a structure is really a template that defines how variables of different data types are to be grouped together under a single name. The template can be used repeatedly to create independent copies of the structure.

In the first example on the opposite page, two copies of the structure employee are created. Each copy is an instance of the structure.

Although this example uses two lines to declare instances of the structure employee, the same results could have been achieved by using a single line as illustrated below:

employee record1, record2;

Multiple instances of a structure can also be declared by creating an *array of instances*. This is illustrated in the second example on the opposite page. Here, the instances are created when the structure is defined.

The name of the instance (record) is followed by the number of instances that are to be contained in the array. In this case, two instances of the structure employee are declared. The number of instances must be enclosed with square brackets. This is called an *index number*.

Each instance can be accessed by using the name of the instance followed by the appropriate index number. In this example, different first names are assigned to each instance. An array of instances of a structure can also be defined outside of the structure's definition. Here's how this is done:

employee record[2];

More than one instance of a structure can be declared by repeating the name of the structure and using a different instance name.

Two instances called record1 and record2 are declared and values are assigned to each data member of the structure.

```
struct employee {
    char first_name[10];
    char last_name[10];
    char emp_num[5];
};

void main( )
{
    employee record1 = {"Bob," "Smith," "30"};
    employee record2 = {"Mary," "Jones," "45"};
}
```

In Memory

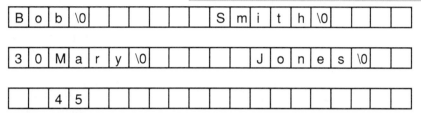

B	o	b	\0						S	m	i	t	h	\0			

3	0	M	a	r	y	\0				J	o	n	e	s	\0		

		4	5														

```
#include <string.h>
struct employee {
    char first_name[10];
    char last_name[10];
    char emp_num[5];
} record[2];
void main( )
{
    strcpy(record[0].first_name,"Bob");
    strcpy(record[1].first_name,"Mary");
}
```

Another way to create multiple instances of a structure is to declare an array of structures.

Remember, the declaration of any array contains the total number of instances. Here, two instances are created.

Reference each array by using the array's index. Remember, an array's index begins with zero.

Assigning Values
to Multiple Instances

Values can be assigned to an array of instances of a structure when the array is declared. This is accomplished by placing values within French braces, as is illustrated in the first example on the opposite page.

Two instances of the employee structure are declared as an array of instances. The name of the array is record. Values are assigned to each instance by using a pair of nested values. Each pair is enclosed with French braces and the data sets are separated by a comma. An outer set of French braces is necessary to enclose the nested pair of data.

Values can also be assigned to each member of the instances individually throughout the program. The assignment does not need to be made when the instance is declared. This technique is shown below:

strcpy(record[1].first_name, "Bob");

In this example shown above, the string copy function strcpy( ) is called to copy the string "Bob" to the first_name element of the second array of the record instances. Remember, the first element of any array begins with zero index number.

A major advantage of working with instances of a structure is that the values contained in one instance can be assigned to another instance by using a simple assignment statement. This is pointed out in the second example.

record2 = record1;

There are only two rules that must be followed. Values must be assigned to the first instance. Both instances must have the same structure definition.

Values can be assigned to multiple instances when each instance is created. Here is another way to create an array of structures. Each set of values is assigned to the appropriate instance of the array of structures.

```
struct employee {
   char first_name[10];
   char last_name[10];
   char emp_num[5];
} ;

void main( )
   {
   employee record[2] = {{" Bob," "Smith", "30"}, {"Mary," "Jones," "45"}};
   }
```

Copying Values of One Instance to Another Instance

Values of members of a structure can be copied to another instance of the same structure by using the assignment operator (=).

Here, the members of record2 contain the same values as that of the members of record1.

```
struct employee {
   char first_name[10];
   char last_name[10];
   char emp_num[5];
} ;
void main( )
   {
   employee record1 = {"Bob","Smith", "30"};
   employee record2;
   record2 = record1;
   }
```

Structures within Structures

A structure can become part of another structure's definition by creating an instance of the structure within the other structureís definition. This technique is shown in the example on the opposite page.

First, a structure, called payroll, is defined as having salary as the only member of this structure. Next, another structure is defined. This is the employee structure that we have used throughout this section of the book.

Notice that the first line within the body of the employee structure declares an instance of the payroll structure. This instance is called comp. This technique is called *nesting structures*.

Although an instance of the payroll structure is declared within the employee structure, no memory is reserved for this instance until an instance of the employee structure is declared. At that time space is reserved in memory for both instances.

Since the instance comp is actually part of the employee structure, the program must reference both the instance of the employee structure and the comp instance when accessing the salary structure member.

Members of the nested structure are treated as members of the outer structure. In this example, members of the nested structure are the first members of the outer structure.

The memory diagram on the opposite page shows the block of memory reserved for the record instance of the employee structure. The first four bytes are for the salary member of the comp instance of the payroll structure.

In this program, two distinct structures are defined: payroll and employee.

However, the employee structure declares an instance of the payroll structure. This is called a nested structure.

An instance of the employee structure is declared. This instance also includes the instance of the payroll structure called comp.

Values are assigned to members of the record instance of the employee structure.

```c
#include <string.h>
struct payroll{
  float salary;
};
struct employee {
    payroll comp;
    char first_name[10];
    char last_name[10];
    char emp_num[5];
};
void main( )
  {
  employee record;
    strcpy(record first_name, "Bob");
    strcpy(record last_name, "Smith");
    strcpy(record emp_num, "30");
    record.comp.salary = 25000;
  }
```

Notice that to assign or reference the value of a member of the nested structure, the name of the instance of the nested structure is used.

In Memory

25000	B	o	b	\0					S	m	i	t	h	\0

					3	0														

Remember ...

○	The size of a float is four bytes.

Passing Elements of a Structure to a Function

An element of a structure can be used throughout C++ as a variable that is not a member of a structure. Non-structure members (variables) are covered in the first chapter of this book.

Therefore, there is functionally no difference between the age variable and the record.age variable shown below. This assumes that the age variable is declared as an integer and the record.age variable is declared as an integer member of the record structure.

$$age = 30;$$
$$record.age = 30;$$

Values of a structure member can be passed as an argument to a function the same way a variable can be passed to a function. This is illustrated in the example on the opposite page. Notice that record.age is passed to the display( ) function when the display( ) function is called.

Only the value of record.age is passed to the function. Therefore, a local variable of the same data type must be declared within the formal argument of the display( ) to accept the value. This is illustrated with the statement shown on the opposite page and below.

$$void\ display\ (int\ age);$$

Both record.age and age have the same value of 30. The record.age member of the instance record receives this value through an assignment statement within the program. The age variable receives this value by passing the record.age element of the instances record to the function display( ).

The memory diagram on the opposite page illustrates that the value 30 appears in two memory locations, although not necessarily sequential locations.

Passing by Value

An element of a structure can be passed to a function by referencing the name of the structure and the element as the argument to the function.

The variable that will hold the argument is declared as the same data type as the element of the structure.

Passing the value of an element actually makes a copy of the value that is assigned to the element.

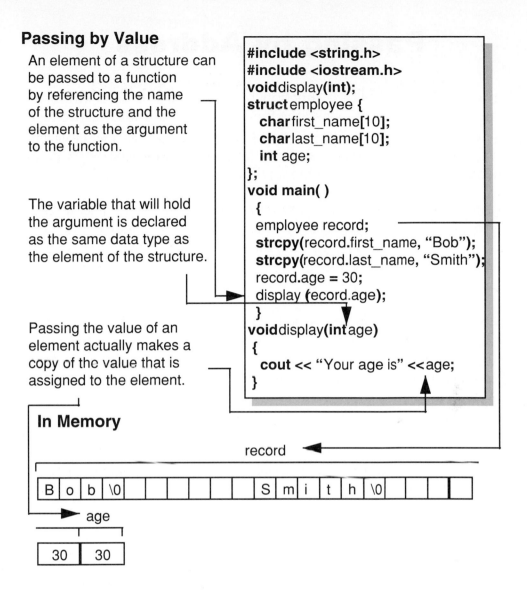

```cpp
#include <string.h>
#include <iostream.h>
void display(int);
struct employee {
    char first_name[10];
    char last_name[10];
    int age;
};
void main( )
{
    employee record;
    strcpy(record.first_name, "Bob");
    strcpy(record.last_name, "Smith");
    record.age = 30;
    display (record.age);
}
void display(int age)
{
    cout << "Your age is" << age;
}
```

In Memory

record

B	o	b	\0							S	m	i	t	h	\0				

age

30	30

Passing by Address

Data can be shared with a function by enclosing the data within the parameter of the function when the function is called. There are two techniques that can be used. These are to pass by value or the *pass by address*, also called *passing by reference*. Both techniques are fully discussed in the previous section, "Passing Elements of a Structure to a Function."

The previous page contains examples of passing an element of a structure to a function by value. That is, only the value of the element is transferred, creating two copies of the value in memory. When the function returns control back to the calling statement, the second copy of the value is removed from memory.

However, a function can be instructed to use a member of an instance of a structure directly. That is, the value of the structure member is not copied. This is made possible by passing the address of the structure member to the function. This technique is illustrated on the opposite page and below.

```
display(&record.age);
```

Recall from the Chapter 2 discussion regarding C++ operators that the ampersand operator (&) references the address of a variable. Without the ampersand operator, the compiler references the value that is represented by the variable.

Within the formal parameter of the function definition there is a pointer variable declared. The asterisk operator (*) is used to declare the variable as a pointer variable. Recall, a pointer variable is a variable that contains an address of another variable. In this case, the address of record.age.

Notice that there is only one copy of the value of the record.age instance in memory. This is because the function uses the same value and does not make a copy of the value.

An address of an element of a structure is passed to a function by referencing the address of the element. This is done by placing an ampersand in front of the reference to the name of the structure and element.

The variable that will hold the argument is declared as a pointer to the same data type as the element.

Passing the address of an element uses the actual value of the element. The value is not copied to another variable.

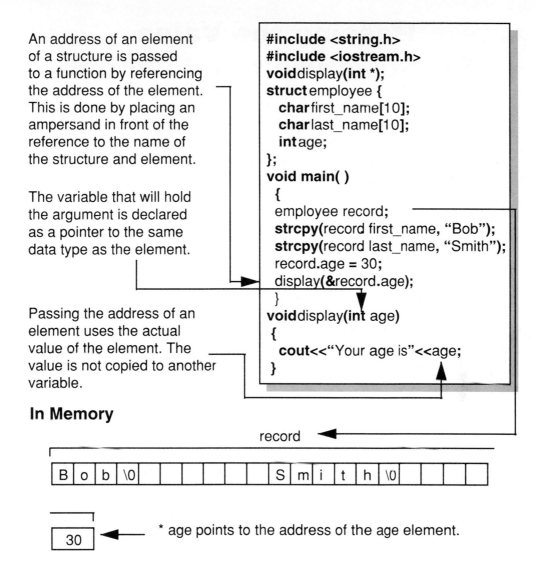

```
#include <string.h>
#include <iostream.h>
void display(int *);
struct employee {
    char first_name[10];
    char last_name[10];
    int age;
};
void main( )
{
    employee record;
    strcpy(record first_name, "Bob");
    strcpy(record last_name, "Smith");
    record.age = 30;
    display(&record.age);
}
void display(int age)
{
    cout<<"Your age is"<<age;
}
```

In Memory

record

B	o	b	\0						S	m	i	t	h	\0			

30

* age points to the address of the age element.

Passing the Value
of a Structure to a Function

C++ programmers frequently have a need to make the entire instance of a structure available to a function. Like working with members of an instance, there are two techniques that are available to give a function access to an instance. These are passing the instance of the structure by value or by address (reference).

The example on the opposite page illustrates the technique of *passing an instance of a structure by value.* That is, only the values of each member of an instance are available to the structure.

In the function call, shown below, the name of the instance called record is passed as the only argument to the display( ) function. Within the formal parameter in the function definition is the declaration of another instance of the same function. In this example, rec2 is the name of the new instance.

display(record);

When the instance rec2 is declared, the compiler automatically copies the values of each member of the record instance to the corresponding member of the rec2 instance.

Members of the new instance, rec2, are referenced by using the dot operator. This is shown within the definition of display( ) on the opposite page and below.

rec2.age;

The memory diagram illustrates how both instances are placed in memory. Keep in mind that although the members of each instance are placed at sequential addresses in memory, both instances may not actually be sequentially located in memory.

The entire structure can be passed as an argument to a function by specifying the name of the instance of the structure as the argument to the function.

Values from the first instance (record) are automatically copied to the second instance (rec2).

```
#include <string.h>
#include <iostream.h>
struct employee {
    char first_name[10];
    char last_name[10];
    int age;
};
void display(employee);
void main( )
{
    employee record;
    strcpy(record first_name, "Bob");
    strcpy(record last_name, "Smith");
    record.age = 30;
    display(record);
}
void display(employee rec2)
{
    cout<<"Your age is"<<rec2.age;
}
```

Notice that the structure is defined before the name of the structure is used in the prototype of the function.

A second instance of the structure is declared within the function.

In Memory

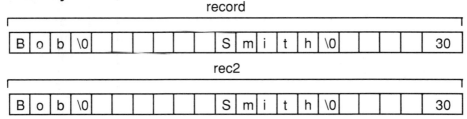

record

| B | o | b | \0 | | | | | | S | m | i | t | h | \0 | | | | 30 |

rec2

| B | o | b | \0 | | | | | | S | m | i | t | h | \0 | | | | 30 |

Passing the Address of a Structure to a Function

There are two ways to pass information to a function. These are by value and by address (reference). The technique for passing a structure by value is presented on the previous pages. This section discusses how to *pass a structure by address*.

In the example on the opposite page, the name of the instance (record) of the structure is passed as an argument to the function display( ). Notice that the name of the function is preceded by the ampersand operator (&). This operator instructs the compiler to reference the address of the instance rather than the value of the instance.

Within the formal parameter of the display( ) function is the declaration of a pointer variable that will hold the address of the first member of the instance record.

The memory diagram on the bottom of the opposite page clarifies these steps. The values contained by each member of the record instances are shown in their proper positions in memory. The value contained by the prec pointer variable is the address of the first element of the first_name character array member of the record instance.

Members of the record instance are referenced from within the display( ) function by using the asterisk (*) operator with the pointer variable prec to instruct the compiler to use the value of the age member of the record instance. This statement is also shown below.

(*prec).age;

The address of the entire structure can be passed as an argument to a function by preceding the name of the instances of the structure with an ampersand.

Notice that a pointer to the name of the structure is used in the function's prototype.

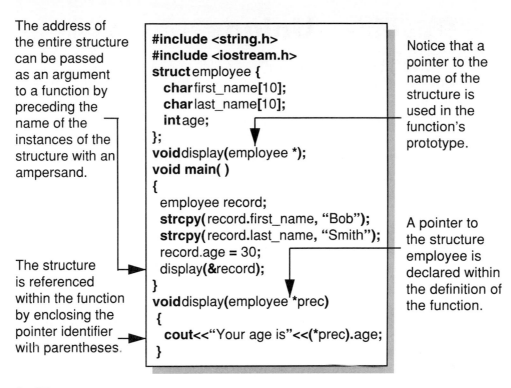

```
#include <string.h>
#include <iostream.h>
struct employee {
    char first_name[10];
    char last_name[10];
    int age;
};
void display(employee *);
void main( )
{
    employee record;
    strcpy(record.first_name, "Bob");
    strcpy(record.last_name, "Smith");
    record.age = 30;
    display(&record);
}
void display(employee *prec)
{
    cout<<"Your age is"<<(*prec).age;
}
```

A pointer to the structure employee is declared within the definition of the function.

The structure is referenced within the function by enclosing the pointer identifier with parentheses.

In Memory

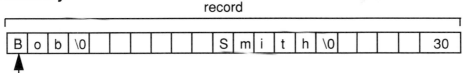

record

| B | o | b | \0 | | | | | | S | m | i | t | h | \0 | | | | 30 |

*prec points to the beginning of the record instance of the employee structure.

Unions

Throughout this chapter, the technique used in C++ to group like and unlike data is explained so that the group can be referenced by a single name. This construct is called a *structure*.

C++ offers another way to group like and unlike data under a single name called a *union*. However, a union has one distinct difference over a structure and that is the way memory is reserved.

In a structure, each member of the structure is reserved in its own memory location, which is a consecutive address to other members of the same instance of the structure.

In contrast, each member of a union occupies the same memory location. This concept can be confusing. How can two members of a union occupy the same memory location? The answer is that they share the space. That is, only one member of a union can be in memory at one time. A union, therefore, is a technique that is used to manage memory.

A union named code is defined on the opposite page using a construct similar to that of a structure. The only difference is that the keyword union is used. There are two members of the code union. These are EmpCode, which is a character, and the integer EmpNum.

An instance of the code union is then declared called dept1. This statement instructs the compiler to reserve a single portion of memory in a size that is appropriate to hold the largest member of the union. That is, the size of an integer.

An integer on a personal computer consists of two bytes and a character one byte. Therefore, only the first byte of the instance dept1 is used when the character member of the union is used by the program.

A union defines a location in memory that can be used by more than one variable. These variables can be of different data types. When an instance of a union is declared, the compiler reserves memory for the largest variable data type that is defined in the union. Only one of the variables can hold a value at the same time.

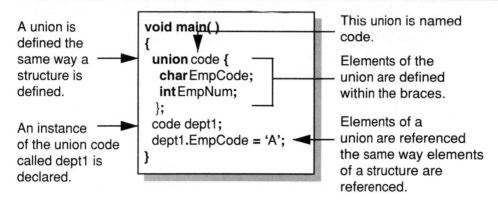

A union is defined the same way a structure is defined.

This union is named code.

Elements of the union are defined within the braces.

An instance of the union code called dept1 is declared.

Elements of a union are referenced the same way elements of a structure are referenced.

```
void main( )
{
    union code {
        char EmpCode;
        int EmpNum;
    };
    code dept1;
    dept1.EmpCode = 'A';
}
```

In Memory

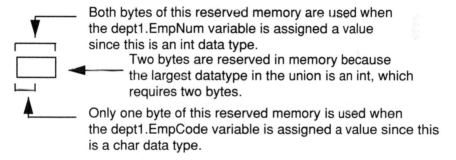

Both bytes of this reserved memory are used when the dept1.EmpNum variable is assigned a value since this is an int data type.

Two bytes are reserved in memory because the largest datatype in the union is an int, which requires two bytes.

Only one byte of this reserved memory is used when the dept1.EmpCode variable is assigned a value since this is a char data type.

Other Ways to Declare an Instance of a Union

In the example on the opposite page, an instance of the union code is declared outside of the definition. Once the declaration statement is executed, each member of the union is referenced by using the dot operator, similar to the technique for referencing a member of an instance of a structure. This is illustrated in the top example on the opposite page.

An instance of a union can also be declared as part of the definition statement as shown in the top example. Here, the dept1 instance is declared by placing the name of the instance between the closed French brace and the semicolon. This technique is the same as declaring an instance of a structure when the structure is defined.

Also, like a structure, an array of instances can be declared by using the name of the instance followed by the number of array elements contained with square brackets.

An array of instances of a union can be declared when the union is defined, as is illustrated in the left example on the opposite page, or by using the tag name of the union, as is shown below.

```
code dept[2];
```

Each array element is referenced by using the appropriate index number within the square brackets, as shown below and on the opposite page.

```
dept[0].EmpCode = 'A';
```

When an instance of the union is declared as part of the function definition, the union does not have to be named (tag name). This is illustrated in the bottom example on the opposite page. Remember, without a tag name, no instance of the union can be declared outside of the definition of the union.

```
void main( )
{
unioncode {
 charEmpCode;
 intEmpNum;
 } dept1;
dept1.EmpCode = 'A';
}
```

An instance of a union can be declared as part of the definition of the union. The name of the instance must appear outside of the last French brace.

An array of instances of a union can be declared when the union is defined by specifying the size of the array within square brackets.

Each instance of the union can be referenced by using the corresponding index number.

```
void main( )
{
union code {
 charEmpCode;
 intEmpNum;
 } dept[2];
dept[0].EmpCode = 'A';
}
```

```
void main( )
{
union {
 charEmpCode;
 intEmpNum;
 } dept1;
dept1.EmpCode = 'A';
}
```

The name of the union is optional when the union is defined, as long as the instance of the union is declared as part of the definition. If the union isn't named, then additional instances of the union cannot be declared within the program.

Enumerations

C++ offers another way to group data and it is called *enumerations*. An enumeration establishes a set of values for an instance of the group. That is, an instance of an enumeration can only have a value that is defined within the group.

The technique of defining enumerations is illustrated in the examples on the opposite page. The enumeration is defined by using the keyword *enum*, followed by the name of the enumeration and values contained within French braces, such as in the definition shown below.

enum DaysOf Week {Sun, Mon, Tues, Wed, Thurs, Fri, Sat};

Each member of the enumeration is an integer that has a value from zero through six. However, a value can be assigned to the integer by using the assignment operator within the definition of the enumerations. This is shown in the bottom example on the opposite page.

Once an enumeration is defined, the name of the enumeration is used to declare an instance of the enumeration. This technique is shown below and on the opposite page.

enum DaysOfWeek day;

When the day is declared as an instance of the enumeration DaysOf Week, no value is assigned to day. Instead, the program must assign the value to day using the assignment value as shown below.

day = Mon;

However, the value assigned to the instance of the enumeration day must be one of the values defined in the definition of the DaysOfWeek enumeration.

Enumeration is another way to group variables. It defines a set of integer constants and specifies the legal values for members of the set. These values can be automatically assigned by the compiler or assigned when the enumeration is declared. Values assigned by the compiler begin with zero and increment according to the maximum number of members of the set.

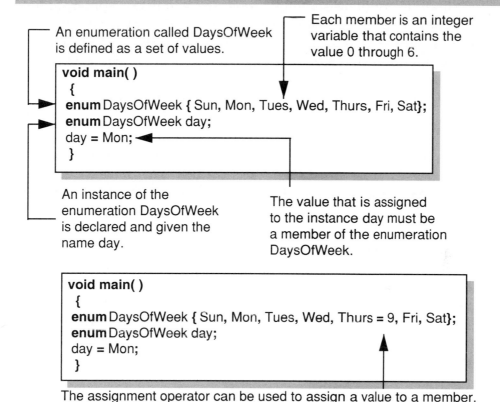

An enumeration called DaysOfWeek is defined as a set of values.

Each member is an integer variable that contains the value 0 through 6.

```
void main( )
{
enum DaysOfWeek { Sun, Mon, Tues, Wed, Thurs, Fri, Sat};
enum DaysOfWeek day;
day = Mon;
}
```

An instance of the enumeration DaysOfWeek is declared and given the name day.

The value that is assigned to the instance day must be a member of the enumeration DaysOfWeek.

```
void main( )
{
enum DaysOfWeek { Sun, Mon, Tues, Wed, Thurs = 9, Fri, Sat};
enum DaysOfWeek day;
day = Mon;
}
```

The assignment operator can be used to assign a value to a member.

Typedefine

In a complex C++ program, the meaning of the data contained in a variable can be unclear. Good programming technique calls for the programmer to give meaningful names to variables. For example, a variable might hold an employee number and work well within the program. However, using the name emp_num for the variable explicitly describes the contents of the variable.

The same concerns arise with the names given to data types in C++. Recall that a *data type* is symbolized in C++ with keywords such as int, char, float, etc. These, too, work perfectly in a program but could be confusing to new C++ programmers to read.

C++ has a feature that permits the programmer to assign another name to these data types by creating a *typedefine*. An example of this is shown below and on the opposite page.

typedef float salary;

In this example, the *typedef keyword* is used to associate the word salary with the data type float. That is, whenever salary is used in the program, the compiler will treat it as a symbol for float. This is illustrated on the opposite page and below.

salary EmpSal;

Here, EmpSal is an instance of data type salary. However, there is no data type called salary in C++. There is a typedef statement that created salary as an alias for the data type symbol float. Therefore, data type salary is really data type float.

Keep in mind that a typedef statement does not remove the original data type symbol. The C++ symbol for the original data type always remains valid.

A typedefine is a way of creating your own name for an existing data type. The statement that defines the new name for the data type must contains three elements. The first is the keyword typedef. Next is the data type that will be referenced by the new name. And finally is the new name itself.

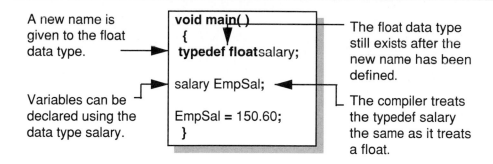

A new name is given to the float data type.

Variables can be declared using the data type salary.

```
void main( )
    {
    typedef float salary;

    salary EmpSal;

    EmpSal = 150.60;
    }
```

The float data type still exists after the new name has been defined.

The compiler treats the typedef salary the same as it treats a float.

Chapter Five

Working with Functions

Anatomy of C++ Program

At the heart of every C++ program is a function. A *function* is an independent block of code that is executed by calling the function name from within a program. A program is built by executing a series of functions in a particular order.

On the opposite page is a sample definition of a function named display_message( ). This function displays a welcome message on the screen and is executed from within a C++ program by using the following statement:

display_message( );

When a function is called, execution of the program transfers to the first instruction that appears within the function's code block. A *function code block* is identified by the open French brace ({) and the close French brace (}). The following is the first statement that is executed when the display_message( ) function is called:

cout << "Welcome to C++.";

A *statement* is the arrangement of keywords and expressions that end with a semicolon (;) and tells the computer to do something. The following are the only two statements that exists in the display_message( ) function:

cout << "Welcome to C++.";
return 0 ;

A program can send data to a function by passing the information as an argument. An *argument* is a value that appears within the parentheses of a function. There are no arguments in the display_message( ) function. Data can be sent back to the program from the function by using the return statement.

C++ programming is an extension of C programming. Syntax that is used in a C program can also be used in a C++ program. There are two main building blocks of a C++ and C program: functions and program statements.

Functions

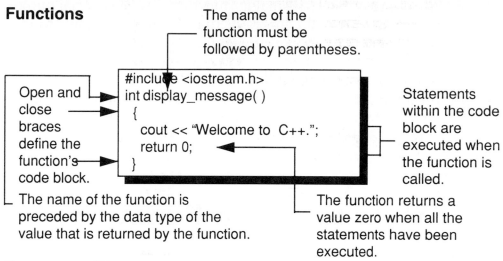

The name of the function must be followed by parentheses.

Open and close braces define the function's code block.

Statements within the code block are executed when the function is called.

```
#include <iostream.h>
int display_message( )
{
    cout << "Welcome to  C++.";
    return 0;
}
```

The name of the function is preceded by the data type of the value that is returned by the function.

The function returns a value zero when all the statements have been executed.

Terms You Should Know ...

	Function	A function is a self-contained unit of the program that performs a specific task.
	Statement	A statement tells the computer to do something and is terminated with a semicolon.
	Argument	An argument is a value placed within a function's parentheses that is used within the function.

The main( ) Function

A C++ program begins with the function main( ). Every C++ must have a main( ) function. Although the main( ) function serves a special purpose in a C++ program, it is still a function. That is, rules that apply to every function also apply to the main( ) function.

The main( ) function must be called main and have a code block identified by the open and close French braces. The main( ) function can receive data as arguments from the command line when the program is executed in the operating system. Likewise, the main( ) function can return a value to the operating system. The main( ) function shown on the opposite page does not perform either of these data transfers.

How to Use a Function

There are three steps that must be performed to use a function in a program. First, there must be a function prototype. A *function prototype* identifies the basic characteristics of the function to the compiler. The following is the prototype for the display_message( ) function. This statement tells the compiler that there is a function called display_message( ) defined in the source code or in a function library. This function has no arguments and returns no value. The keyword *void* indicates that no data type will be used in the data transfer.

```
void display_message(void);
```

Next, there must be a *function definition*. A function definition contains the block of code that will be executed when the function is called by the program. This is shown on the opposite page.

Finally, the function's name must be called from within the main( ) function or from another function that is called by the program.

The main( ) Function

The entry point into every C++ program is the main( ) function.

Library or customized functions are called from within the main( ) function.

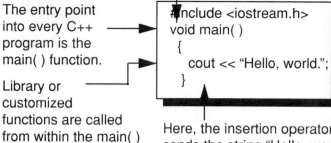

```
#include <iostream.h>
void main( )
{
    cout << "Hello, world.";
}
```

The keyword void tells the compiler that the main( ) function will not return a value after the function executes.

Here, the insertion operator (<<) sends the string "Hello, world." to the cout object which displays the string.

How to Use a Function

The function prototype must be declared before the function is called.

The function is called by using the function name within a statement.

The function definition is created outside the main( ) function.

```
#include <iostream.h>
void display_message(void);
void main( )
{
    display_message( );
}.

void display_message( )
{
    cout << "Hello, world." ;
}
```

The function prototype must contain the data types of the argument values and the return value. Only the data type keyword is necessary, not the name of the argument.

Terms You Should Know ...

○	Function Prototype	A function prototype tells the compiler the data types to expect when the function is called.
○	String	A string is a series of characters that ends, with a null character (\0).

Passing Arguments

Data can be passed to a function by value or by reference. This chapter will discuss passing by value. The section in Chapter 4 "Passing Elements of a Structure to a Function" illustrates passing by reference. *Passing by value* means that a copy of a value is used by the function. This is compared to *passing by reference* where the same value is used by the function.

There are three requirements to pass a value as an argument to a function. First, the data type of the value must be indicated within the parentheses of the function prototype. Data types were discussed in Chapter 1.

Next, a variable must be declared of the same data type within the parentheses of the function definition. A *variable* is an alias that the programmer provides for a place in computer memory that will hold a value. The function definition add_bonus( ) in the example on the opposite page declares the bonus as an integer variable.

```
void add_bonus(int bonus);
```

The variable bonus is then used within the function whenever the programmer needs to reference the value that is passed to the function by the function call. The copy of the value that is passed to a function is destroyed when the last line of the function is executed. Memory used for that value is freed.

Finally, the value that is passed to the function must be placed within the parentheses of the function call. The value can be a literal value, such as the integer shown in the example on the opposite page, or a variable.

Passing Multiple Arguments

More than one value can be passed to a function by separating the arguments with commas. This is illustrated on the opposite page.

Passing Arguments

The function prototype contains the function name and the data type of the argument.

The variable representing the value passed to the function is declared within the parentheses when the function is defined.

The bonus amount is passed as an argument to the add_bonus( ) function.

The value passed to the function is automatically assigned to the bonus variable.

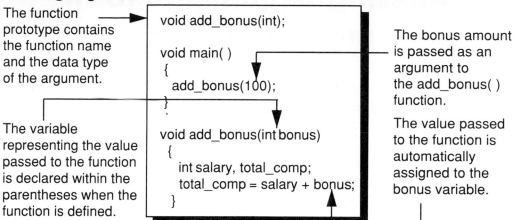

```
void add_bonus(int);

void main( )
{
    add_bonus(100);
}

void add_bonus(int bonus)
{
    int salary, total_comp;
    total_comp = salary + bonus;
}
```

Passing Multiple Arguments

Each argument must be identified in the function prototype.

Each argument must be declared within the parentheses in the function definition.

Arguments are separated by a comma.

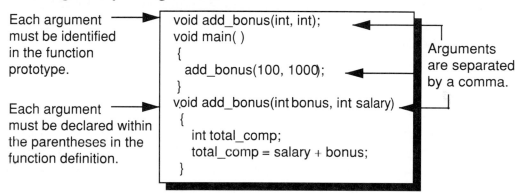

```
void add_bonus(int, int);
void main( )
{
    add_bonus(100, 1000);
}
void add_bonus(int bonus, int salary)
{
    int total_comp;
    total_comp = salary + bonus;
}
```

Terms You Should Know ...

○	Variable	A variable is a symbolic name that is used to identify a value.

Passing Arguments to the main( ) Function

The main( ), as discussed earlier, has the same capabilities as any function in C++—in addition to a few unique features, such as being the entry point to the C++ program. Therefore, values can be passed to the main( ) function.

An executable version of a C++ program resides in an *operating system environment*, such as UNIX, DOS, Windows NT, OS2 or Windows95. Execution of the program takes place by entering the name of the program at the operating system prompt, then by pressing the Enter key. Values can be passed to the program by specifying those arguments to the right of the program name on the command line when the program is executed. This is shown below where the program name is myprg and the argument is Anne.

c:>myprg Anne

Within the parenthesis of the main( ) function two variables are declared. The first variable is called argc and contains the number of arguments that have been entered at the command line. The name of the program is considered an argument. Therefore, every C++ program has one argument according to the argc variable.

The argv variable is an array of pointers. An array is a series of variables of the same data type that can be referenced by using a single name. A pointer is a variable that holds an address of another variable. Arrays are discussed in Chapter 3 and Pointers are discussed in Chapter 10.

A programmer can use the argument passed to the main( ) function by using the appropriate element of the argv[ ] array variable. An element is one value in the series of values referenced by the array. An element can be referenced by placing the corresponding order of the argument within the brackets of the argv[] array. The 1 is used to reference Anne in the example on the opposite page. Array element numbers begin with zero.

Program name. ⎯⎯⎯⎯⎯⎯⎯⎯⎯⎯⎯⎯ ⎯⎯ Command line argument.

Command line. ⎯⎯⎯⎯⎯▶ myprg.exe Anne

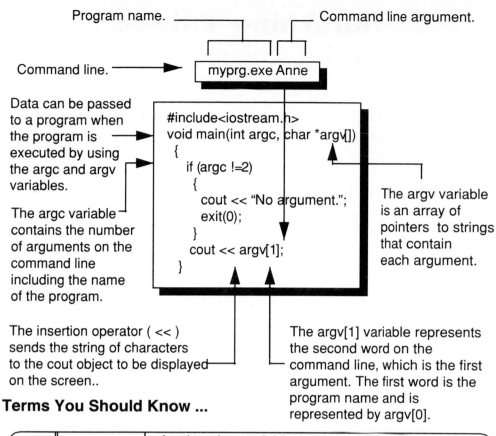

Data can be passed to a program when the program is ⎯⎯▶ executed by using the argc and argv variables.

The argc variable contains the number of arguments on the command line including the name of the program.

```
#include<iostream.h>
void main(int argc, char *argv[])
{
    if (argc !=2)
    {
        cout << "No argument.";
        exit(0);
    }
    cout << argv[1];
}
```

The argv variable is an array of pointers to strings that contain each argument.

The insertion operator (<<) sends the string of characters to the cout object to be displayed on the screen..

The argv[1] variable represents the second word on the command line, which is the first argument. The first word is the program name and is represented by argv[0].

Terms You Should Know ...

○	Pointer	A pointer is a variable that contains the memory address of another variable.
○	Array	An array is a series of variables that use the same variable name. Each variable is identified by an index number. The first variable is given index zero.

Returning Values

Functions are modules of code that perform a particular action. Some functions require additional data from outside the function to complete their task. The outside data is passed to the function as an argument, as is illustrated on previous pages. After completing the task some functions return a value to the main( ) function or to another function.

There are three steps required to return a value from a function. First, the data type of the return value must be specified to the left of the function name in the function prototype. This is illustrated below.

int add_bonus(int);

Next, the data type of the return value must be specified to the left of the function name in the function definition, as is shown here.

int add_bonus(int bonus);

Then, the returning value must be specified to the right of the return keyword. The return statement is shown below. The final step occurs in the function call.

return 0 ;

Functions Calling Functions

A function can be called within another function (remember main( ) is a function) by using the name of the function and passing values, if any, in a statement. An assignment operator is used in the statement if a value is being returned by the function, as shown here. The return value is assigned to return_code.

return_code = add_bonus(100);

Returning Values

The data type of the returning value must be identified in the function prototype.

The statement that calls the function assigns the return value to a variable.

The definition of the function must include the data type of the return value.

The value that is returned by the function is placed in the return statement.

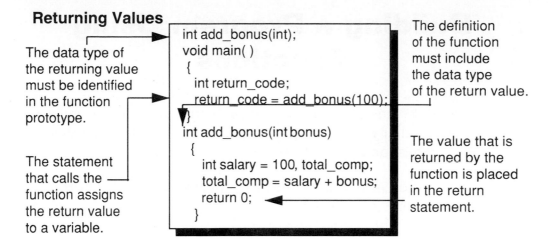

```
int add_bonus(int);
void main( )
{
    int return_code;
    return_code = add_bonus(100);
}
int add_bonus(int bonus)
{
    int salary = 100, total_comp;
    total_comp = salary + bonus;
    return 0;
}
```

Functions Calling Functions

Two function prototypes are declared.

The first function is called within the main( ) function.

The second function is called within the first function.

The value passed to the first function is also passed to the second function.

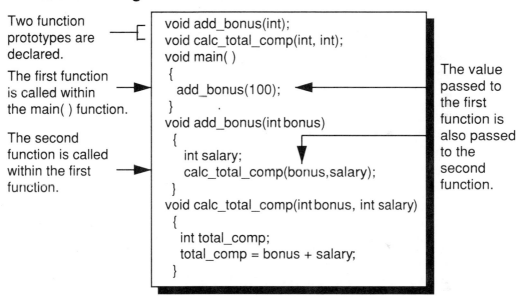

```
void add_bonus(int);
void calc_total_comp(int, int);
void main( )
{
    add_bonus(100);
}
void add_bonus(int bonus)
{
    int salary;
    calc_total_comp(bonus,salary);
}
void calc_total_comp(int bonus, int salary)
{
    int total_comp;
    total_comp = bonus + salary;
}
```

Building a Program Using Functions

A program is designed to solve a real problem. The problem must be divided into smaller parts so that each part of the problem can then be solved by a corresponding C++ function.

Once each function is identified, the algorithm for solving that portion of the problem can be interpreted into C++ statements. An *algorithm* is the term used to describe the method of solving a problem.

Each function requires three steps: the function prototype, the function definition and the function call. The function prototype can be placed within the source code of the program or in the application's header file. In the example on the opposite page, function prototypes are placed in the myheader.h file and copied into the program at compile time by using the #include directive, as shown here. Any unique file name can be given to the application's header file, as long as the name complies with the operating systemís rules for file names. In addition, any number of header files can be created for an application.

#include <myheader.h>

The function definition is included at the end of the file. Functions can also be placed in other source code files that will be joined together when the program is compiled and linked. They can also be placed in an application library. A *library* is precompiled code that is linked with a program to create an executable program.

Each function is called in the appropriate sequence in the main( ) function or in other functions. Most functions, including the main( ) function, should have a return value. The return value will let the calling program (or the operating system in the case of the main( ) function) know if the function successfully completed the operation.

The myheader.h file contains the function prototype for AddBonus( ).

By looking at the return value of the program, you will know if the program was able to add a bonus to the salary.

The AddBonus( ) function adds a bonus to the salary only if the correct employee number is passed to the function. Otherwise, a zero is returned.

```c
#include <myheader.h>
int main( )
   {
     int EmpNum, ReturnValue;
     float EmpSalary, ResultsAddBonus;

     EmployeeNumber = 4;
     EmployeeSalary = 1000;

     ResultsAddBonus = AddBonus(EmpNum,EmpSalary);
     if (ResultsAddBonus == 0)
         ReturnValue = 1;
     else
         ReturnValue = 0;
     return ReturnValue;
   }
 float AddBonus(int EmpNum, float EmpSalary)
   {
     float TotalComp;

     if(EmpNum == 4)
       TotalComp = EmpSalary + 100;
     else
       TotalComp = 0;
     return TotalComp;
   }
```

Tricks of the Trade

Always return the results from functions and the program. This is the best way to indicate a successful operation or identify where an error occurs.

Program Statements

The C++ language is composed of keywords, operators, and classes that can be formulated into an instruction that the compiler will understand. This instruction is called a *statement* and must end with a semicolon (;) as is illustrated here.

```
cout << "Hello, world.";
```

White Space Characters

C++ statements can be written in the source code in various structured styles. A *structured style* refers to each statement being written on one line and some statements being indented to show a visual relationship with other statements.

The flexibility of the manner in which C++ source code can be written is achieved because of the *white space rule*. This rule states that the compiler will ignore white space characters. *White space characters* are the space character, carriage return character, line feed character, tab character and formfeed character.

Therefore, these characters can be used freely in the source code to make the code more readable to the programmer without affecting the compiled program. The use of white space characters is a key building block of structured programming.

However, there is an important exception to the white space rule. That is, a string cannot be divided by a white space character. *For example, the program statement on the following page is not permitted in* C++. The backslash (\ ) character can be used to overcome this problem. This technique is illustrated on the opposite page.

```
cout << " Hello,
world";
```

Program Statements

A statement tells the computer to do something. Here, the computer is told to print a message on the screen. ⟶

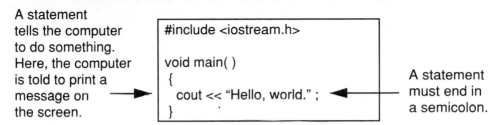

```
#include <iostream.h>

void main( )
{
   cout << "Hello, world." ;
}
```

◄— A statement must end in a semicolon.

White Space Characters

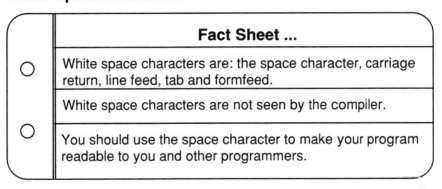

Fact Sheet ...

○ White space characters are: the space character, carriage return, line feed, tab and formfeed.

White space characters are not seen by the compiler.

○ You should use the space character to make your program readable to you and other programmers.

Tricks of the Trade

Here is how a statement that contains a string can span more than a single line. ⟶

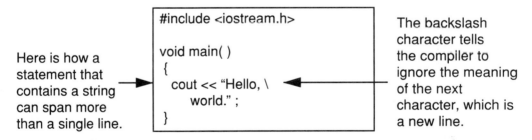

```
#include <iostream.h>

void main( )
{
   cout << "Hello, \
      world." ;
}
```

◄— The backslash character tells the compiler to ignore the meaning of the next character, which is a new line.

Preprocessor Directives

Several steps occur when C++ source code is created into an executable program. This transformation begins when the source code is reviewed by the preprocessor, which changes the code. Next it is on to the compiler where the source code is rewritten into assembler language and finally to the linker where the machine-readable version is joined with other compiled programs to create the executable code.

The first step in the building process is called *preprocessing*. This is where a program called the *preprocessor* examines the source code and modifies the code as instructed by preprocessor directives. A *preprocessor directives* is an instruction that a programmer places within the source code for use by the preprocessor.

A *preprocessor directive* is distinguished from a compiler statement in three ways. A preprocessor directive begins with a pound sign (#), must be contained on a single line of the source code and does not end with a semicolon (;).

For example, the #include < > ,which is used in many examples so far in this chapter, is a preprocessor directive. This tells the preprocessor to copy the contents of the specified header file into the source code at this point in the program.

Therefore, the preprocessor will replace this directive with the entire contents of the specified file. In the examples on the opposite page, the iostream.h file will be copied into the program replacing the #include <iostream.h>. Likewise, the contents of myheader.h file will replace the #include <myheader.h> in the source code after preprocessing has occurred.

As will be seen in the next few pages, a programmer can use preprocessor directives to make a program smaller and more efficient.

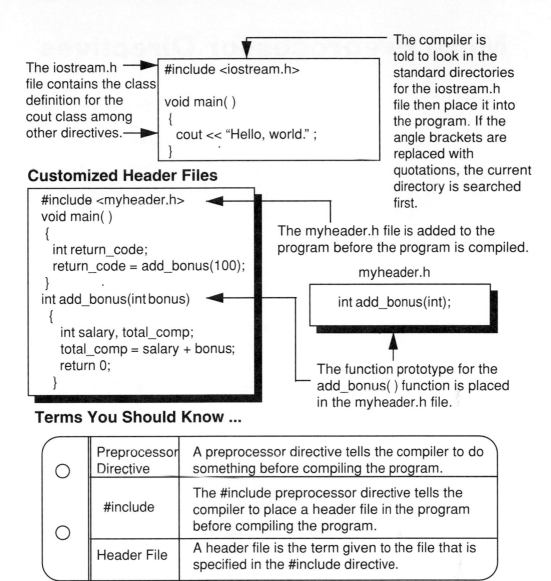

The iostream.h file contains the class definition for the cout class among other directives. ➤

```
#include <iostream.h>

void main( )
{
    cout << "Hello, world." ;
}
```

The compiler is told to look in the standard directories for the iostream.h file then place it into the program. If the angle brackets are replaced with quotations, the current directory is searched first.

Customized Header Files

```
#include <myheader.h>
void main( )
{
    int return_code;
    return_code = add_bonus(100);
}
int add_bonus(int bonus)
{
    int salary, total_comp;
    total_comp = salary + bonus;
    return 0;
}
```

The myheader.h file is added to the program before the program is compiled.

myheader.h

```
int add_bonus(int);
```

The function prototype for the add_bonus( ) function is placed in the myheader.h file.

Terms You Should Know ...

	Preprocessor Directive	A preprocessor directive tells the compiler to do something before compiling the program.
	#include	The #include preprocessor directive tells the compiler to place a header file in the program before compiling the program.
	Header File	A header file is the term given to the file that is specified in the #include directive.

More Preprocessor Directives

There are 12 preprocessor directives that can be used with C++ programs. These will be presented throughout the remainder of this chapter. One of the most commonly used preprocessor directives is #define.

The *#define directive* tells the preprocessor to search the source code for a specific series of characters, then replace those characters with one or more characters that are identified in the #define directive. This technique is similar to the search and replace feature that is available in many editors.

Two #define directives are used in the example on the opposite page. These are also illustrated below. The first #define directive instructs the compiler to examine each line of the source code for the word TRUE. When this word is found, the preprocessor will remove TRUE from the source code and replace it with 1. The same procedure is followed for the second #define directive except the word FALSE is replaced with a 0.

```
#define TRUE 1
#define FALSE 0
```

The #define preprocessor directive enables a programmer to use words that are meaningful to a programmer within the source code instead of symbols that are preferred by the compiler. In this example, the words TRUE and FALSE convey a clearer meaning than the integers 1 and 0.

Another reason for using the #define directive is to reduce memory overhead. Variables can be used for the same purpose as the #define directive in the previous example. This is illustrated below. However, memory must be reserved for the variables, which is not the case with the #define directive.

```
int TRUE, FALSE:
TRUE = 1;
FALSE = 0;
```

In addition to the #include preprocessor directive, 11 others can be used to build flexibility into your program. These are: #define, #if, #else, #elif, #endif, #ifdef, #ifndef, #undef, #line, #error and #pragma.

#define

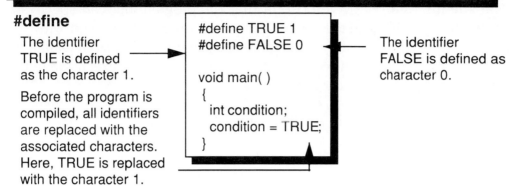

The identifier TRUE is defined as the character 1.

Before the program is compiled, all identifiers are replaced with the associated characters. Here, TRUE is replaced with the character 1.

```
#define TRUE 1
#define FALSE 0

void main( )
{
    int condition;
    condition = TRUE;
}
```

The identifier FALSE is defined as character 0.

Fact Sheet ...	
○	#define definition is not terminated with a semicolon.
	Character sequences that contain spaces must be within quotations.
○	Once a #define definition is created it can be used as part of other #define definitions.
	No substitution will occur if the identifier is used within quotations.

Terms You Should Know ...

○	#define	Defines an identifier and zero or more characters . All occurrences of the Identifier in the program are replaced with the characters.
○	Macro Name	A macro name is the term used to name the identifier in a #define definition.

#define with Arguments

The #define directive is verbose in that the programmer can specify an argument. In the example shown below, an argument is used with the #define directive. This use of a #define directive is called *macrosubstitution* and is used in place of a compiled function to speed the execution of the program.

#define MIN(a,b) (a < b) ? a : b

In this example, the preprocessor is told to search the source code for the character series MIN(a, b). The symbols a and b are place-holders for any symbol that is used in the source code within the MIN parentheses. As shown on the opposite page, a and b are place-holders for x and y.

When the preprocessor encounters the MIN(a, b) characters in the source code, the preprocessor replaces these characters with the expression that appears to the right of the MIN(a, b) in the #define directive, which is shown below.

(a < b) ? a : b

This expression is an *inline if statement*. It states that the value of the expression is the value of a if the value of a is less then the value b, otherwise the value of the expression is the value of b. This expression is covered in depth in Chapter 6.

Notice that the use of MIN(x, y) in the source code resembles a function call where the return value of the function is assigned to the variable z. However, if the sole purpose of the function is to determine the greater of two values, then there is no need to create a function. Macrosubtitution using the #define directive will handle this task without using additional memory.

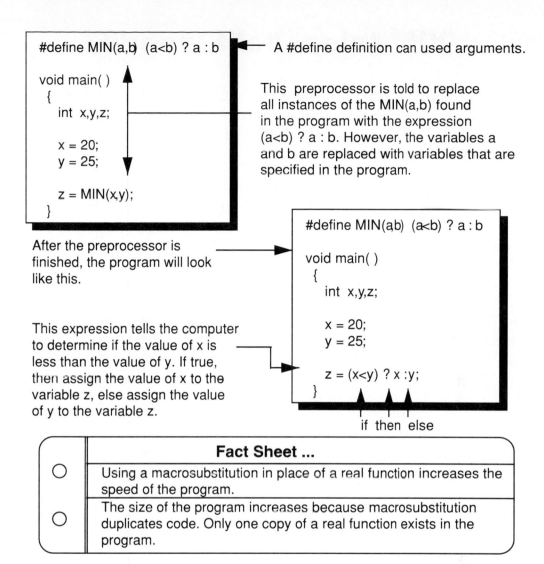

```
#define MIN(a,b)  (a<b) ? a : b
```

A #define definition can used arguments.

```
void main( )
{
    int  x,y,z;

    x = 20;
    y = 25;

    z = MIN(x,y);
}
```

This preprocessor is told to replace all instances of the MIN(a,b) found in the program with the expression (a<b) ? a : b. However, the variables a and b are replaced with variables that are specified in the program.

After the preprocessor is finished, the program will look like this.

```
#define MIN(a,b)  (a<b) ? a : b

void main( )
{
    int  x,y,z;

    x = 20;
    y = 25;

    z = (x<y) ? x :y;
}
            if  then  else
```

This expression tells the computer to determine if the value of x is less than the value of y. If true, then assign the value of x to the variable z, else assign the value of y to the variable z.

Fact Sheet ...

O Using a macrosubstitution in place of a real function increases the speed of the program.

O The size of the program increases because macrosubstitution duplicates code. Only one copy of a real function exists in the program.

#if, #else, #elif, #endif

An important objective of writing a C++ program is to be able to reduce duplication of source code. This may not become an issue when writing a program that is designed to be used by a single operating system or a single end user of the program.

However, the demand by end users for customized versions of a program has placed programmers in a difficult situation. For example, 99% of the C++ source code for a program might be the same regardless if the program runs in a UNIX or DOS environment. This means that one percent of the code is unique to each of these operating systems. Must the programmer write two versions of the source code?

No! There is no need to do this if the #if, #else, and #elif preprocessor directives are used. As illustrated in the examples on the opposite page, C++ statements are placed within the #if ... #endif preprocessor conditional directives. These directives are similar in functionality as the if..else program control statements in C.

First, the #define directive will search the source code for the ENVIRON-MENT series of character, then replace those characters with 1. Next, the preprocessor #if directive evaluates the definition of ENVIRONMENT. If the definition is true, then only the C++ statements within the block remain in the source code. Statements in the #else directive block are removed. The opposite occurs if the definition does not evaluate to 1.

The #elif directive is used to have the preprocessor conduct more than one evaluation within an #if..#endif block.

This technique allows the programmer to alter which segments of the source are compiled by changing the definition of a single #define directive.

#if, #else, #endif

Preprocessor conditional directives are used to determine which portion of the code is compiled.

The preprocessor evaluates the substituted value in the #define directive, then places the proper statement in the program for compiling.

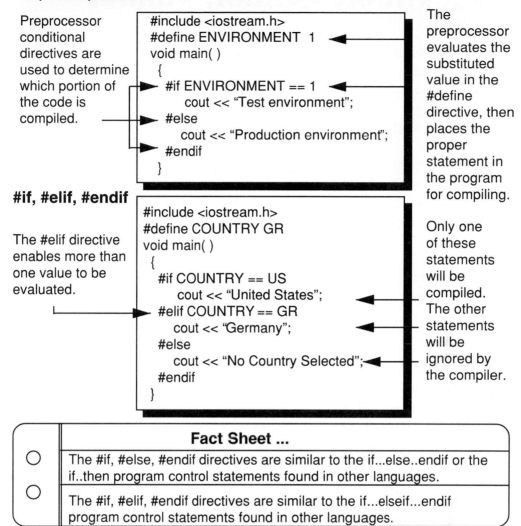

```
#include <iostream.h>
#define ENVIRONMENT  1
void main( )
   {
     #if ENVIRONMENT == 1
          cout << "Test environment";
     #else
          cout << "Production environment";
     #endif
   }
```

#if, #elif, #endif

The #elif directive enables more than one value to be evaluated.

Only one of these statements will be compiled. The other statements will be ignored by the compiler.

```
#include <iostream.h>
#define COUNTRY GR
void main( )
   {
     #if COUNTRY == US
          cout << "United States";
     #elif COUNTRY == GR
          cout << "Germany";
     #else
          cout << "No Country Selected";
     #endif
   }
```

Fact Sheet ...

○ The #if, #else, #endif directives are similar to the if...else..endif or the if..then program control statements found in other languages.

○ The #if, #elif, #endif directives are similar to the if...elseif...endif program control statements found in other languages.

#ifdef, #ifndef, #undef

In the previous examples, the preprocessor is given instructions to insert a particular block of code into the program if a macro is defined a specific way. However, in many situations, the programmer does not care how the macro is defined. Instead, the programmer is only concerned that a macro is defined.

A different technique is used in this situation. The programmer can direct the preprocesor to include a block of code into the program based upon the existence or lack of a macro definition. The actual definition of the macro is irrelevant to the programmer.

In the top example on the opposite page, the program calculates the total compensation value. Two expressions are found in the program, however, only one of them will be compiled.

The first expression uses the BONUS macro as part of the calculation. BONUS contains the percentage increase in the salary value that is used to determine total compensation. A compiler error will occur if this statement is used in the program without BONUS being defined.

However, the programmer uses the *#ifdef directive*, which instructs the preprocessor to include this statement only if BONUS is defined. Otherwise, the preprocessor prevents this statement from being compiled.

Since the program is still required to calculate total compensation, the programmer provides an alternative statement. The *#ifndef directive* places this statement into the compiled program if BONUS is not defined. Notice that the second statement does not use BONUS in the calculation.

The *#undef directive* is used to remove a previously defined macro.

#ifdef, #ifndef

The preprocessor is given instructions to follow if the #define directive for the BONUS macro is not defined in the program.

After the substitution, this statement reads:
total_comp = salary * 1.10.

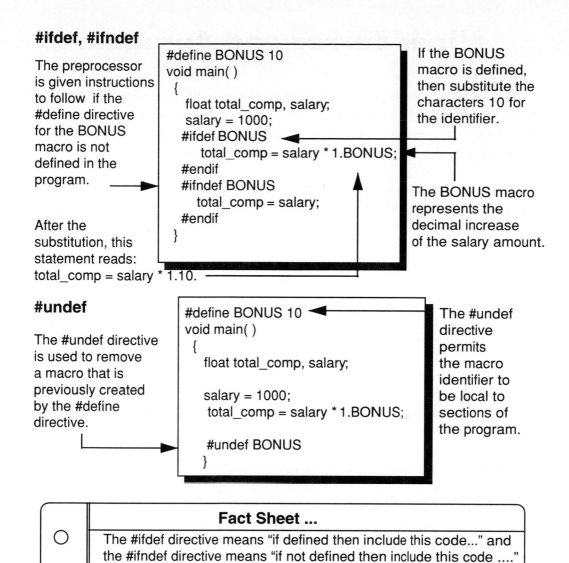

```
#define BONUS 10
void main( )
  {
    float total_comp, salary;
    salary = 1000;
  #ifdef BONUS
      total_comp = salary * 1.BONUS;
  #endif
  #ifndef BONUS
      total_comp = salary;
  #endif
  }
```

If the BONUS macro is defined, then substitute the characters 10 for the identifier.

The BONUS macro represents the decimal increase of the salary amount.

#undef

The #undef directive is used to remove a macro that is previously created by the #define directive.

```
#define BONUS 10
void main( )
  {
    float total_comp, salary;

    salary = 1000;
    total_comp = salary * 1.BONUS;

    #undef BONUS
  }
```

The #undef directive permits the macro identifier to be local to sections of the program.

Fact Sheet ...

The #ifdef directive means "if defined then include this code..." and the #ifndef directive means "if not defined then include this code ...."

#line, #error and #pragma

The preprocessor has three other directives that C++ programmers find useful to incorporate into their programs. The first of these directives explained on the opposite page is the *#line directive*. This directive is used to establish the beginning value of the line counter.

When the preprocessor encounters the #line directive, forthcoming lines are renumbered. In the illustration on the opposite page the first line of the program is identified as line 100 rather than line 1, which is the default value.

Programmers use the #line directive to make messages that refer to line numbers (i.e., syntax errors and compiler warnings) meaningful. For example, major selections of the program can be assigned a series of line numbers that are out of sequence with other portions of the program.

A programmer may want to assign each function a block of 100 lines. The first function begins with 100, the second function with 200, and so forth. When an error occurs, the programmer will know by looking at the line number which function contains the error. Many editors have a search feature that will move the cursor to a specified line number and allow the programmer to correct the problem.

The *#error directive* displays a message and the programmer supplies tokens when the directive is processed. #error directives are handled differently for each compiler. Therefore, consult the compiler manual for more detailed information on how the use the #error directive.

The *#pragma directive* is used to activate particular features of a compiler from within the program. This too is handled differently for each compiler. Refer to the compiler manual to learn the proper use of this directive in a program.

The compiler counts the number of lines in a program. The counter usually begins with zero. The #line directive sets the starting number for the counter.

```
#line 100

void main( )
  {
    float total_comp, salary;

    salary = 1000;
     total_comp = salary * 1.BONUS;
    }
```

In this example, the first line of the compiled program is numbered line 100.

Fact Sheet ...

#line

The #line directive is used primarily for debugging a program.

#error

The #error directive is also used for debugging a program.

When the compiler encounters the #error directive in the program, compilation stops.

The #error directive is followed by a message that is displayed when the compiler encounters the #error directive.

The message must not be enclosed within quotations. Example: #error stopped.

#pragma

The #pragma directive is used to give instructions to the compiler.

For example, the #pragma directive instructs the the compiler to trace the program while the program is executing.

Refer to the compiler manual for the proper compiler options.

Making a C++ Program

This chapter provides an introduction to C++. I began by showing how real problems are broken down into small pieces then translated into C++ functions. Each function has statements that are used to solve a piece of the problem.

Once all of the functions have been built, the programmer must call each function in the proper sequence in the program to achieve the desired result—having the computer solve the real problem.

All the functions and statements that compose the program are entered into a source code file using an editor. An editor is similar to a word processor. The source code file is saved using the cpp file extension (C Plus Plus).

Next, the programmer must have the compiler create the executable version of the program. This is accomplished in several ways depending on the compiler that is being used. The first method is to invoke the compiler and linker from the command line. The cl command is commonly used by some compiler makers, as shown here. This command will result in the creation of an executable program unless there are errors in the program then error messages are displayed. Check the proper command for your compiler.

cl myprog.cpp

Another way to build an executable version of a C++ program is by using the integrated develop environment (IDE), which is available with many compilers. Such compilers allow the programmer to compile and link the program from a pull-down menu.

A number of compilers use a make program to manage the compilation of source code. A *make program* is an executable program that recompiles only those files that need to be recompiled. Read the compiler's documentation for more details about make.

Create a program using an editor then save the program file under a name that has a cc, cpp, or cxx file name extension. Check your compiler manual for the proper file extension for your compiler.

The file that contains the source code for the program must be compiled and linked. Here, the cl command is used to execute the compiler and linker. Your compiler might be executed a different way. The compiler manual will show you how to compile and link your program.

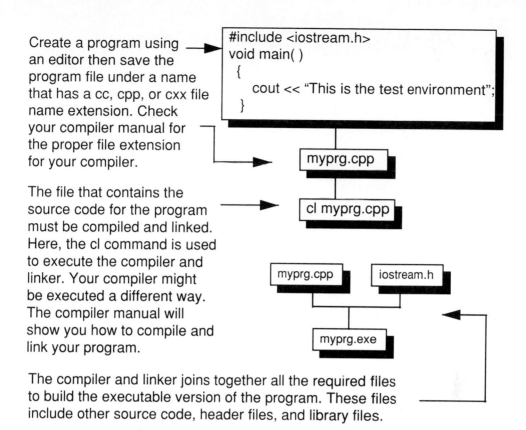

```
#include <iostream.h>
void main( )
{
    cout << "This is the test environment";
}
```

myprg.cpp

cl myprg.cpp

myprg.cpp   iostream.h

myprg.exe

The compiler and linker joins together all the required files to build the executable version of the program. These files include other source code, header files, and library files.

Terms You Should Know ...

○	Compiler	A compiler converts source code into object code, which is in a machine readable form.
○	Linker	A linker joins together the program's object code with library object code to create an executable program.
	Library	A library is a collection of ready-to-run functions.

Chapter Six

Working with Program Control

Program Control Statements

The main( ) function is the entry point in a C++ program. From here the program executes statements in the order the statements appear in the main( ) function. When the program finishes executing the last statement in main( ), the program ends and control is returned back to the operating system.

The sequential execution of statements is called *program flow*. A programmer can redirect the flow of the program by calling a function or by using a program control statement. When a function is called within the main( ) function, the flow of execution temporarily leaves the main( ) function and continues with the first statement in the function that is called by the program. When the last statement in the called function is executed, control returns to the next statement in the main( ) function.

A *program control statement* redirects the order in which statements are executed within the main( ) function and other functions throughout the program. There are several kinds of program control statements, all of which are discussed in this chapter.

if

On the opposite page there are two examples of the *if program control statement*. The if statement evaluates an expression contained within the parentheses. If the expression evaluates true, then the statement(s) in the code block of the if statement is executed. If the expression evaluates false, then the statement(s) in the code block of the if statement is not executed.

In the top example, a single statement is executed if the value of variable a is 1. However, in the second example, multiple statements are executed if the same condition exists. If more than one statement is to be executed, then the statements must be enclosed within French braces. These braces are not necessary if a single statement is executed.

A program control statement redirects the flow of a program based upon the
results of a conditional test. The result is either false or true, where false
is zero value and true is a non-zero value. There are two general types of
program control statements. These are *conditional statements* and loops. A
conditional statement executes a portion of the code if the condition is met. A
loop executes one or more statements a number of times based upon the condition.

if

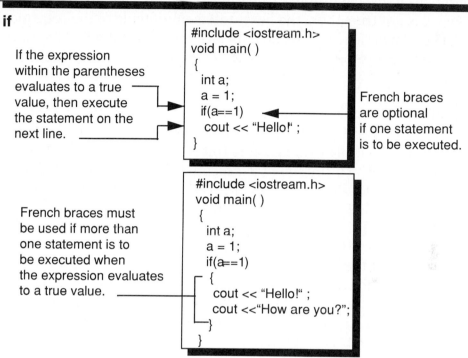

If the expression
within the parentheses
evaluates to a true
value, then execute
the statement on the
next line.

```
#include <iostream.h>
void main( )
{
  int a;
  a = 1;
  if(a==1)
    cout << "Hello!" ;
}
```

French braces
are optional
if one statement
is to be executed.

French braces must
be used if more than
one statement is to
be executed when
the expression evaluates
to a true value.

```
#include <iostream.h>
void main( )
{
  int a;
  a = 1;
  if(a==1)
    {
      cout << "Hello!" ;
      cout <<"How are you?";
    }
}
```

if ... else

The if statement is used to redirect the regular flow of the program by skipping one or more statements in the program. By itself the if statement means if this condition is true then execute this statement(s). If the statement is not true, then the next statement outside of the code block of the if statement is to be executed. In fact, the next statement below the if statement in the program is always executed even if the expression evaluates true.

An if statement can be used in conjunction with the *else statement* to control which statements are executed when the expression evaluates true and false. That is, if the expression is true, then the statement(s) within the code block of the if statement is executed. However, if the expression is false, then the statement(s) within the code block of the else statement is executed. A combination of an if statement and an else statement guarantees that either set of statements is executed but not both.

In the example at the top of the opposite page the if... else combination is illustrated. Notice that only a single statement is executed in the code block of each of these statements. No French brace is required. If the value of variable a equals one, then "Hello!" is displayed on the screen otherwise "Goodbye!" is displayed.

However, the French braces are required when multiple statements are to be executed in either the code block of the if statement or the else statement. This is illustrated in the bottom example on the opposite page. Only the if statement or else statement that contains the multiple statements needs to be delimited by French braces—not both.

In this example, "Hello! How are you?" is displayed on the screen if the value of a is one else the message "Goodbye! See you soon!" is displayed on the screen.

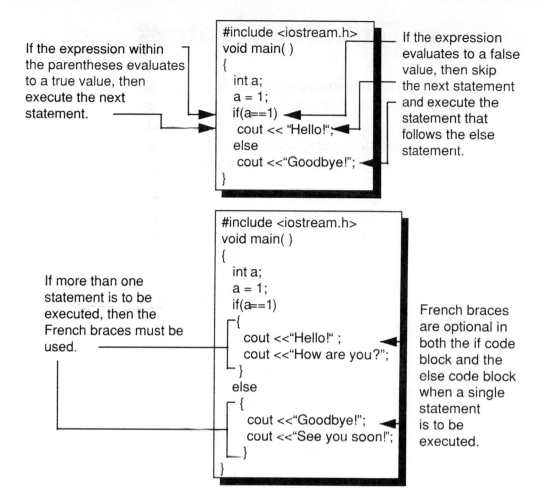

If the expression within the parentheses evaluates to a true value, then execute the next statement.

```
#include <iostream.h>
void main( )
{
    int a;
    a = 1;
    if(a==1)
        cout << "Hello!";
    else
        cout <<"Goodbye!";
}
```

If the expression evaluates to a false value, then skip the next statement and execute the statement that follows the else statement.

If more than one statement is to be executed, then the French braces must be used.

```
#include <iostream.h>
void main( )
{
    int a;
    a = 1;
    if(a==1)
    {
        cout <<"Hello!" ;
        cout <<"How are you?";
    }
    else
    {
        cout <<"Goodbye!";
        cout <<"See you soon!";
    }
}
```

French braces are optional in both the if code block and the else code block when a single statement is to be executed.

The ? Operator

It is hard to conceive that a question mark is an operator in C++ but it is. The question mark is called the *ternary operator* and performs the functionality of an inline if statement. An example of the ternary operator is shown in the top example in the opposite page and below.

$$b = a > 15 ? 3 : 0;$$

The ternary operator evaluates the expression that appears to the left of the operator. In this example, the expression of a > 15 is evaluated first. This expression will be either true or false.

If the expression is true, then the value or expression that appears between the ternary operator and the colon is assigned to the variable b. The value or expression to the right of the colon is assigned to b if the expression is false.

In this example, the value of a is 15. Therefore, the expression evaluates to a false and the value zero is assigned to the variable b.

Nested if

An if statement can be included within another if statement. This is referred to as *nested if statements* and is illustrated in the example at the bottom of the opposite page.

The expression in the second if statement is evaluated only if the expression in the first if statement is true. That is, variable a must equal one otherwise the second if statement is not executed. An alternative to this example of a nested if statement is to combine both expressions into one if statement.

The ? Operator
(if...then...else)

The ternary operator.

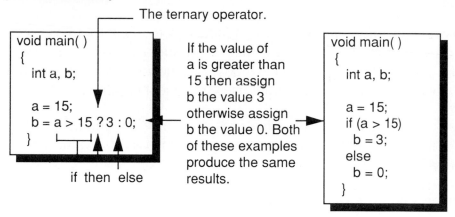

```
void main( )
{
    int a, b;

    a = 15;
    b = a > 15 ? 3 : 0;
}
```

if then else

If the value of a is greater than 15 then assign b the value 3 otherwise assign b the value 0. Both of these examples produce the same results.

```
void main( )
{
    int a, b;

    a = 15;
    if (a > 15)
        b = 3;
    else
        b = 0;
}
```

Nested if

More than one if statement can be used to evaluate two expressions. The second if statement is placed within the if statement code block.

```
#include <iostream.h>
void main( )
{
    int a, b;
    a = 1;
    b = 2;
    if(a==1)
    {
        if (b==2)
        {
            cout <<"Hello!" ;
            cout <<"How are you?";
        }
    }
}
```

If the expression in the first if statement evaluates to a true value, the expression in the second if statement is evaluated.

if ... else if

On the previous page, the if statement is nested to allow for two expressions to be evaluated. There is another technique used in C++ to evaluate more than one expression. This method is shown on the top example on the opposite page. This example uses the else if statement.

The *else if statement* combines the features of an else statement with that of an if statement. In this example, the expression a==1 is evaluated first in the if statement.

If this expression is false, then the else if statement is executed. Another expression b==3 must evaluate to true if the statements within the body of the else if statement are to be executed.

Multiple Conditions

The if statement and the else if statement can evaluate more than one expression by using the logical operators. For example, at the bottom of the opposite page, the AND operator (&&) is used to join the two expressions in the if statement. Here, both expressions must evaluate true before the statements within the body of the if statement are executed.

Alternatively, the OR operator (||) can replace the AND operator (&&) in the if statement. This is illustrated below. Statements within the body of the if statements are executed if either expression is true. The only way in which these statements are not executed is if both statements are false.

```
if (a==1 || b==2)
```

if ... else if

If the expression in the if statement evaluates to a true value, then execute these statements.

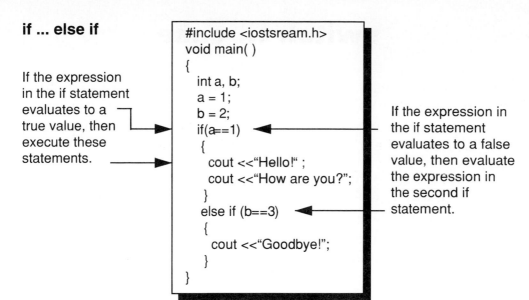

```
#include <iostsream.h>
void main( )
{
    int a, b;
    a = 1;
    b = 2;
    if(a==1)
    {
        cout <<"Hello!" ;
        cout <<"How are you?";
    }
    else if (b==3)
    {
        cout <<"Goodbye!";
    }
}
```

If the expression in the if statement evaluates to a false value, then evaluate the expression in the second if statement.

Multiple Conditions

Any valid expression can be used within the if statement parentheses.

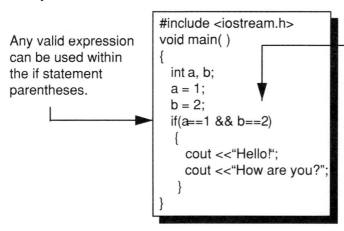

```
#include <iostream.h>
void main( )
{
    int a, b;
    a = 1;
    b = 2;
    if(a==1 && b==2)
    {
        cout <<"Hello!";
        cout <<"How are you?";
    }
}
```

Here, the logical operator AND is used to tell the compiler that both conditions must evaluate true before the body of the if statement is executed.

switch ... case

A typical C++ program is required to change the flow of the program many times during the execution of the program. The most common method for redirecting the flow is to call functions. Another frequently used method is the if statement, which is discussed on the previous pages.

However, there is a practical limit to the number of if statement's that can be used sequentially in the program. For example, assume that the program needs to execute unique statements if the value of variable a is equal to 1 or 2 or 3. This will require three if statements or a combination of if statements and else if statements.

Now imagine if the program had to change flow in one of 20 directions based upon 20 different values of the variable a. This series of if statements will become unwieldy. C++ offers another technique to deal with multiple decisions. This is called the switch ... case statement.

The *switch ... case statement* accepts a single value in the switch statement then compares that value with other values that are defined in the case statement. This is illustrated on the opposite page. In this example, variable a is placed between the parentheses of the switch statement.

The value of variable a is then compared to the value specified in each case statement. The first case statement contains the value one, which is followed by the colon. Beneath this case statement are statements that will be executed if the value of variable a is equal to the value one. The last statement in this block is the keyword break. This instructs the compiler to stop and to execute the statement that follows the closed French brace of the switch ... case statement. The same sequence applies to the remaining case statements. If, however, none of the case statements matches the variable a, then the statements beneath the *default* keyword are executed.

switch ... case

A switch ... case statement compares the results of an expression with constant values.

If the value of variable a is the integer value one, then this block is executed.

The break statement is used to identify the end of the block for the compiler.

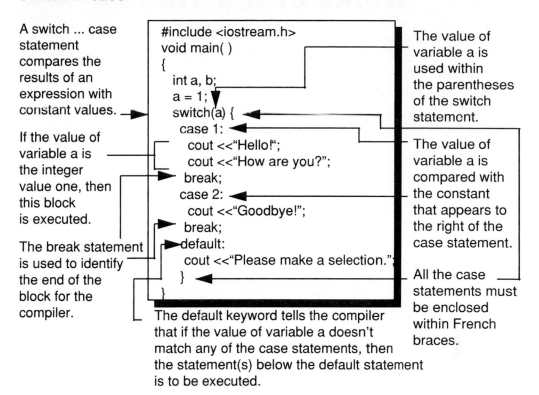

```cpp
#include <iostream.h>
void main( )
{
    int a, b;
    a = 1;
    switch(a) {
    case 1:
        cout <<"Hello!";
        cout <<"How are you?";
        break;
    case 2:
        cout <<"Goodbye!";
        break;
    default:
        cout <<"Please make a selection.";
    }
}
```

The value of variable a is used within the parentheses of the switch statement.

The value of variable a is compared with the constant that appears to the right of the case statement.

All the case statements must be enclosed within French braces.

The default keyword tells the compiler that if the value of variable a doesn't match any of the case statements, then the statement(s) below the default statement is to be executed.

Fact Sheet ...

○ The switch...case statement can test only for equality.

○ Each constant within the case statements must be unique.

Tricks of the Trade

Many C++ programs display a menu on the screen then wait for the user to enter a response. The response is then evaluated and the proper segment of the program is executed. This technique is illustrated on the opposite page where a simple, two option menu is displayed and the user is prompted to enter the corresponding letter of the desired menu option.

The *cin object* and the *extraction operator* are used to read the response from the keyboard. This is illustrated below. The value of the response is stored in the selection variable. Next, the switch ... case statement is used to evaluate the response and redirect the flow of the program.

cin >> selection;

If the user chooses the letter A, then the statement beneath the first case statement is executed. In this example, the message "Hello!" is displayed on the screen. In a typical program, the case statement would probably call a function. A function can contain complex statements that do not lend themselves to being placed directly within the case statement.

If the user selects the letter B, then the statement beneath the second case statement is executed. In this example, the message "Goodbye!" is displayed on the screen.

Notice that the switch ... case statement does not include a default statement. A *default statement* is optional. If a default statement is not included in the switch ... case statement then the value specified within the parentheses of the switch statement must be matched, otherwise the switch ... case statement has no practical effect on the program.

The switch ... case statement is the most common technique that is used to react to characters entered at the keyboard. You'll see this method used whenever a program asks the user to select an option from a menu that is displayed on the screen.

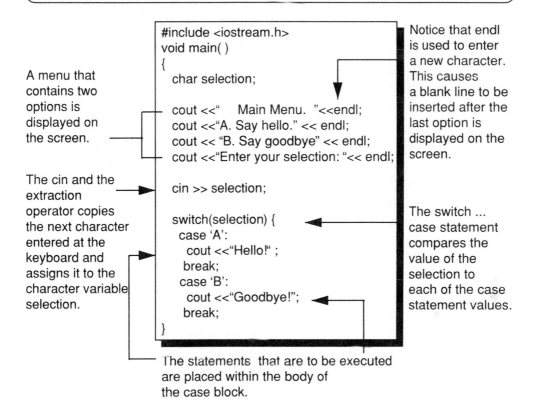

A menu that contains two options is displayed on the screen.

The cin and the extraction operator copies the next character entered at the keyboard and assigns it to the character variable selection.

```cpp
#include <iostream.h>
void main( )
{
  char selection;

  cout <<"    Main Menu.  "<<endl;
  cout <<"A. Say hello." << endl;
  cout << "B. Say goodbye" << endl;
  cout <<"Enter your selection: "<< endl;

  cin >> selection;

  switch(selection) {
    case 'A':
      cout <<"Hello!" ;
     break;
    case 'B':
      cout <<"Goodbye!";
     break;
  }
}
```

Notice that endl is used to enter a new character. This causes a blank line to be inserted after the last option is displayed on the screen.

The switch ... case statement compares the value of the selection to each of the case statement values.

The statements that are to be executed are placed within the body of the case block.

for Loop

A *loop* is a construct in C++ that repeatedly executes one or more statements. The number of times statements are executed depends on the type of loop that is used and the expression used in the loop. The first loop that is explored is the *for loop*.

The for loop executes a code block a specific number of times. This is illustrated on the opposite page. Within the parentheses of the for loop are three statements. The first statement assigns the starting count for the loop. This statement assigns zero to the variable i.

The center statement determines the end count when the for loop stops executing. In this example, the for loop continues to execute as long as the value of variable i is less than 7. When the value of i is equal to 7, then the for loop ends and the program continues with the statement after the end of the for loop.

The third statement within the parentheses of the for loop increments the counter. That is, the incremental operator (++) is used to add one to the current value of variable i. In the top example, the incremental operator is positioned after the variable i. This means that for each value of the counter, statements within the code block of the for loop are executed. After the loop has completed the cycle, the counter variable is incremented and the second expression is evaluated.

However, in the bottom example, the incremental operator is placed before the incremental operator. This sequence causes the value of variable i to be incremented before the for loop is executed. Therefore, the value of variable i in the DaysOfWeek[i] array is one and not zero as is the case in the top example.

A general rule to follow is that if the incremental operator is positioned before the variable, then one is added to the variable before the loop is executed. If this operator follows the variable, then one is added after the loop is executed.

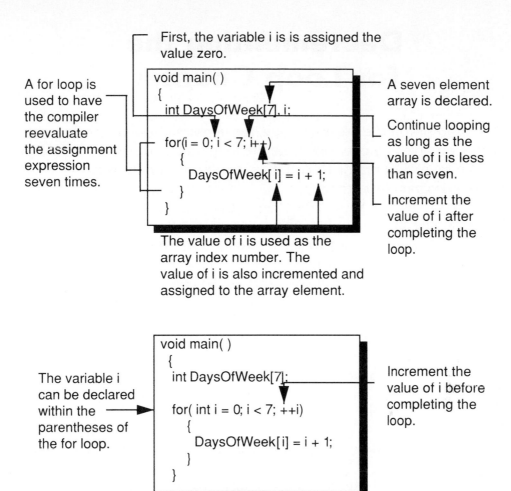

First, the variable i is is assigned the value zero.

A for loop is used to have the compiler reevaluate the assignment expression seven times.

A seven element array is declared.

Continue looping as long as the value of i is less than seven.

Increment the value of i after completing the loop.

```
void main( )
{
    int DaysOfWeek[7], i;

    for(i = 0; i < 7; i++)
    {
        DaysOfWeek[ i] = i + 1;
    }
}
```

The value of i is used as the array index number. The value of i is also incremented and assigned to the array element.

The variable i can be declared within the parentheses of the for loop.

Increment the value of i before completing the loop.

```
void main( )
{
    int DaysOfWeek[7];

    for( int i = 0; i < 7; ++i)
    {
        DaysOfWeek[ i] = i + 1;
    }
}
```

Decrementing the for Loop Counter

In the example on the previous page, the *incremental operator* increases the counter variable i by one each time the loop executed. The for loop used the incremental operator to count up to the maximum value at which time the program exits the loop.

The *decremental operator* (--) can also be used in a for loop to count down to the minimum value at which the program will break out of the loop. The minimum value of i is set in the second statement in the for loop. Here the for loop is exited if the value of the counter variable i is equal to zero.

This technique is illustrated in the examples on the opposite page. The rules that apply to the placement of the incremental operator also apply to the decremental operator.

In the top example, the decremental operator is positioned after the variable i. This will cause the value of variable i to decrease by one after the statements within the code block of the loop are executed once.

In comparison, the bottom example shows the decremental expression where the decremental operator is positioned before the variable i. This will cause the program to decrease the value of i before executing the code block of the for loop once. That is, the value of variable i during the first cycle of the loop is 6, not 7, as is the case in the first example.

Notice that the examples on the opposite page and on the previous page use the for loop to assign a value to an element of the array DaysOfWeek[]. The counter variable i is used as the index number of the array. This technique enables the program to efficiently initialize elements of the array.

$$DaysOfWeek[i] = i - 1;$$

A for loop can be used to count backwards by setting the initial value of the variable i to the maximum value.

```
void main( )
{
    int DaysOfWeek[7], i;

    for(i = 7; i>=0; i--)
    {
        DaysOfWeek[ i] = i - 1;
    }
}
```

The compiler is told to decrement the value of the variable i after completing the loop.

The for loop ends when the value of the variable i is equal to zero.

```
void main( )
{
    int DaysOfWeek[7], i;

    for(i = 7; i>=0; --i)
    {
        DaysOfWeek[ i] = i - 1;
    }
}
```

The compiler is told to decrement the value of the variable i before completing the loop.

Another Way to Use a for Loop

Previous pages showed examples of the for loop that contained open and closed French braces. Statements that are to be executed when the loop is executed are placed within these braces. However, the French braces are not required if there is only a single statement that is to execute within the loop.

The top example on the opposite page illustrates this technique. Here, there is a single statement that increments the array DaysOfWeek[]. No French braces are used. This initialization statement is executed seven times.

A Nested for Loop

A for loop can be included in another for loop as shown in the center example on the opposite page. This is referred to as *nested for loops*. In this example, for every iteration of the outer for loop, the inner for loop is executed seven times.

Notice that this program initializes a multidimensional array. The array salesreps is declared as three sets of seven elements. The outer loop controls the counter for the top level of the array. That is, the three sets. The inner loop controls the counter for the bottom level of the array. That is, the seven elements.

An Infinite Loop

The for loop statements can be removed from the parentheses to create an endless loop. This is shown in the bottom example on the opposite page. Notice that both semicolons must remain within the parentheses. In this example, the value of a is incremented infinitely. In a typical C++ program, an exit( ) or break statement is used to escape from the loop. These are discussed later in this chapter.

Another Way to Use a for Loop

if a single
statement is
to be executed
within a for
loop, then the
French braces
are optional.

```
void main( )
{
    int DaysOfWeek[7];

    for( int i = 0; i < 7; i++)
        DaysOfWeek[ i] = i + 1;
}
```

A Nested for Loop

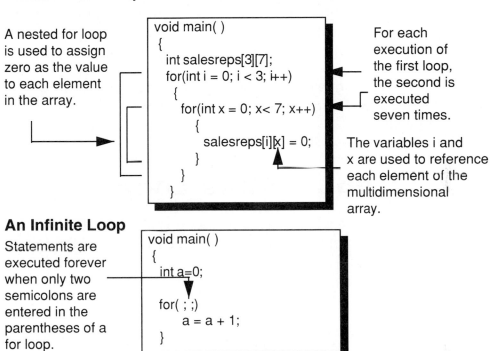

A nested for loop
is used to assign
zero as the value
to each element
in the array.

```
void main( )
{
    int salesreps[3][7];
    for(int i = 0; i < 3; i++)
    {
        for(int x = 0; x< 7; x++)
        {
            salesreps[i][x] = 0;
        }
    }
}
```

For each
execution of
the first loop,
the second is
executed
seven times.

The variables i and
x are used to reference
each element of the
multidimensional
array.

An Infinite Loop

Statements are
executed forever
when only two
semicolons are
entered in the
parentheses of a
for loop.

```
void main( )
{
    int a=0;

    for( ; ;)
        a = a + 1;
}
```

while Loop

The *while loop* executes statements within the code block of the while loop only if the expression within the parentheses evaluates to true. If the expression is false, then statements within the code block of the loop are ignored and control passes to the statement that follows the end of the while loop.

This is illustrated in the example on the opposite page. First, the variable counter variable i is initialized to zero. The expression within the while loop determines if the value of variable i is less than seven. If this is true, then the statements within the French braces are executed.

After the last statement within the while loop is executed, control of the program returns to the top of the loop. This is where the expression is once again evaluated. As long as this expression is true, the while loop will continue to execute.

do ... while Loop

Another version of the while loop is the do ... while loop. The *do ... while loop* executes the statements within the French braces as long as the expression in the while statement evaluates to true. The major difference between a while loop and a do ... while loop is that the statements within the code block of a do ... while loop must be executed at least once.

The condition in a do ... while loop is examined at the bottom of the loop. When program control enters this loop, the program has no idea whether or not this expression is true or false. Therefore, statements within the body of the do ... loop are executed.

However, once program control reaches the while statement and the expression evaluates false, the program continues with the next statement following the while statement. That is, the program breaks out of the loop.

while loop

The while loop continues to execute statements within the code block of the loop as long as the expression within the parentheses evaluates to a true value.

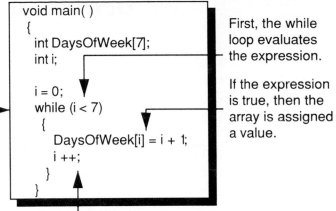

```
void main( )
{
    int DaysOfWeek[7];
    int i;

    i = 0;
    while (i < 7)
    {
        DaysOfWeek[i] = i + 1;
        i ++;
    }
}
```

First, the while loop evaluates the expression.

If the expression is true, then the array is assigned a value.

The value of the integer i is incremented. The compiler then moves to the beginning of the loop and evaluates the expression again.

do ... while loop

The do ... while loop functions very similarly to the while loop except the the expression is evaluated after the code block of the loop executes at least once.

```
void main( )
{
    int DaysOfWeek[7];
    int i;

    i = 0;
    do {
        DaysOfWeek[ i ] = i+ 1;
        i ++;
    } while (i < 7 );
}
```

The array is assigned a value then the integer variable i is incremented before the compiler determines if the value of variable i is less than the value 7.

break

Most of the loops illustrated in this chapter curtail operations when the test expression evaluates to false. For example, the while loop on the previous page continues to execute statements within the body of the loop as long as the value of variable i is less than seven.

Another way to terminate the loop is to use the break statement. The *break statement* immediately ends the looping cycle just as if the test expression evaluates to false. This technique is illustrated in the top example on the opposite page. Here, the loop will continue to execute until variable i equals seven.

However, there is an if statement within the loop. The if statement evaluates the expression contained with the parentheses. If the expression is true, then the break statement is executed. That is, if variable i has a value of 5, the break statement terminates the while loop.

When the break statement is issued, statements that are below the break statement but still are within the code block of the while loop are not executed. Instead, control is transferred to the statement immediately following the closed French brace of the loop.

exit( )

C++ provides another technique for terminating a loop—and the program. This is by calling the *exit( ) function*. When this function is called, the program ends just as if program execution reached the closed French brace of the main( ) function.

A C++ program can return a value to the operating system when the program terminates by using the return statement. The same effect is achieved by passing the return value to the exit( ) function as shown on the opposite page.

break

The break statement can be used to exit a switch ... case statement and to exit a loop. Whenever the compiler sees a break statement, it automatically executes the statement that follows the loop. ⟶

```
void main( )
{
   int DaysOfWeek[7];
   int i;

   i = 0;
   while (i < 7)
     {
        DaysOfWeek[i] = i + 1;
        i ++;
        if(i== 5)       ◄────
          break;
     }
}
```

Here, the if statement is asked to evaluate the value of the integer i. If the value of i is 5, then the break statement is executed, exiting the while loop.

exit( )

The exit() function is used to to exit the program immediately. Statements that follow the exit( ) function are ignored.

```
void main( )
{
   int DaysOfWeek[7];
   int i;

   i = 0;
   while (i < 7)
     {
        DaysOfWeek[i] = i + 1;
        i ++;
        if(i== 5)        ◄────
          exit(2);
     }
}
```

An integer value can be passed to the exit( ) function. This value is automatically displayed on the screen when the program ends. A zero value indicates that the program ended without an error. A value greater than zero indicates an error.

continue

There are situations when execution of the program should return to the top of the loop immediately without executing the remaining statements in the loop. This is depicted in the top example on the opposite page. Here, the while loop is executing statements within the code block of the loop until the value of variable i is equal to seven.

However, with each iteration of the loop, the if statement evaluates whether or not the value of variable i is equal to five. If this expression is true, then the *continue statement* is executed. Immediately, the program moves to the top of the loop. The statement that increments variable i is not executed. Instead the expression within the while loop is evaluated again.

goto

The goto statement is another way to change the normal flow of a program. The *goto statement* requires two components. These are the goto statement and the label that defines the segment of the program that will be executed when the goto statement is called.

In the example on the bottom of the page, the last three statements in the program define the label called error. The label name (error) must be followed by a colon. When the if statement determines that the variable i is equal to five, the goto statement is called referencing the name of the label (error) in the statement. Execution of the program immediately jumps to the error label and continues executing program statements within that section of the program.

A word of caution. Although goto statements seem to be an easy and fast method to redirect execution of the program to various portions of the program, avoid using the goto statement. Extended use of the goto statement can lead to an unreadable and an unmaintainable program.

---

continue

The continue statement tells the compiler to skip the rest of the statements within the body of the loop and continue at the top of the loop.

```
void main( )
{
  int DaysOfWeek[7];
  int i;

  i = 0;
  while (i < 7)
    {
      DaysOfWeek[ i ] = i + 1;
      if(i == 5)
        continue;
      i++;
    }
}
```

Here, the value of the integer i will never increase beyond the value five. Once the value of variable i is five, the continue statement is executed.

goto

The goto statement enables control of the program to jump to another statement that is identified with a label.

```
#include <iostream.h>
void main( )
{
  int DaysOfWeek[7], i = 0;
  while (i < 7)
    {
      DaysOfWeek[ i ] = i + 1;
      i ++;
      if(i ==5)
        goto error;
    }
  goto end;
  error:
   cout <<"Detected an error.";
   exit(2);
  end:
}
```

Here, the goto statement tells the compiler to jump to the line that contains the label error, then execute the next statements.

Chapter Seven

Working with Objects and Classes

- Classes
- Declaring an Instance of a Class
- Hiding Data Using the Access Specifier
- The Constructor
- Overloading the Constructor
- The Destructor
- Defining a Function Member Outside the Class Definition

Classes

C++ is a language designed to interpret real life objects, such as a student registration form, into syntax that the computer can understand. Real life objects have two characters. These are data and functionality. In the case of a student registration form, the data portion of this object consists of information about the student. The functional characteristics of a student registration form are many, including data validation.

In languages that are not object-oriented, data and functionality are treated separately. For example, in the C language, the data characteristics about an object is associated in a number of ways including the use of a structure. However, the functional characteristics are not directly associated with the object. That is, any part of the program can use these functions.

In C++, a *class* is used to define the relationship between data and functions. In the class definition illustrated on the opposite page, both passing_grade and getgrade( ) are members of the class course. These are called *data member* and *function member*, respectively.

The *class definition* is a template that informs the compiler what an instance of the class will look like when an instance is declared in the program. A template does not reserve memory. The compiler reserves memory when an instance of the class is declared. An *instance* of a class is called an object.

Access to members of a class is controlled by the class definition. In the example on the opposite page, both the data and function member are defined beneath the *public access specifier*, which makes these class members available to the class itself, to other classes, and to other segments of the program.

Later in this chapter you will see how to limit access to class members by using other access specifiers.

C++ is called an object-oriented language because C++ has a way of grouping both data and function together into a class. A class is a template similar to that of a structure and union. An instance of a class is called an object and only then is memory reserved for the class.

Class Definition

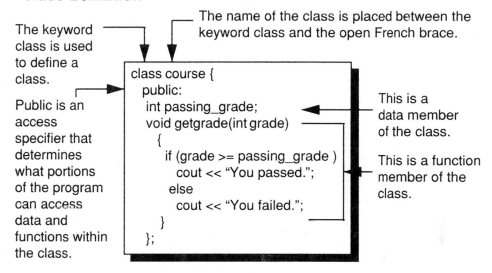

The name of the class is placed between the keyword class and the open French brace.

The keyword class is used to define a class.

Public is an access specifier that determines what portions of the program can access data and functions within the class.

```
class course {
    public:
    int passing_grade;
    void getgrade(int grade)
      {
        if (grade >= passing_grade )
          cout << "You passed.";
        else
          cout << "You failed.";
      }
};
```

This is a data member of the class.

This is a function member of the class.

Terms You Should Know ...

Class	A collection of data and functions.
Data Member	A variable that is a member of a class.
Function Member	A function that is a member of a class.

Declaring an Instance
of a Class

The class definition shown above the main( ) function in the example on the opposite page does not reserve memory. This simply defines the class called course. Memory is reserved by declaring an instance of the class in the program. An instance is a copy of the template.

An instance of a class is declared by specifying the name of the class followed by the name of the instance. This is illustrated on the opposite page where the first statement in the main( ) function declares an instance of the class course. The name of this instance is cs101, which is referred to as an object of the course class.

Each instance of a class contains unique memory locations for data members of the instance. For example, there could also be another instance of course declared with the name of cs102. Both instances will have memory reserved for the passing_grade data member. Each instance has its own copy of the passing_grade data member.

However, instances of the same class share function members. That is, there is only a single copy of getgrade( ) in memory. The compiler tracks which instance calls the function member so that the function uses only data members that are associated with that instance.

Members of an instance that are defined within the public access specifier of the class can be used in the program by specifying the name of the instance, the dot operator and the name of the member of the instance. In the example on the opposite page, the passing_grade members of the instance cs101 are assigned the value 70 by using the dot operator and the assignment operator. Likewise, the next statement calls the function member by using the dot operator. Notice that a value is passed to the function. Data members and function members are used the same way in a program as if they were not associated with an instance. Only the calling convention is different.

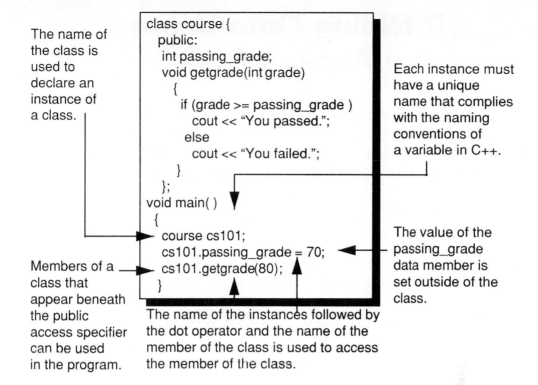

The name of the class is used to declare an instance of a class.

```
class course {
    public:
      int passing_grade;
      void getgrade(int grade)
        {
          if (grade >= passing_grade )
            cout << "You passed.";
          else
            cout << "You failed.";
        }
};
void main( )
  {
    course cs101;
    cs101.passing_grade = 70;
    cs101.getgrade(80);
  }
```

Each instance must have a unique name that complies with the naming conventions of a variable in C++.

Members of a class that appear beneath the public access specifier can be used in the program.

The name of the instances followed by the dot operator and the name of the member of the class is used to access the member of the class.

The value of the passing_grade data member is set outside of the class.

Terms You Should Know ...

○	Instance	An instance is a copy of a class. Only when an instance is declared is memory reserved.
○	Dot Operator	The dot operator separates the name of the instance from the member of the class that is being accessed in the program.

Hiding Data Using the Access Specifier

An advantage of using C++ and classes is that use of data members and function members can be controlled from within the class definition. This is made possible through the use of the *access specifier*. On the previous pages, the public access specifier is used to inform that compiler that any class or any part of the program can use the data member and function member of the course class.

However, the example on the opposite page limits access to the data member of this class by using the *private access specifier*. The private access specifier tells the compiler that those members defined beneath the private access specifier cannot be used by any part of the program that is outside of the class. This means that only function members of the class can use any member that is defined in the private section of the class definition.

This is clearly illustrated in the example on the opposite page. Here, the data member of the class is defined in the private sector of the class. Only the getgrade( ) function is able to use this data member. If the following statement is included in the main( ) function, as is the case on the previous page, the compiler will signal an error that the data member is not accessible from within the main( ) function.

cs101.passing_grade = 70;

This technique is called *hiding data*. Although the term data is used, this same technique is also used to hide function members. If the getgrade( ) function is defined beneath the private access specifier, then a compiler error will occur if the program shown on the next page is compiled.

The need to hide members of a class becomes important in complex applications where many programmers are using the same class. Restricting use of members prevents inadvertent bugs from entering the application.

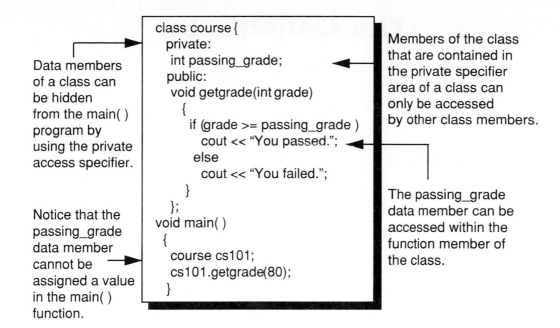

Data members of a class can be hidden from the main( ) program by using the private access specifier.

Notice that the passing_grade data member cannot be assigned a value in the main( ) function.

```
class course {
    private:
     int passing_grade;
    public:
     void getgrade(int grade)
     {
        if (grade >= passing_grade )
          cout << "You passed.";
        else
          cout << "You failed.";
     }
};
void main( )
{
    course cs101;
    cs101.getgrade(80);
}
```

Members of the class that are contained in the private specifier area of a class can only be accessed by other class members.

The passing_grade data member can be accessed within the function member of the class.

Terms You Should Know ...

○	Private	Private is an access specifier that limits access only to class members from within the class.
○	Public	Public is an access specifier that permits access to class member by other members in the class, other classes, and from within the main( ) or other functions in the program.

The Constructor

Whenever an instance of a class is declared, the compiler can be instructed to automatically execute a particular function member of the class. This function is called the *constructor*. The constructor takes the same form as other function members with one exception: the name of the function must be the same as the name of the class.

Notice that in the example on the opposite page there are two function members. These are course( ) and getgrade( ). The course( ) function member shown below is the constructor for the course class. Each time an instance of the course class is created, the compiler immediately calls the course( ) function.

course ( )

A constructor is used for housekeeping chores, such as to reserve a block of memory or to initialize data members. This is the case in the program shown on the next page. The constructor contains a single statement that assigns the value 70 to the data member passing_grade.

When the first statement in the main( ) function is executed, the compiler creates an instance of the course class called cs101. Before the next statement is executed, however, the compiler calls the course( ) function to initialize the passing grade for course cs101.

Constructors are optional. An instance of a class will operate properly without the use of a contructor. Only use a constructor in a class where data members must be initialized or if a block of heap memory must be reserved for data members of the class. Avoid using a constructor unnecessarily. The definition of a constructor within a class when a constructor is unwarranted clutters the definition of the class and makes it difficult for the programmer to read.

A constructor is a member function that is called automatically when an instance of the class is created. A constructor can be used to initialize data members and reserve memory.

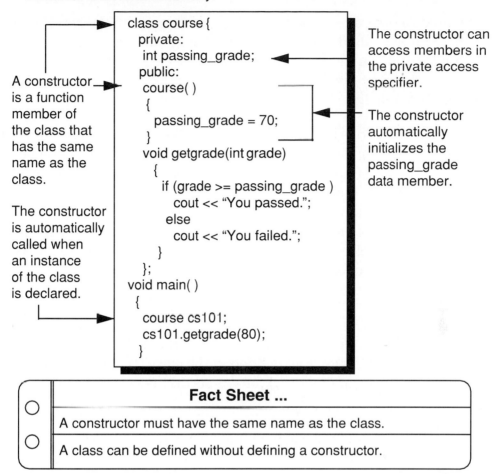

A constructor is a function member of the class that has the same name as the class.

The constructor is automatically called when an instance of the class is declared.

```
class course {
    private:
    int passing_grade;
    public:
    course( )
    {
        passing_grade = 70;
    }
    void getgrade(int grade)
    {
        if (grade >= passing_grade )
            cout << "You passed.";
        else
            cout << "You failed.";
    }
};
void main( )
{
    course cs101;
    cs101.getgrade(80);
}
```

The constructor can access members in the private access specifier.

The constructor automatically initializes the passing_grade data member.

Fact Sheet ...

A constructor must have the same name as the class.

A class can be defined without defining a constructor.

Overloading the Constructor

C++ enables a program to create multiple functions with the same name. This technique is called *overloading*. In the C programming language, functions are identified to the compiler by the name of the function. However, in C++ functions are identified by using the name of the function and the formal parameters list.

Therefore, the functions maxvalue( ) and maxvalue(int) are considered the same function in C and different functions in C++. C++ treats the name of the function and the number and type of the parameters as the identifier of the function. A function can have a different number of parameters or the same number of parameters but the parameters are of different data types. For example, maxvalue(int) and maxvalue(char) have the same number of parameters but the parameters are different data types, which makes each function unique.

A constructor is a function member of a class and therefore has all the characteristics of any function. That is, a constructor can be overloaded. This technique is illustrated in the example on the opposite page. Notice that there are two constructors defined in the class. The first constructor does not require a parameter while the second constructor requires a parameter.

Which constructor is called when an instance of the class is created? The answer depends on whether or not a value is passed to the instance when the instance is created. If a value is not passed to the instance, then the constructor without the parameter is called by the compiler. This constructor establishes a default value for the passing_grade data member.

However, in the example on the opposite page, the value 75 is passed when the instance is declared. The compiler searches the class definition for a constructor that contains an integer parameter. When found, the value 75 is passed to the constructor, which then initializes the passing_grade data member for the instance.

C++ recognizes a function by the uniqueness of the function name and formal arguments.

There can be more than one function—and constructor—with the same name in a C++ program as long as the formal parameter lists are different. This concept is called overloading.

Functions that have the same name must have either a different number of arguments or the same number of arguments but the arguments must be of different data types.

Here, the constructor is overloaded. This allows the programmer to use the constructor without the parameter to set the default passing grade. The programmer also has the option to specify the passing grade as an argument to the constructor.

```cpp
class course {
   private:
    int passing_grade;
   public:
    course( )
     {
       passing_grade = 70;
     }
    course(int grade)
     {
       passing_grade = grade;
     }
    void getgrade(int grade)
     {
       if (grade >= passing_grade )
         cout << "You passed.";
       else
         cout << "You failed.";
     }
   };
void main( )
   {
     course cs101(75);
     cs101.getgrade(80);
   }
```

Fact Sheet ...

The compiler matches the name of the constructor and the formal parameter list to determine which constructor to use.

The Destructor

The compiler can call a specific function whenever the instance of the function is terminated. This function is called a destructor. A destructor is nearly identical to that of a constructor except that name of the constructor must begin with a tilde (~) and have the same name as the class.

This technique is illustrated in the example on the opposite page. Here, there is a constructor called course( ) and a destructor called ~course( ). The destructor in this example displays a message "Goodbye" on the screen. In a typical C++ application, the destructor is used to free heap memory that was reserved by the constructor when the instance of the class was declared.

The destructor is called whenever the instance of the class loses scope. The scope of an instance is determined by the position of the declaration statement within the program. Scope is also determined by the code block within which the declaration statement is called. Remember, a code block begins with an open French brace ({) and ends with a closed French brace (}).

Code blocks can be used throughout a program, therefore, be careful when declaring instances of a class. If the declaration of the instance is made within the main( ) function's code block, then the instance remains alive throughout the life of the program. The destructor is called immediately preceding the termination of the program.

On the other hand, if the instance is declared within a function other than the main( ) function, then the destructor is executed after the last statement in the function. The instance loses scope when the function terminates. The same effect occurs when a code block associates with an if statement, while statement or any code block where an instance of a class is declared.

A destructor is a member function that is called automatically when an instance of the class is destroyed. A destructor can be used to release reserved memory.

An instance of a class is destroyed when the instance loses scope. If the instance is declared globally, then scope of the instance ends when the program ends. If the instance is declared locally, the instance ends when the code block ends. ⟶

```
class course {
   private:
    int passing_grade;
   public:
    course( )
    {
      passing_grade = 70;
    }
    ~course( )
    {
      cout << "Goodbye.";
    }
    void getgrade(int grade)
    {
      if (grade >= passing_grade )
        cout << "You passed.";
      else
        cout << "You failed.";
    }
  };
void main( )
  {
    course cs101;
    cs101.getgrade(80);
  }
```

The constructor.

The destructor.

The instance cs101 is declared locally to the main( ) function.

Defining a Function Member Outside the Class Definition

As can be imagined, a class definition can become confusing when many functions are defined as members of the class. Function definitions simply clutter the text that defines the class. C++ provides a technique that eliminates this clutter while maintaining the integrity of the class definition.

This technique requires that the definition of the function member be created outside of the class definition. This is shown in the example on the opposite page. The definition of the class called course contains two members. The first is passing_grade, which is a data member, and the getgrade( ) function, a function member.

However, within the class definition there is a reference to the function getgrade(). The actual definition of the function takes place outside of the class definition. The reference within the class definition is the function prototype, which is the same syntax as the function's header statement. This statement must end with a semicolon.

The definition of the function must begin with the name of the class and be followed by the *scope resolution operator* (::), and by the name of the function. This is shown on the opposite page.

Notice that the header statement of the function definition does not end with a semicolon. Except for the reference to the name of the class and the scope resolution operator, the function member definition is the same whether the function is defined inside or outside of the class definition.

Always declare function members of a class outside of a class unless the class contains only a simple function. Data members, however, must be defined with the definition of the class.

Member functions of a class can be defined within the class definition or defined outside of the class definition. The member function definition must include the name of the class followed by the scope resolution operator then the name of the class.

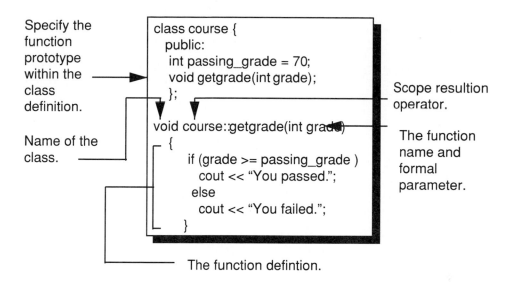

Specify the function prototype within the class definition.

Name of the class.

```
class course {
    public:
    int passing_grade = 70;
    void getgrade(int grade);
};

void course::getgrade(int grade)
{
    if (grade >= passing_grade )
        cout << "You passed.";
    else
        cout << "You failed.";
}
```

Scope resultion operator.

The function name and formal parameter.

The function defintion.

Tricks of the Trade

Avoid defining complex member functions within the definition of the class. This makes the class definition difficult to read.

Chapter Eight

Working with Overloading

- Overloading
- Overloading a Function Using Different Data Types
- Overloading a Unary Operator
- Overloading a Binary Operator
- Operators that Can and Cannot Be Overloaded

Overloading

Functions are identified in C++ by their complete header. The header includes the name of the function and any parameters that are contained within the function's parentheses. The complete function header must be unique for every function otherwise there is a compiler error.

This concept is different than the technique for identifying functions in the C language. In C, functions are uniquely identified by just the function name. The formal parameter list of the function is not used to identify the function.

Using the same name for multiple functions is referred to as *overloading a function*. This technique is illustrated in the example on the opposite page. Here, there are two functions called raise( ). The first function does not contain any formal parameters. The second function is passed an integer.

The compiler is not confused as to which function to execute when the statement raise( ) is encountered in the program. The compiler references the function whose header matches the function calling statement. For example, when raise() is called, the compiler realizes that no parameter is passed to the function; therefore, there is only one function with the name raise( ) that is without a formal parameter.

The same logic is followed by the compiler the second time raise( ) is called except this time, the value 300 is passed to the function. The compiler then logically executes the raise( ) function that contains a single formal parameter that is an integer.

An overloaded function can have the same name. It must also have a unique combination of number of parameters and type of parameters. That is, functions can have the same number of parameters but of different data types. For example, there could be a function raise(char) that will not conflict with raise(int) because the data type is different.

C++ enables the programmer to give functions and operators multiple funcitonality while maintaining the integrity of the function name and operator symbol.

Overloading a Function

Function prototypes

The raise( ) function is overloaded. There are two functions with the same name but with different arguments.

The compiler identifies which function to use by evaluating the function name and the arguments.

In the first function call no arguments are used therefore the default value is displayed. An argument is used in the second function call to set the value of the raise.

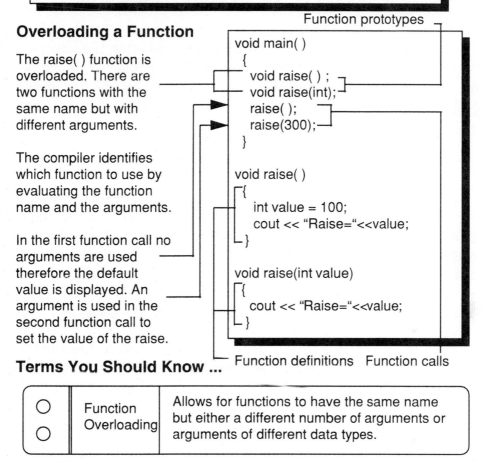

```
void main( )
{
    void raise( ) ;
    void raise(int);
    raise( );
    raise(300);
}

void raise( )
{
    int value = 100;
    cout << "Raise="<<value;
}

void raise(int value)
{
    cout << "Raise="<<value;
}
```

Function definitions   Function calls

Terms You Should Know ...

	Function Overloading	Allows for functions to have the same name but either a different number of arguments or arguments of different data types.

Overloading a Function Using Different Data Types

In the example on the opposite page and shown below, the raise( ) function is overloaded by using the same function name but changing the data type of the value passed to each function. In the first case, the raise( ) function is passed a float then the function is passed an integer.

```
void raise(float);
void raise(int);
```

Notice that these functions are defined outside of the main( ) function. Only the function prototypes are placed within main( ). When the function is called, the compiler will examine the data type of the value passed to the function. If the data type is an integer, then the raise(int) function is executed. If a float data type is passed, then the raise(float) function is executed. However, if a value of a different data type is passed, such as a character data type, then the compiler will display an error.

Overloading functions enables programmers to reduce the number of functions that must be learned by other programmers. In a traditional C program, raise(int) and raise(float) must have two distinct function names. Learning these names and names of other functions can become time-consuming and confusing for many programmers.

With overloading, however, the programmer needs only to know the single function called raise( ), which can accept either an integer value or a float value. Regardless of the value of the parameter passed to the function, the function names remain the same.

A word of caution. Avoid unnecessary function overloading in a program. Only use overloading when this feature will add clarity to the program and reduce the number of similarly named functions.

The raise function is overloaded.

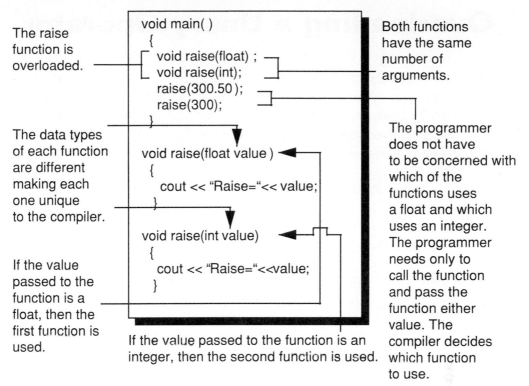

Both functions have the same number of arguments.

```
void main( )
{
    void raise(float) ;
    void raise(int);
    raise(300.50 );
    raise(300);
}

void raise(float value )
{
    cout << "Raise="<< value;
}

void raise(int value)
{
    cout << "Raise="<<value;
}
```

The data types of each function are different making each one unique to the compiler.

If the value passed to the function is a float, then the first function is used.

The programmer does not have to be concerned with which of the functions uses a float and which uses an integer. The programmer needs only to call the function and pass the function either value. The compiler decides which function to use.

If the value passed to the function is an integer, then the second function is used.

Terms You Should Know ...

○ ○	Data Type	A data type describes the type of value that will be placed in a particular memory location. Data types are declared using keywords such as int.

Overloading a Unary Operator

In addition to functions, the overloading feature of C++ can be used to overload operators. This means that the functionality of an operator can be changed by overloading the operator in the program. This technique is illustrated on the opposite page where the functionality of the unary operator ++ is enhanced.

An operator is overloaded by creating an operator function. In this example, the operator++( ) function is created as a member of the class display. Notice that the keyword operator must be followed by the C++ operator that is to be overloaded and then parentheses.

A code block then follows where statements that specify the new functionality for the operator are defined. In this example, the counter data member of the class is incremented by one.

Notice that the compiler executes the new functionality of the incremental operator only if the incremental operator is used with an instance of the class. This is illustrated in the main( ) function of the example. First, an instance of a class display called a is declared. When the instance is declared the constructor display( ) automatically initializes the counter data member of the class to zero.

Next, the ++a statement is executed. The compiler notices that a is an instance of a class and not a numeric data type. Therefore, the compiler uses the overloaded functionality of the incremental operator. If the incremental operator is used on an operand that is not the instance of the class, then the traditional functionality of the incremental operator is executed.

A word of caution! Unnecessary operator overloading can cause confusion for the programmer who must modify your application. Make sure that comments in the program indicate that the operator is overloaded.

Operator overloading enables a programmer to give new functionality to the standard operators used in C++. The operator keyword must precede the operator that is to be overloaded. The new functionality for the operator is placed within the operator function code block.

The counter variable is hidden.

The incremental operator is overloaded.

This function displays the value of the counter variable.

The overloaded incremental operator is used to manipulate the instance of the display class.

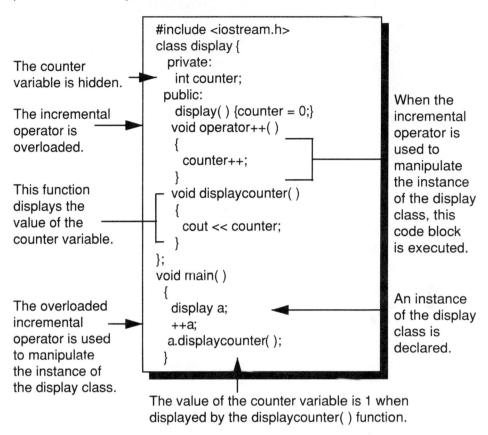

```
#include <iostream.h>
class display {
  private:
    int counter;
  public:
    display( ) {counter = 0;}
    void operator++( )
    {
      counter++;
    }
    void displaycounter( )
    {
      cout << counter;
    }
};
void main( )
{
  display a;
  ++a;
  a.displaycounter( );
}
```

When the incremental operator is used to manipulate the instance of the display class, this code block is executed.

An instance of the display class is declared.

The value of the counter variable is 1 when displayed by the displaycounter( ) function.

Overloading a Binary Operator

The technique for overloading a binary operator is a little different than overloading a unary operator. Conceptually, both involve the same process in that the existing functionality of the operator is enhanced. However, the code block of the binary operator function differs from that of the unary operator function.

In the example on the opposite page, the addition operator (+) is overloaded. This operator requires two operands. One of the operands is passed to the addition operator function and is a different instance of the same class. The second operand is the data member of the current instance of the class.

Inside the code block of the addition operator( ) function another instance of the class is declared. This instance is called temp and is used within the addition operator( ) function to hold the results of the manipulation by the addition operator. The temp instance of the class is then returned.

The second statement in the main( ) function uses the addition operator to add data members of instances of a and b the results of which are assigned to the data member of instance c. All these instances are of the same class.

The value of the data member of instance b is passed to the addition operator function of instance a. The values of the data members of both instances are added and the sum is assigned to the temp instance of the same class. The temp instance is returned by the addition operator function, which is in turn assigned to the data member of the instance c.

The last statement in the main( ) function calls the displaycounter( ) function of the c instance of the display class. This function displays the value of the counter member of the c instance to the screen. Although this example performed a single addition equation, multiple data members can be manipulated by using a single overloaded addition operator in a statement.

A temporary instance of the same class is declared.

The temporary instance is then returned and assigned to instance c.

Add the value of the counter variable of instance b to the counter variable of instance a then the sum is assigned to counter variable of instance c.

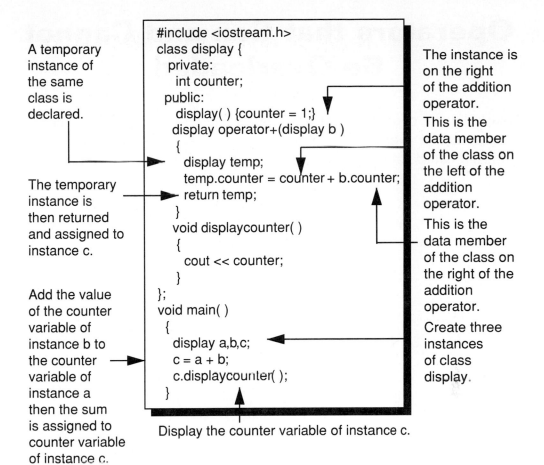

```cpp
#include <iostream.h>
class display {
  private:
    int counter;
  public:
    display( ) {counter = 1;}
    display operator+(display b )
    {
      display temp;
      temp.counter = counter + b.counter;
      return temp;
    }
    void displaycounter( )
    {
      cout << counter;
    }
};
void main( )
{
  display a,b,c;
  c = a + b;
  c.displaycounter( );
}
```

The instance is on the right of the addition operator.

This is the data member of the class on the left of the addition operator.

This is the data member of the class on the right of the addition operator.

Create three instances of class display.

Display the counter variable of instance c.

Operators that Can and Cannot Be Overloaded

Nearly all the operators that are available in C++ can be overloaded. A few cannot be overloaded. Tables on the opposite page contain operators that can be overloaded and operators that cannot be overloaded.

Can Be Overloaded

+	~	/=	<<=	--
-	!	%=	==	->*
*	=	^=	!=	,
\	<	&=	<=	->
%	>	|=	>=	[ ]
^	+=	<<	&&	( )
&	-=	>>	||	new
|	*=	>>=	++	delete

Cannot Be Overloaded

```
.
.*
::
?:
sizeof
```

Helpful Tips ...

Be sure the overloaded functionality remains intuitive to the user.

Overloaded unary operators (++) can be implemented as pre- or postincrement.

Overloaded unary operators should be defined as a member of a class.

Be sure that the compiler that is being used supports overloading a particular operator used in the program.

Chapter Nine

Working with Inheritance

- Inheritance
- Access Specifiers
- More About Inheritance
- Multiple Inheritance
- Ambiguity in Multiple Inheritance
- Containership Class
- Levels of Inheritance

Inheritance

Members of a class can be used by members of another class through the technique of *inheritance*. The class that is inherited by another class is referred to as a *base class*. The class that inherits the other class is called the *derived class*. This technique is illustrated in the example on the opposite page.

The class course is the base class that is inherited by the class student. Class student is the derived class. A derived class can use any member of the base class that is defined beneath the *protected* and *public access specifier* of the base class.

In this example, the derived class student inherits the pass_grade data member of the base class course and the function member course( ), which is the constructor of the base class.

A base class is defined similarly to classes that have been defined in the previous chapter with one exception. A base class must contain the protected access specifier section of the class definition to control which members of the class can be used by derived classes. Only derived classes can use members that are defined in the protected access specifier section of the base class.

A derived class is defined by specifying the name of the class followed by a colon, then the name of the base class from which the derived class will inherit class members. This is shown on the opposite page where the student class is defined as a derived class from the course class.

Notice that the student class displays the value of the pass_grade data member of the course class. The pass_grade data member, which is defined in the protected section of the base class, is available to the derived class and the base class but not to other parts of the program.

Members of a class can utilize data members and function members from another class by inheriting members. Inheritance enables subsequent classes to access but not control members of another class.

Single Inheritance

The protected access specifier defines members that can be used by derived classes.

A derived class is a class that inherits from another class.

A base class is inherited by another class.

This class is inherited by the student class.

This class inherits the course class.

All public members of the base class will remain public in the derived class.

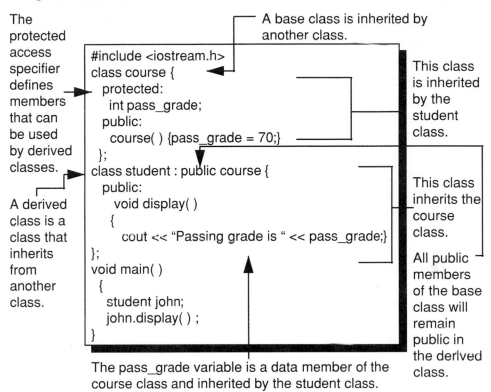

```
#include <iostream.h>
class course {
  protected:
    int pass_grade;
  public:
    course( ) {pass_grade = 70;}
};
class student : public course {
  public:
    void display( )
    {
      cout << "Passing grade is " << pass_grade;}
};
void main( )
{
  student john;
  john.display( ) ;
}
```

The pass_grade variable is a data member of the course class and inherited by the student class.

Access Specifiers

C++ has three access specifiers. These are *private, protected* and *public*. Each access specifier limits the access to class members that are defined beneath the corresponding section of the class. Class member defined in the private access specifier section of the class can only be accessed by other members of the same class. That is, a function member of another class or the program itself can use data and function members that are defined beneath the private section of a class.

In contrast, members of a class that are defined beneath the protected access specifier section of the class can be accessed by members of the class and by members of derived classes. Any member beneath the protected access specifier section is inherited by a derived class. Other classes and the program itself cannot directly use members that are beneath the protected access specifier section of a class.

This technique is shown on the opposite page where the pass_grade data member of the class course is used by the derived class student.

Any member beneath the public access specifier section of a class can be accessed by members of the same class, by members of the derived class, and by any part of the program. This technique is illustrated in the last statement of the main( ) function on the opposite page.

Here, the display( ) function is used directly in the program although this function is a member of class student. Notice, however, that an instance of a class must be referenced in the program before the member can be accessed. In this example, an instance called john is declared then the dot operator is used to call the display( ) function member of the instance john. The program cannot directly reference the function member using the statement display( );.

The chart on the opposite page illustrates the limitations of each of the three access specifiers.

Divides classes into sections that provide limited access to class members.

Data members defined in the protected section can be accessed by derived classes and its own class.

Data members defined in the private section can be accessed by its own class.

Data members defined in the public section can be accessed outside the class.

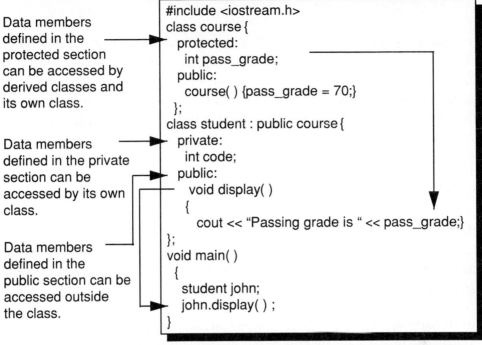

```cpp
#include <iostream.h>
class course {
  protected:
    int pass_grade;
  public:
    course( ) {pass_grade = 70;}
};
class student : public course {
  private:
    int code;
  public:
    void display( )
    {
        cout << "Passing grade is " << pass_grade;}
};
void main( )
{
    student john;
    john.display( ) ;
}
```

	Access Specifier	Accessible from own class	Accessible from derived class	Accessible from outside class
○	private	Yes	Yes	Yes
○	protected	Yes	Yes	No
	public	Yes	No	No

More About Inheritance

An advantage of inheritance is that characteristics of one class can be enhanced by another class without changing the basic characteristics of the base class. For example, a base class called course can have a data member that contains the passing grade for the course. A derived class called professor can use this passing grade or change the passing grade for the professor's section of the course.

Although the class professor may change the passing grade for the professor's section, the default passing grade that is contained in the base class remains unchanged. That is, the derived class can change or enhance the passing grade characteristics of the class course but cannot change the characteristic in the base class. The value of the passing grade in the class course is not affected by modifications made by a base class.

Inheritance allows a programmer to utilize code that is developed by another programmer. In the previous example, the programmer who developed the base class called course specified the fundamental characteristics of the course, one of which is the passing grade.

However, the programmer who created the derived class called professor did not have to be concerned with that basic specification. Instead, the programmer inherited all those characteristics from the base class called course then only needed to focus on enhancing those characteristics.

The benefit of inheritance is realized in complex applications, such as software that is used to design tires. For example, a programmer might be responsible for building a tire—which is a class in C++. Another programmer enhances the tire class by creating a truck tire class. The truck tire class inherits all the basic characteristics of a tire class, then enhances those characteristics to reflect the needs of a truck tire.

Terms You Should Know ...

	Inheritance	The process of creating new classes from existing classes.
	Base Class	The class that will be inherited by one or more classes.
	Derived Class	The class that inherits members from one or more classes.
	Access Specifier	A keyword that defined access to members of a class.
	private	An access specifier that grants access only to members of its class.
	protected	An access specifier that grants access to its own class members and derived class members.
	public	An access specifier that grants access to its own class, derived classes and from outside its class.

Fact Sheet ...

Members of the base class that are used by a derived class remain unchanged.
A derived class can enhance the capabilities of members of the base class.
Inheritance allows for reusable code that can be enhanced without touching the members of the base class.
Reverse inheritance does not exist. A base class cannot inherit members from a derived class.

Multiple Inheritance

Examples on the previous pages illustrate *single inheritance*. This is where a derived class inherits the characteristics of a single base class. C++ enables classes to inherit characteristics from more than one base class. This is referred to as *multiple inheritance*.

A derived class can inherit from more than once base class by extending the derived class definition header with the comma operator. The name of the derived class is followed by a colon, then the name of the first base class, the comma operator and the name of the second base class.

This technique is illustrated in the example on the opposite page. Here, the class student is derived from both the class course and the class recorded. Members of both class course and class recorded that are defined beneath the protected access specifier section of these classes are inherited by the class called student.

Notice that within the main( ) function an instance of the student class called john is declared. The program then calls the display( ) function for the instance john. This function is a member of the class student and displays the passing grade for the course, which is inherited by class student from class course.

Next, the program calls the final_grade( ) function of the instance john. This function is inherited by the class student from class recorded. The final_grade( ) function is passed the student's grade, which then determines the corresponding final grade and displays the results on the screen.

A word of caution! Avoid inheriting from too many base classes. This can lead to confusion when reading the program. Some programmers have set a practical limitation of five base classes. Therefore, use this number as a guideline when developing the class structure for your own applications.

Multiple inheritance occurs when a class is derived from more than one base class.

The first base class determines the passing grade for the course.

The second base class determines the final grade for the course.

The student class is derived from both the course and the recorded classes.

john is an instance of the derived class.

final_grade( ) is inherited from the recorded class.

```cpp
#include <iostream.h>
class course {
    protected:
        int pass_grade;
    public:
        course( ) {pass_grade = 70;}
};
class recorded {
    public:
        void final_grade(int grade)
        {
            if (grade > 89 )
                cout << "Final grade is " << 4;
            if (grade > 79 && grade < 90)
                cout << "Final grade is " << 3;
            if (grade > 69 && grade < 80)
                cout << "final Grade is " << 2;
        }
};
class student : public course, public recorded{
    public:
        void display( ) {cout << "Passing grade is " << pass_grade;}
};
void main( )
{
    student john;
    john.display( ) ;
    john.final_grade(80);
}
```

The pass_grade variable is inherited from the course class.

Ambiguity in Multiple Inheritance

Problems can arise when a derive class inherits from more than one base class. A typical problem is that the derive class and the base classes have members with the same name. The confusion arises when the program references the class member.

The example on the opposite page illustrates this problem. Here, there are three classes. The class junior is derived from class sophomore and class freshman. All three classes contain a function member called display( ). The program creates an instance of the junior class called student. However, there could be confusion if the program uses the following statement. Which display( ) function is called?

```
student.display( );
```

In this case, the display( ) function member of class student is executed by the compiler. How could the display( ) function member of the other classes be called?

The program statement must explicitly specify the display( ) function member by using the name of the base class followed by the scope resolution operator then specify the name of the function member. This technique is illustrated below and on the opposite page.

```
student.freshman::display( );
```

This statement clarifies which member of a base class is to be called. Notice that this statement still must reference the instance of the derived class. In this example, the instance of the derived class is student.

The compiler might become confused when an instance of a derived class references a member function that has identical names in the base classes. Avoid conflicts by using unique names for class members or by explicitly calling a function member from a base class.

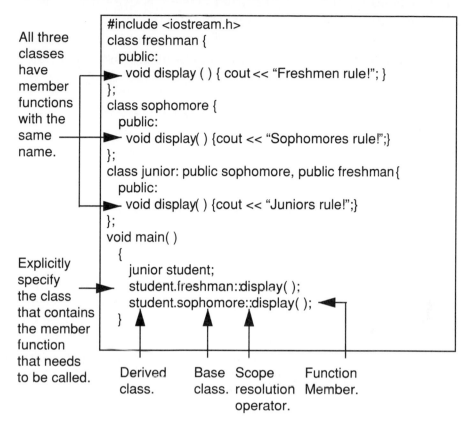

All three classes have member functions with the same name.

```
#include <iostream.h>
class freshman {
    public:
        void display ( ) { cout << "Freshmen rule!"; }
};
class sophomore {
    public:
        void display( ) {cout << "Sophomores rule!";}
};
class junior: public sophomore, public freshman{
    public:
        void display( ) {cout << "Juniors rule!";}
};
void main( )
    {
        junior student;
        student.freshman::display( );
        student.sophomore::display( );
    }
```

Explicitly specify the class that contains the member function that needs to be called.

Derived class.

Base class.

Scope resolution operator.

Function Member.

Containership Class

The idea of building classes from other classes is explored in detail on the previous pages of this chapter by using the technique of inheritance. Another way of building on existing classes is to use a containership class. A *containership class* is a class that contains an instance of another class.

The major difference between base class-derive class inheritance and a containership class is that only public members of the contained class can be used by the containership class. This concept is clearly illustrated on the opposite page.

Notice that an instance of the course class called cs101 is declared within the class student. The class course is the contained class and the class student is the containership class. If the class called course had protected members, then the class student could not access those members. However, if the class student is derived from the class course, then the protected members, if there were any, could be accessed from within the class student.

A containership class has the same access to members of the contained class as does the program itself. Practically, there is no difference between declaring an instance of the contained class (course) from within the containership class (student) or from within the program (main( )).

Public members of the contained class can be accessed from within the containership class by referencing the name of the instance of the contained class as shown below. Public members can also be accessed from the program by first referencing the instance of the containership class. This is illustrated in the example on the opposite page. Both the instance of the containership class and the instance of the contained class must be referenced to directly access a public member of the contained class.

cs101.display( );

A containership class contains an object of another class. Once the object is declared in the class, the class can use public members of the object.

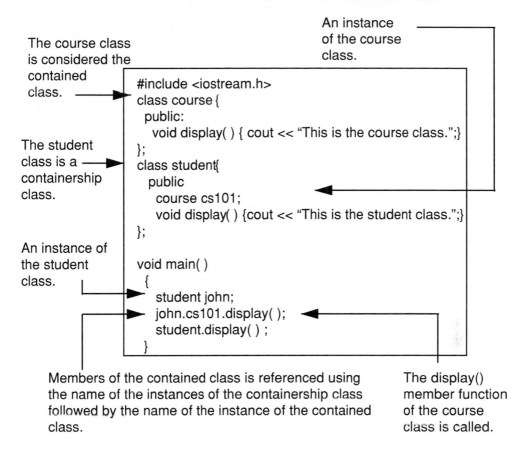

An instance of the course class.

The course class is considered the contained class.

The student class is a containership class.

An instance of the student class.

```
#include <iostream.h>
class course {
    public:
        void display( ) { cout << "This is the course class.";}
};
class student{
    public
        course cs101;
        void display( ) {cout << "This is the student class.";}
};

void main( )
    {
        student john;
        john.cs101.display( );
        student.display( ) ;
    }
```

Members of the contained class is referenced using the name of the instances of the containership class followed by the name of the instance of the contained class.

The display() member function of the course class is called.

Levels of Inheritance

There are two techniques that can be used to inherit characteristics from more than one class. The topic of multiple inheritance is presented earlier in this chapter. In that section, several base classes are used to create a derived class. The derived class then inherits characteristics for each of the base classes.

Another technique of multiple inheritance is to use multiple levels of inheritance. *Multiple levels of inheritance* is created when a derived class is inherited by another derived class. That is, the initial derived class becomes a base class to another derived class.

This technique is illustrated on the opposite page. The class called course is a base class that is inherited by class recorded. Class called recorded is the derived class, derived from class course. The derived class student is derived from the class recorded.

Class student inherits all of the protected members of the class recorded, which includes all the protected members of the class course. Therefore, class student inherits all the protected members of the class course without class student being derived from class course.

This chaining effect enables each class in the chain to enhance the characteristics of the previous classes. For example, the first base class can define a tire. The first derived class enhances this definition to define a car tire. The next derived class in this chain enhances the car tire definition to include the definition of a car tire for a Nissan Sentra.

The programmer who creates the class that defines the tire for the Nissan Sentra is not concerned about the fundamental design of a car tire. The programmer is only concerned about the difference between the previously defined car tire and a tire for a Nissan Sentra. Likewise, if a change is made to the fundamental design of a car tire, this change will automatically be incorporated into the car tire for the Nissan Sentra since this characteristic is inherited.

A derived class can inherit from another derived class.

```cpp
#include <iostream.h>
class course {
  protected:
    int pass_grade;
  public:
    course( ) {pass_grade = 70;}
};
class recorded : public course {
  public:
    void final_grade(int grade)
      {
        if (grade > 89 )
          cout << "Final grade is " << 4;
        if (grade > 79 && grade < 90)
          cout << "Final grade is " << 3;
        if (grade > 69 && grade < 80)
          cout << "final Grade is " << 2;
      }
};
class student :public recorded {
  public:
    void display( ) {cout << "Passing grade is " << pass_grade;}
};
void main( )
  {
    student john;
    john.display( ) ;
    john.final_grade(80);
  }
```

The course class is a base class.

The recorded class is both a derived class from the course class and a base class.

The student class is a derived class from the recorded class.

Working with Pointers

- Pointers
- Using Pointers in Expressions
- Incrementing Pointers
- Decrementing Pointers
- Pointer Math
- Tricks of the Trade
- An Array of Pointers
- Pointers-to-Pointers
- Pointer-to-a-Function
- Tricks of the Trade

Pointers

The concept of *pointers* can be confusing to understand; however, this chapter provides a clear explanation of how to use pointers. In the previous chapters it was stated that data is stored in memory by assigning a value to a variable. Before the assignment is made, the variable must be declared as a particular data type and assigned a name.

A declaration of a variable does two things. First, the declaration statement reserves a memory location that is large enough to hold a value of the specific data type. For example, a variable that is a char data type is one byte on a personal computer. An integer is two bytes on the same computer.

Every memory location is identified internally by the computer by using the memory's address. Although the address, which is a numeric value, is meaningful to the computer, the address is difficult to use directly by the programmer. Instead of referring to data by using the address of its memory location, programmers use the variable name. The name of a variable is an alias for the address of the memory location that contains the data.

A *pointer* is a variable that holds an address of a memory location. That is, the value contained in a pointer variable is the address of another variable. This is illustrated on the opposite page. Pointer variable b contains the memory address of integer variable a.

The *asterisk operator* (*) is used to declare a pointer variable. This is shown in the first statement in main( ) on the opposite page. The *ampersand operator* (&) is used to reference the address of a variable. In this example, the ampersand operator appears to the left of the variable a. Here, the compiler is instructed to assign the address of variable a to pointer variable b. The asterisk operator (*) is also used to reference the value of the address pointed to by the pointer. This is shown in the last statement of the program where the value of variable a is displayed on the screen.

Variables are references to locations in the computer's memory where a value is stored. Each memory location is identified by a unique number called an *address*. A pointer is a variable that contains the memory address of another variable.

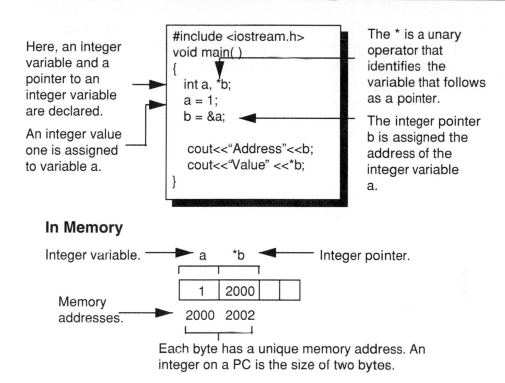

Here, an integer variable and a pointer to an integer variable are declared.

An integer value one is assigned to variable a.

```
#include <iostream.h>
void main( )
{
    int a, *b;
    a = 1;
    b = &a;

    cout<<"Address"<<b;
    cout<<"Value" <<*b;
}
```

The * is a unary operator that identifies the variable that follows as a pointer.

The integer pointer b is assigned the address of the integer variable a.

In Memory

Integer variable. ⟶ a   *b ⟵ Integer pointer.

| 1 | 2000 | | |

Memory addresses. ⟶ 2000 2002

Each byte has a unique memory address. An integer on a PC is the size of two bytes.

Using Pointers in Expressions

Let's review the correct usage of the ampersand operator (&) and the asterisk operator (*). When a variable is used in an expression, the compiler recognizes that the variable name is really a symbol for an address in memory. The compiler assumes that when the variable name is used that the programmer is referencing the value that is contained at that address rather than the address itself. This is illustrated below assuming that both variable a and variable c are integers.

c = a;

However, a programmer can reference the value stored at an address in memory or the address itself. By using the name of the variable, the programmer accesses the value located at that address. By using the ampersand operator (&) to the left of the variable name, the programmer can reference the address of that memory location. This is illustrated on the opposite page and below. Variable b is a pointer and variable a is an integer.

b = &a;

A fair question to ask is, why should a programmer reference an address of a memory location? As is illustrated in Chapter 5, there are occasions when the same data is shared with another section of the program. The most efficient method to accomplish this task is to use a pointer. That is, reference the address of the data rather than the value of the data.

A pointer variable contains an address of another variable. This address can be used by the program by referencing the name of the pointer variable as illustrated in the first display statement on the opposite page. The value of that address (the address contained in the pointer variable) is used in the program by placing the asterisk (*) operator to the left the pointer variable name. This is shown in the last statement on the opposite page.

Terms You Should Know ...

○	*	The asterisk is the unary operator that returns the value of the variable that is located at the address that follows.
○	&	The ampersand unary operator returns the address of the variable that follows.
	unary operator	A unary operator requires only one operand.

Using Pointers in Expressions

A pointer can be used in any expression. However, the program must indicate if the pointer refers to the address itself or the value contained at that address.

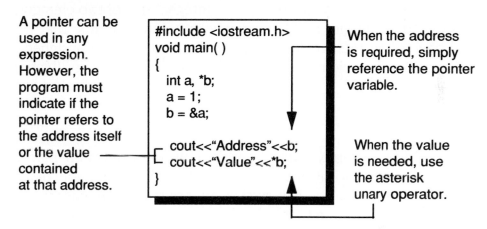

```
#include <iostream.h>
void main( )
{
   int a, *b;
   a = 1;
   b = &a;

   cout<<"Address"<<b;
   cout<<"Value"<<*b;
}
```

When the address is required, simply reference the pointer variable.

When the value is needed, use the asterisk unary operator.

Incrementing Pointers

A pointer is a variable that contains an address of a location in memory. Memory addresses are numeric values that are sequential. In the memory diagram on the opposite page, the first memory location is address 2000. The next address is 2001, then 2002 and so on. What happened to memory address 2001 in this diagram? Address 2000 contains an array element that is the size of an integer data type. An integer data type on a personal computer is two bytes in size. Therefore, data stored at address 2000 takes up two bytes. However, only the first address of the value is referenced. The compiler knows that the value extends to the next byte.

In the example on the opposite page, an integer array of two elements is declared and an integer pointer variable (a pointer variable that holds the address of an integer data type). The pointer is then assigned the address of the first element of the array. This statement is illustrated below.

$$b = \&a[0];$$

Remember, when an array is declared, elements of the array are placed in consecutive memory locations. This is illustrated in the memory diagram on the opposite page. The values that are assigned to elements of the array are stored alongside each other in memory. Notice that the value of the pointer variable b is the address 2000, the address of the first element of the array.

The second element of the array can be referenced by incrementing the pointer variable b. The incremental operator (++) is used with the pointer variable b as shown on the opposite page. This operator increases the value of the pointer by one. The results are shown in the bottom portion of the memory diagram. But this value is 2002 and not 2001! The value of the pointer is increased not by one address but by the size of the data type. In this case, the address holds an integer that requires two bytes. Therefore, the address value is increased by two rather than one.

Incrementing Pointers

The value of a pointer contains an address that can be changed by adding integers to the address.

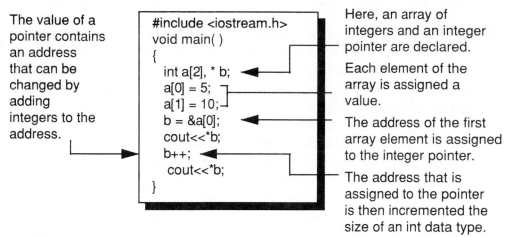

```
#include <iostream.h>
void main( )
{
    int a[2], * b;
    a[0] = 5;
    a[1] = 10;
    b = &a[0];
    cout<<*b;
    b++;
    cout<<*b;
}
```

Here, an array of integers and an integer pointer are declared.

Each element of the array is assigned a value.

The address of the first array element is assigned to the integer pointer.

The address that is assigned to the pointer is then incremented the size of an int data type.

In Memory

Before Incrementing the pointer.

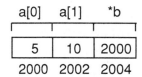

a[0]	a[1]	*b
5	10	2000
2000	2002	2004

After incrementing the pointer.

a[0]	a[1]	*b
5	10	2002
2000	2002	2004

Decrementing Pointers

The *decremental operator* (--) can also be used with a pointer to move to the previous data. Remember, when the value of a pointer is either incremented or decremented, the value of the address contained in the pointer changes according to the size of the data type and not to the next sequential address.

For example, assume that the address 2002 is the address of the first element of a character array. This address is assigned to a pointer. The pointer is decremented. Since the size of the data type of the array is a character, the value of the address in the pointer is reduced by one address. The new value is 2001. This is because the size of a character is a byte of memory and each memory address references one byte.

Now, change this scenario to reflect the example illustrated on the opposite page. In this case, the data type of the data contained in the address 2002 is an integer. An integer in this example requires two bytes of memory or two memory addresses. Therefore, when the decrement operator is applied to the pointer, the resulting value of the pointer is 2000.

When either the incremental or decremental operator is used with a pointer, the compiler knows that the unit of change is the number of bytes that is required by the data type and not simply the memory address. In fact, this is true for any arithmetical operation that is performed on a pointer. This concept is referred to as *pointer arithmetic*.

The compiler knows the unit of change in an expression involving pointer arithmetic by referring to the data type declaration of the pointer variable.

The value of a pointer contains an address that can be changed by subtracting integers from the address.

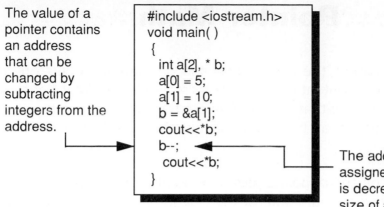

```
#include <iostream.h>
void main( )
{
  int a[2], * b;
  a[0] = 5;
  a[1] = 10;
  b = &a[1];
  cout<<*b;
  b--;
   cout<<*b;
}
```

The address that is assigned to the pointer is decremented by the size of an int data type.

In Memory

Before decrementing the pointer.

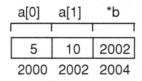

a[0]	a[1]	*b
5	10	2002
2000	2002	2004

After decrementing the pointer.

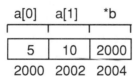

a[0]	a[1]	*b
5	10	2000
2000	2002	2004

Pointer Math

So far in this chapter, the incremental and decremental operators are used to change the contents of the address stored in a pointer. These are not the only operators that can manipulate the value of a pointer. Any arithmetical operator can be used to change the address contained in a pointer variable.

In the example on the opposite page, the addition operator (+) is used to add two to the current value of the pointer variable b. The original value of pointer variable b is 2000. After the addition operation, the value is 2004. Why isn't the address 2002?

Remember, all arithmetic operations on pointers are performed in measurement of the size of the data type. In this example, the integer is the data type and has a size of two bytes. Therefore, adding two to the value of pointer variable b is adding two integer sizes or four bytes.

Although any arithmetical operator can be used in pointer arithmetic, keep in mind that memory addresses are whole numbers. Any mathematical operation that results in a fractional value cannot be used with the contents of a pointer variable.

Assume that the value of a pointer variable is 3005. That is, an address of another variable. The multiplication operator (*) can be used to multiply the address by three, which results in the value 90015. However, it would be inappropriate to divide this value by two since the result is 45007.5. There isn't a location in memory that has an address with a decimal place.

Simple addition and subtraction are sufficient to perform pointer arithmetic in most C++ applications. Avoid using complex expressions that could result in an invalid memory address.

The programmer can use integer arithmetic to change the contents of a pointer.

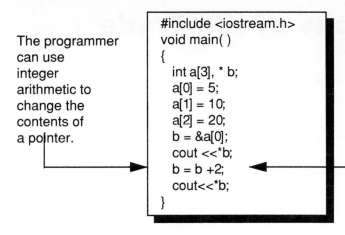

```
#include <iostream.h>
void main( )
{
    int a[3], * b;
    a[0] = 5;
    a[1] = 10;
    a[2] = 20;
    b = &a[0];
    cout <<*b;
    b = b +2;
    cout<<*b;
}
```

Here, the address that is contained in the pointer is increased by two integer addresses. Remember, an integer requires two bytes.

In Memory

Before the pointer addition.

a[0]	a[1]	a[2]	*b
5	10	20	2000
2000	2002	2004	2006

After the pointer addition.

a[0]	a[1]	a[2]	*b
5	10	20	2004
2000	2002	2004	2006

Tricks of the Trade

An array is a collection of data of the same data type that can be referenced by the same name. That is, the name of the variable. Each data type in the collection is called an element and can be treated the way that a variable of the same data type is treated in the program.

The number of elements in the collection is determined by the index value that is placed within square brackets when the array is declared. In the example on the opposite page, three elements are in the array named a. Each element of the array is referenced by using the name of the array followed by the appropriate index number, which is contained within square brackets.

Index numbers begin with zero. That is, the first element of the array is referenced by using the index number zero. The last element is referenced by using the index number two in the example on the opposite page.

On the previous page, an element of an array is referenced by using a pointer variable. This is possible by preceding the array element with an ampersand operator, as is illustrated below. The pointer variable then contains the address of the array element. In the following example, variable b is a pointer.

$$b = \&a[0];$$

There is another technique that can be used to assign the address of the first element of the array to a pointer variable. This is by using the name of the array without specifying an array element, as shown in the example on the opposite page and shown below. The name of the array without brackets refers to the address of the first element.

$$b = a;$$

The address of an array can be assigned to a pointer by specifying the name of the array without an index value. For example, the address of the first element in the array names[5] can be referenced simply by using the word name.

The address of the first element in the array a is assigned to the integer pointer b. ——▶

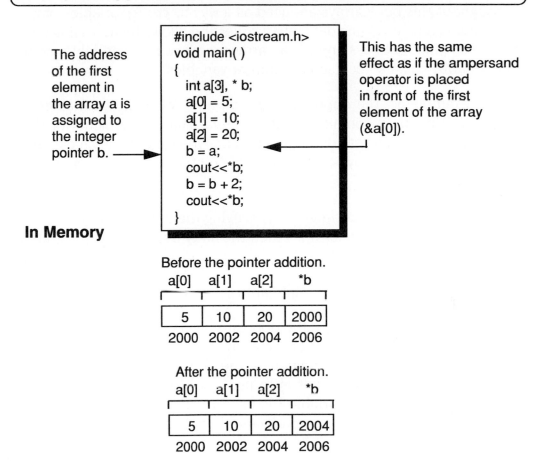

```
#include <iostream.h>
void main( )
{
    int a[3], * b;
    a[0] = 5;
    a[1] = 10;
    a[2] = 20;
    b = a;
    cout<<*b;
    b = b + 2;
    cout<<*b;
}
```

This has the same effect as if the ampersand operator is placed in front of the first element of the array (&a[0]).

In Memory

Before the pointer addition.

a[0]	a[1]	a[2]	*b
5	10	20	2000

2000 2002 2004 2006

After the pointer addition.

a[0]	a[1]	a[2]	*b
5	10	20	2004

2000 2002 2004 2006

An Array of Pointers

Throughout this book arrays are used as a way to group variables of the same data type. Arranging data into a collection allows for accessing data efficiently since data assigned to an array are placed sequential in memory. An array can also be used for pointer variables.

In the example on the opposite page, an array of pointer variables is declared. This array contains three pointers. That is, elements of this array can hold an address of an integer data type variable. Each element is a pointer and the array is a collection of pointers commonly referred to as an *array of pointers*.

An array of pointers is declared by specifying the data type keyword followed by the asterisk operator (*) then the array itself. This is illustrated below.

int *a[3];

Notice that in the example on the opposite page the address of variable b is assigned to each element of the array. The results of this operation is illustrated in the memory diagram at the bottom of the page. Another way to achieve the same result is to use a for loop. This is illustrated below. Here the counter variable i is used to specify the array element that will be assigned the address of variable b. The array a is an array of pointers.

```
for (i = 0; i <3, i++)
  {
     a[i] = &b;
  }
```

Pointers can be grouped by creating an array of pointers.

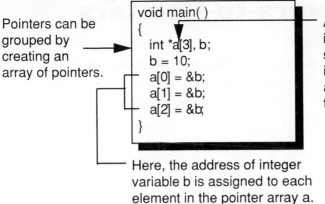

```
void main( )
{
    int *a[3], b;
    b = 10;
    a[0] = &b;
    a[1] = &b;
    a[2] = &b;
}
```

An array of pointers is declared using the same technique as is used to declare an array of any data type.

Here, the address of integer variable b is assigned to each element in the pointer array a.

In Memory

b	*a[0]	*a[1]	*a[3]
10	2000	2000	2000

2000 2002 2004 2006

Did You Know ...

By using the name of an array of pointers without the index reference, you can access the address of the first element of the array. This is called pointing to a pointer.

Pointers-to-Pointers

A pointer is a variable and has a location in memory. That is, a pointer variable is located at an address in memory. Therefore, another pointer variable can contain the address of a pointer variable. This concept is called *a pointer-to-a-pointer*.

Using a pointer-to-a-pointer is confusing for many C++ programmers. However, the example on the opposite page will simplify this concept. In this example, three variables are declared and all of them are of the integer data type.

The first is a regular variable called a. The second is variable b. The asterisk operator (*) indicates that this variable is a pointer variable that will contain the address of an integer data type. Lastly is the variable c. The double asterisk operator signals that the variable is a pointer to a pointer.

Notice that variable a is assigned the value 10. Pointer variable b is then assigned the address of variable a. And the pointer-to-a-pointer variable c is assigned the address of pointer b. The result of this operation is illustrated in the memory diagram at the bottom of the opposite page.

Pointers-to-pointers are used to minimize data transfer in memory during the operation of a program. For example, instead of copying data or moving data during a sort routine, the addresses of the data can be moved then a program statement can reference the address to display the appropriate data. The actual data remains at the original location in memory.

The proper use of pointers-to-pointers increases the efficiency of C++ programs that manipulate large amounts of data in computer memory.

A pointer is a variable that contains the address of another variable. A pointer-to-a-pointer is a pointer variable that contains the address of another pointer variable. This is called *multiple indirection*.

Here, integer variable a, integer pointer b, and an integer pointer-to-a-pointer are declared.

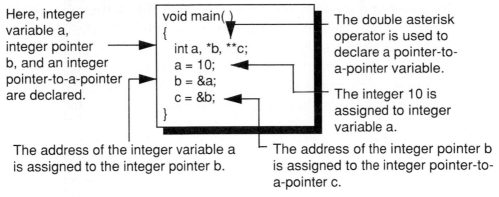

The double asterisk operator is used to declare a pointer-to-a-pointer variable.

The integer 10 is assigned to integer variable a.

The address of the integer variable a is assigned to the integer pointer b.

The address of the integer pointer b is assigned to the integer pointer-to-a-pointer c.

In Memory

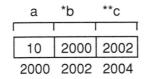

a	*b	**c
10	2000	2002
2000	2002	2004

Terms You Should Know ...

○	Single Indirection	Single indirection is where the variable called by the program contains the address of another variable. That variable contains the desired value.
○	Multiple Indirection	Multiple indirection is where the variable called by the program contains the address of another variable. That variable contains the address of the variable that contains the desired value.

A Pointer-to-a-Function

Data is stored at a memory location as is seen throughout this chapter. However, other portions of a program also reside in memory. When a C++ program is compiled and linked, the program is divided into several segments, two of which are the data segment and the code segment. The data segment contains data that is used by the program. The code segment contains functions that compose the program.

Recall that a pointer is a variable that holds an address. The address can be a location of a regular variable, of a pointer or of a function. The address of a function is actually the address of the entry point to that function. Referencing the address of a function has the same effect as calling the function. This is illustrated in the example on the opposite page.

Notice that the program declares a pointer variable to a function as a character data type. Once the pointer is declared, the address of the pointer is assigned to the function. This is illustrated below. Only the name of the function is used and not the parentheses. The function is cast as a character pointer.

Funcp = (char *) EmpNum;

The function is called by using the pointer. This technique is shown below. The asterisk operator is followed by the function name, both of which are contained within parentheses to assure proper order of execution. The a in parentheses below is a variable that is being passed to the function. Variable a is an integer that has the value 5.

(*EmpNum) (a);

This technique has the same effect as using EmpNum(a) within the program.

Any function can be called by referencing the address of the function using a pointer-to-a-function. All functions are assigned a physical location in the computer's memory, which can be identified by a specific address. This is actually the address of the beginning of the function, which is called the entry point into the function. A programmer can reference the address of a function by using the name of the function without the parentheses.

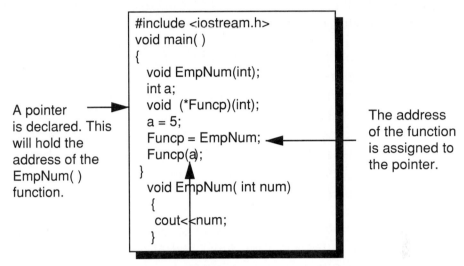

A pointer is declared. This will hold the address of the EmpNum( ) function.

```
#include <iostream.h>
void main( )
{
   void EmpNum(int);
   int a;
   void  (*Funcp)(int);
   a = 5;
   Funcp = EmpNum;
   Funcp(a);
}
   void EmpNum( int num)
   {
    cout<<num;
   }
```

The address of the function is assigned to the pointer.

Arguments to the function are passed within the parentheses.

Tricks of the Trade

The use of pointer variables enables a C++ program to use memory more efficiently. Instead of moving data around memory the program can reference the address of the data. However, there is a major drawback in using pointers. That is, a pointer variable always points to something in memory—including garbage.

All pointer variables should be initialized by the program immediately after they are declared otherwise bugs can occur in the program. A typical bug occurs when a pointer variable is used within a statement without the pointer variable first being initialized. The program is then accessing an address of memory where unknown data exists. Bugs caused by uninitialized variables are hard to detect. This is because the memory location pointed to by the pointer variable might actually have what appears to be good data.

Assume that a pointer variable is expected to contain the address of an integer but the pointer variable is not initialized. However, the pointer variable does contain a dummy address assigned by the compiler. The dummy address might be pointing to a memory address where an integer is stored—but not the integer the program expects to access. When the program executes the statement containing the uninitialized pointer variable, the dummy address is accessed and an integer that seems to be correct is used in the statement.

The example on the opposite page illustrates several techniques for initializing pointer variables. Integer pointer variable b is assigned the address of integer variable a. Likewise, character pointer variable d is assigned the address of character variable c. Notice that both the integer variable and the character variable are also initialized.

The character variable is initialized with the null character. A null character is represented by a backslash followed by a zero enclosed in single quotation marks ('\0'). The backslash instructs the compiler to ignore the normal meaning of the next character. In this case, the next character is a zero.

The misuse of pointers is probably the source of most bugs with a program. Make sure to always initialize each pointer immediately after the pointer is declared. Uninitialized pointers contain garbage that could bring a program crashing down.

Immediately after declaring an integer variable and an integer pointer, both are assigned a value.

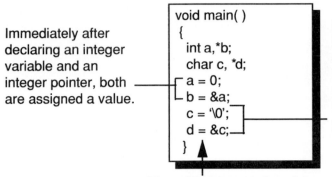

```
void main( )
{
    int a,*b;
    char c, *d;
    a = 0;
    b = &a;
    c = '\0';
    d = &c;
}
```

Here, a null character is assigned to the character variable c. The address of this variable is assigned to the character pointer.

The addresses assigned to each pointer can be changed at anytime throughout the program.

Did You Know ...

Initializing the first element of a character array with a null character can reduce errors in a program. Nearly every function that operates on a string recognizes the null character as the end of the string. A string function stops then returns control back to the next statement in your program when a null character is read from the string.

Working with Virtual Functions

Creating a Virtual Function

A *virtual function* can be considered a place-holder for functions of a derived class. The word *virtual* means that something appears to be real but really is not real. In this case, a function member of the base class appears to be a real function member but it is not.

A virtual function is declared using the same technique as is used for any function member except the name of the function precedes the keyword *virtual*. This is illustrated in the example shown on the opposite page. Here the function member display( ) is declared as a virtual function.

All virtual functions must be contained in a base class. In this example, the class student is the base class to the class professor. Notice that both classes contain a function member called display( ). Each function member displays a unique message on the screen.

Within the main( ) function, a base class pointer is created as an instance of the class student. Here, the base class pointer is called john. An instance of the derived class professor is also declared and called mary.

A base class pointer points to the starting address of an instance of either the base class itself or of a derived class. The example on the opposite page assigns the address of the instance of the derived class mary to the base class pointer john.

Once the base class pointer is assigned an address of a derived class, the base class pointer can be used to access any member of the class. In this case, the base class pointer john is calling in the display( ) function of the derived class. This example could have created an instance of the class student as an object, then assigned, the address of that instance to the base class pointer john. The program can use john to call the base class version of display( ).

A virtual function is a function that appears real to parts of the program but does not really exist and is redefined by derived classes.

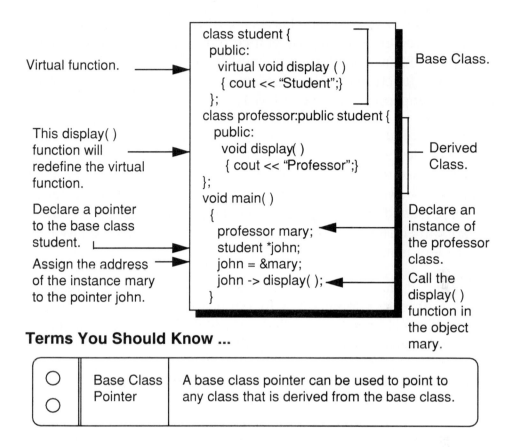

Virtual function. ➞

This display( ) function will ➞ redefine the virtual function.

Declare a pointer to the base class student. ➞

Assign the address ➞ of the instance mary to the pointer john.

```cpp
class student {
   public:
      virtual void display ( )
      { cout << "Student";}
};
class professor:public student {
   public:
      void display( )
      { cout << "Professor";}
};
void main( )
{
   professor mary;
   student *john;
   john = &mary;
   john -> display( );
}
```

Base Class.

Derived Class.

Declare an instance of the professor class.

Call the display( ) function in the object mary.

Terms You Should Know ...

○ ○	Base Class Pointer	A base class pointer can be used to point to any class that is derived from the base class.

Without Redefining
a Virtual Function

In the previous example, two classes are defined: the base class student and the derived class professor. Notice that the derived class redefined the display( ) function that is defined in the base class. That is, the derived class function member display( ) changed the functionality of the base class function member display( ).

Another technique for using virtual functions calls for the derived class not to redefine the virtual function in the base class. This method is illustrated in the example on the opposite page. Here, the same two classes are defined, however, the class professor does not contain a function member called display(). Instead, the class professor has a function member named show( ). Therefore, the function member display( ) in the class student is never redefined.

The impact of this technique becomes apparent when the base class pointer is used to reference the function member. In this example, an instance of the class student called mary is declared as is an instance of the derived class professor.

The address of the mary object is assigned to the base class pointer john. The program then calls the function member display( ).

That's true, but the object mary inherits the function member from the class student, which does define a function member called display( ). Therefore, the virtual function member display( ) of the base class is called when the base class pointer john references the display( ) function.

A base class pointer references members of the current derived class first before accessing the virtual function member of the base class. An instance of the base class need not be declared to call the virtual function.

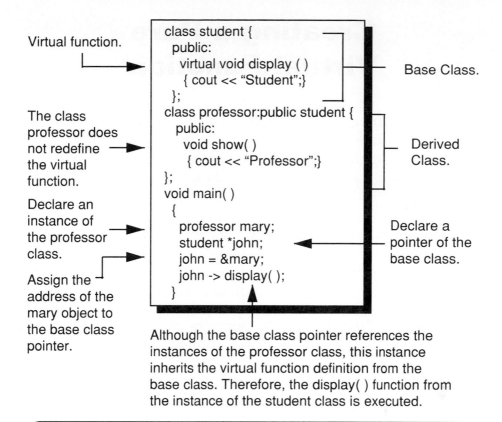

Virtual function.

The class professor does not redefine the virtual function.

Declare an instance of the professor class.

Assign the address of the mary object to the base class pointer.

```
class student {
  public:
    virtual void display ( )
      { cout << "Student";}
};
class professor:public student {
  public:
    void show( )
      { cout << "Professor";}
};
void main( )
  {
    professor mary;
    student *john;
    john = &mary;
    john -> display( );
  }
```

Base Class.

Derived Class.

Declare a pointer of the base class.

Although the base class pointer references the instances of the professor class, this instance inherits the virtual function definition from the base class. Therefore, the display( ) function from the instance of the student class is executed.

Helpful Tips ...

A function that is declared to be a virtual function remains a virtual function throughout the inheritance hierarchy from the point in the program where the function is defined.

Creating a Pure Virtual Function

So far in this chapter, we have explored creating a virtual function that contains at least one statement with the body of the function. There is another type of virtual function called a *pure virtual function*. A pure virtual function does not contain any statements within the body of the function.

A pure virtual function is declared the same way as is described in the previous pages. The keyword virtual is the prefix to the name of the function member. However, no statements are contained with the body of the function. In fact, a pure virtual function does not have any body.

This technique is illustrated on the opposite page. Notice that beneath the public access specifier of the class student, the display( ) function member is defined as a pure virtual function. There is no body to this function. Instead, the assignment operator is used to assign the value zero to the function. This signifies that this is a pure virtual function.

The remainder of this example is the same as in the previous illustration in this section. An instance of the class professor called mary is declared and an instance of class student called john is declared as a base class pointer.

The address of mary is assigned to the base class pointer john. The program then uses john to call to the function member display( ) of the instance mary.

Derived classes must redefine the body of a virtual function of the base class. A compile-time error will occur if an instance of the derive class calls a pure virtual function that has not yet been defined. Therefore, the program on the opposite page could not successfully compile if the function member display( ) of the class professor is renamed. This forces the program to call the pure virtual function member display( ) from the class student that does not have any body.

A pure virtual function is a virtual function that does not contain a function definition. All derived classes must provide a function definition for the pure virtual function.

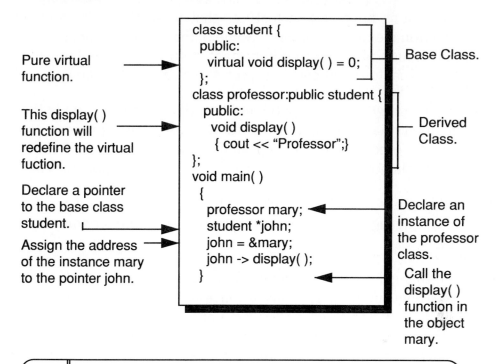

Pure virtual function. ————▶

This display( ) function will redefine the virtual fuction. ————▶

Declare a pointer to the base class student. ————▶

Assign the address ————▶
of the instance mary to the pointer john.

```
class student {
  public:
    virtual void display( ) = 0;   ] ── Base Class.
};
class professor:public student {
  public:
    void display( )
    { cout << "Professor";}
};
void main( )
{
  professor mary;  ◀————
  student *john;
  john = &mary;
  john -> display( );
}
```

Base Class.

Derived Class.

Declare an instance of the professor class.

Call the display( ) function in the object mary.

Helpful Tips ...

Make sure that all redefinitions of a virtual function use the same return value, function name and argument list as the virtual function, otherwise a compiler error will occur.

More about Virtual Functions

Virtual functions have certain features that make them different from other function members of a class. Some of these features are discussed on the previous pages. Another important feature of a virtual function is when the virtual function becomes part of the executable program.

When a C++ program is compiled and linked, the source code is joined with the appropriate C++ libraries to form an executable program. When the program executes, all the information about nonvirtual function members is already known and is included in the executable program.

This technique is called *early binding*, which is a mainstay of most programming languages. All of the code is made part of the program at compile time.

However, this is not the case when the program uses a virtual function. Since a virtual function is really a place-holder for another function, information about the real function is not known at compile time. The real function is already part of the executable program and the compiler will call the right function by using a pointer to an array of pointers to function at run time.

This technique is called *late binding*. That is, the virtual function holds the place for the real function during compile time, then the real function takes this reserved position during run time.

Each of these techniques offers a trade-off. In early binding where a virtual function is not used, the run-time version of the program executes faster than a program that uses late binding. This is because the real function is already in place in the program. However, this technique limits the flexibility of switching reference to functions using the base class pointer. A program that uses late binding provides flexibility but slows the execution process due to the late binding.

Fact Sheet ...

Classes that contain a pure virtual function are called an *abstract class*. There can never be an object created from an abstract class. Abstract classes are designed to be base classes that are inherited by derived classes.

Redefining a virtual function is similar to overloading a function. However, the term overloading is not used because the prototype of the redefined virtual function must be identical to the prototype of the virtual function.

Virtual functions are resolved by using late binding. This means that the object that contains the virtual function and the object's functions are resolved at runtime.

Terms You Should Know ...

	Early Binding	Objects and the objects' functions are linked to the program at compile time because all of the information is known about the object at that time.
	Late Binding	Objects and the objects' functions are linked to the program at runtime when the compiler calls the right function by using a pointer to an array of pointers to functions. Late binding can slow down the running of the program.

Friend Functions

C++ offers another type of function called a *friend function*. A friend function is a function that has been granted access to the private and protected members of a class. This technique is illustrated on the opposite page.

In this example, the program defines class student as having a data member called grade that is hidden beneath the private access specifier. This class also declares the display( ) function as a friend function by using the keyword friend followed by the name of the friend function.

Notice that the display( ) function is not defined as a member of the class student. The display( ) function is actually a stand-alone function that is not a member of any class.

The definition of the display( ) function is contained below the definition of the class student in the program. This function displays the value of the grade variable on the screen. However, the variable grade is not declared in the display( ) function but is declared as a private data member of the class student.

The display( ) function can utilize any member of the class student since the class student has recognized the display( ) function as a friend function. A compiler error will occur if the display( ) function is not declared as a friend function to the class student.

The program creates an instance of the class student called john. Next, the program uses the dot operator to call the assign_grade( ) function member of the instance john passing the value 80 to this function. The assign_grade( ) function assigns the integer passed to the function to the variable grade. Finally, the program calls the display( ) function to display the grade on the screen. Notice that the dot operator is not required to call the display( ) function since this function is not a member of any class—just a friend to the class student.

> A friend function is a function that is defined outside of a class and has access to the private and protected members of a class.

Creating a Friend Function

The keyword friend is used to identify a friend function inside the public section of the class definition.

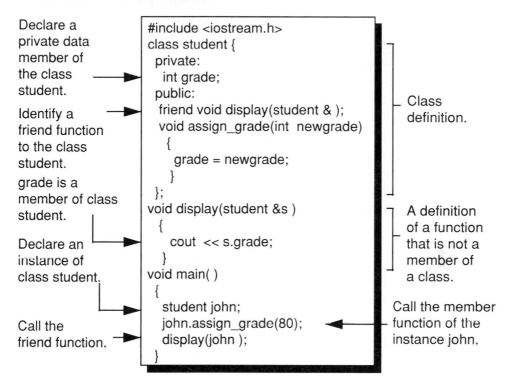

Declare a private data member of the class student. →

Identify a friend function to the class student. →

grade is a member of class student.

Declare an instance of class student. →

Call the friend function. →

```
#include <iostream.h>
class student {
  private:
    int grade;
  public:
    friend void display(student & );
    void assign_grade(int  newgrade)
    {
      grade = newgrade;
    }
};
void display(student &s )
{
    cout  << s.grade;
}
void main( )
{
    student john;
    john.assign_grade(80);
    display(john );
}
```

Class definition.

A definition of a function that is not a member of a class.

Call the member function of the instance john.

Creating a Friend Function from a Function Member

In the previous example, a function that was not a member of a class is declared as a friend function to a class. The same rights can be given to a function member of another class. This technique is illustrated on the opposite page.

Here, the display( ) function member of the class report is declared as a friend function of the class student. Notice that the friend keyword is used in the first statement beneath the public access specifier. This statement declares that the display( ) function is a friend function.

The friend function must be explicitly declared. That is, the function name must be preceded by the name of the class of which the function is a member and by the scope resolution operator. This is shown on the opposite page and below.

friend void report::display( );

Once the friend function is declared, the function member display( ) can then use the private, protected and public portions of the class student. In this example, the function member of the class report displays the grade integer variable, which is a private data member of the student class.

This program creates an instance called john of the class student and an instance called rpt of the class report. The dot operator is used to call the assign_grade( ) member function of the instance john. Notice that the an integer is passed to this function that assigns this value to the variable grade.

Finally the dot operator is used again to call the display( ) function member of the class rpt. This function displays the value of the variable grade on the screen.

Any function that is a function member of a class can also be a friend function of another class. The keyword friend must be used as well as the the name of the class that contains the friend function.

Forward reference to the class student.

Identify a friend function to the class report.

grade is a member of class student.

Declare an instance of class student.

Call the friend function that uses the private data member of instance john.

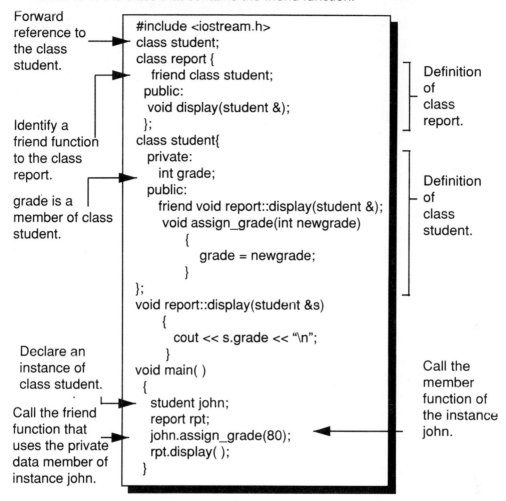

```
#include <iostream.h>
class student;
class report {
    friend class student;
  public:
   void display(student &);
  };
class student{
   private:
      int grade;
   public:
      friend void report::display(student &);
      void assign_grade(int newgrade)
         {
              grade = newgrade;
         }
  };
void report::display(student &s)
      {
          cout << s.grade << "\n";
      }
void main( )
   {
     student john;
     report rpt;
     john.assign_grade(80);
     rpt.display( );
   }
```

Definition of class report.

Definition of class student.

Call the member function of the instance john.

Forward Reference of a Class

The program declared the display( ) function member of the report class as a friend function to the class student. However, there is a problem with this declaration. The compiler does not know about the class report when the declaration within the class student is made.

The compiler will complain and display an error message. There is a dilemma for the programmer. Another compiler error will occur if the class report is defined before the class student. This is because the display( ) function member of the class report references the variable grade. This variable is not defined yet.

Overcoming this problem is simple by including a *forward reference statement* to the class report. This is shown in the second line of the program and below.

class report;

Since the semicolon follows the class name, the compiler realizes that this is not a class definition but simply a reference to a class that will be defined later in the program. The compiler will then hold off reporting errors when a reference is made to an item than is not defined until the first pass of the source code is made.

The compiler makes the assumption that the definition of the unresolved item is defined in the class that is referenced but not defined yet in the program.

Forward referencing of a class uses a technique similar to function prototyping. A function prototype, discussed early in this book, informs the compiler that there will be a function defined. Of course, the function prototype statement provides the compiler with more information about the function than is supplied with the forward reference of a class.

When a function member of a class becomes a friend function of another class, the compiler becomes confused. The class definition references a member of another class before the other class is defined. The compiler must be told about the other class by placing a forward reference statement in the program.

The forward reference statement tells the compiler that there will be a class called student defined later in the program.

The class report makes reference to the class student before the student class is defined.

```
#include <iostream.h>
class student;
class report {
    friend class student;
  public:
    void display(student &);
  };
class student{
    private:
      int grade;
    public:
      friend void report::display(student &);
      void assign_grade(int newgrade)
        {
            grade = newgrade;
        }
};
void report::display(student &s)
    {
        cout << s.grade << "\n";
    }
void main( )
  {
    student john;
    report rpt;
    john.assign_grade(80);
    rpt.display( );
  }
```

Definition of class report.

Definition of class student.

Working with Keyboard Input—Screen Output

Keyboard Input—Screen Output

C++ offers many methods to read information from the keyboard and display information on the screen. Since C++ is a superset of the C language, all of the library functions for keyboard input and screen output are available in C++. In addition, the C++ library offers other techniques to achieve similar results.

A simple way to read a character from the keyboard is to use the *getchar( )* *function*. This technique is illustrated on the opposite page and shown below. The getchar( ) function does not require an argument and the return value of the function is the next character that is contained in the keyboard buffer. The keyboard buffer is a segment of memory that is used to temporarily store characters entered from the keyboard.

letter = getchar( );

In the example shown on the next page, the program uses the *printf( )* *function* to display a prompt on the screen that asks the user to enter a character at the keyboard. The getchar( ) function is then called. This function reads a character from the keyboard buffer and returns the value to the calling statement. Next, the program assigns this returned value to the character variable letter. An EOF *value* is returned if there is an error detected by the function.

Besides returning the value to the statement, the getchar( ) function also displays the character on the screen. This feature is *called echo*. This means that the programmer does not need to use a screen output function to display the value of the character variable letter on the screen. There are other keyboard input functions that do not echo the character to the screen. These are discussed later in this chapter.

When the getchar( ) function reads the keyboard buffer, the character that is read by the function is removed from the keyboard buffer and placed into the program's data segment of memory.

Nearly every program that you'll write requires that data be moved into and out of the computer. This is commonly referred to as data input—output. In this chapter you'll explore the routines that are used to read data from the keyboard and display data on the screen.

Read a Character from the Keyboard with Echo getchar( )

The getchar( ) function reads a single character from the keyboard. This character is automatically displayed on the screen. The getchar( ) function doesn't accept any arguments and returns the character that is read from the keyboard. Some compilers require that the stdio.h header file be included in programs that use the getchar( ) function.

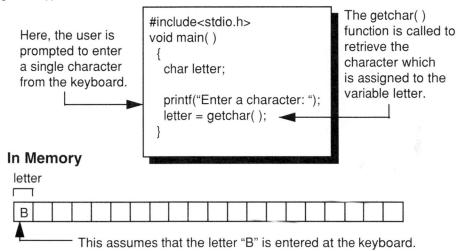

Here, the user is prompted to enter a single character from the keyboard.

```
#include<stdio.h>
void main( )
  {
    char letter;

    printf("Enter a character: ");
    letter = getchar( );
  }
```

The getchar( ) function is called to retrieve the character which is assigned to the variable letter.

In Memory

letter

| B | | | | | | | | | | | | | | | | | | | | | | |

This assumes that the letter "B" is entered at the keyboard.

Reading a Character from the Keyboard without Echo getch( )

There are applications that require that the input from the keyboard remain confidential, such as in a program that prompts the user to enter a password. Therefore, the getchar( ) function discussed on the previous page cannot be used.

Instead, the programmer can use the *getch( ) function*. The getch( ) function, not an ANSI function but available on DOS, performs the same function as the getchar( ) function except that the character that is read from the keyboard is not automatically displayed on the screen. This function simply reads and removes the character from the keyboard buffer and returns the value of the character to the calling statement. Notice that the getch( ), like the getchar( ), function does not require any arguments.

An example of this technique is showed below and in the program on the next page. Here, the program declares a character variable called letter, then prompts the user to enter a letter at the keyboard. The getch( ) function is called to read that letter without displaying the letter on the screen. The value of the letter is then assigned to the character variable letter.

```
letter = getch( );
```

A word of caution! The getch( ) function cannot be used to read CTRL C. Also, this function must be called twice to read the value of a keyboard function key or a cursor movement key. The first time the getch( ) function is called, a zero is returned. The second time the key code value is called.

All programs that call the getch( ) function must use the conio.h header file. This file contains the function prototype for the function.

C++ Programmer's Notebook

The getch( ) function reads a single character from the keyboard. This character is not automatically displayed on the screen. The getch( ) function doesn't accept any arguments and returns the character that is read from the keyboard. Some compilers require that the conio.h header file be included in programs that use the getch( ) function.

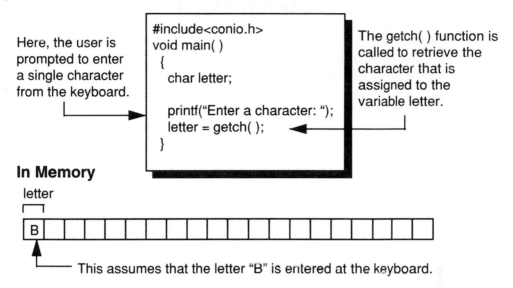

Here, the user is prompted to enter a single character from the keyboard.

```
#include<conio.h>
void main( )
  {
    char letter;

    printf("Enter a character: ");
    letter = getch( );
  }
```

The getch( ) function is called to retrieve the character that is assigned to the variable letter.

In Memory

letter

B																							

This assumes that the letter "B" is entered at the keyboard.

Did You Know ...

Both the getchar( ) function and the getch( ) actually return an integer that is interpreted as an ASCII value and not as an integer. Each character on the keyboard has a corresponding ASCII value.

Displaying a Character on the Screen
putchar( )

A single character can be displayed on the screen by using the *putchar( ) function*. The putchar( ) receives the character that is to be displayed on the screen as an argument. An EOF value is returned if the putchar( ) function cannot display the character.

In the example on the next page, the putchar( ) function displays the character 'A' on the screen. First the program declares a character variable called letter. Next, the variable is assigned the character 'A.'

Notice that the character is within single quotation marks. This instructs the compiler to use the ASCII value of the character 'A.' The ASCII value is an integer that when assigned to a character variable is interpreted as a character rather than a numeric value.

A word of caution! Do not place the character within double quotation marks. Double quotation marks instructs the compiler that the value within the double quotation marks should be treated as a string. Remember, a string is a character array where the last character is a null character. This is not the same as a single character.

The program calls the putchar( ) function from within an if statement. This allows the program to determine if the putchar() function is successful displaying the character on the screen. If the function fails, an EOF value is returned and is trapped by the if statement.

Here is a trick that should be used in every application. Create an error file in the application. Whenever an error is detected, write the error to the file. In the case of the putchar( ) function, an error could not be displayed on the screen since the screen caused the error. An error file, however, records the error.

The putchar( ) function displays a single character at the current cursor position. The character that is to be displayed on the screen is passed as an argument to to the putchar( ) function. Some compilers require that the stdio.h header file be included in programs that use the putchar( ) function. The putchar( ) function returns the character that it displayed on the screen or an EOF if an error is detected.

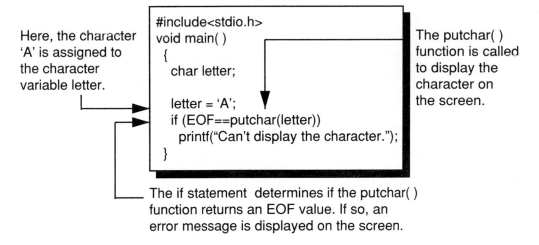

Here, the character 'A' is assigned to the character variable letter.

```
#include<stdio.h>
void main( )
  {
    char letter;

    letter = 'A';
    if (EOF==putchar(letter))
      printf("Can't display the character.");
  }
```

The putchar( ) function is called to display the character on the screen.

The if statement determines if the putchar( ) function returns an EOF value. If so, an error message is displayed on the screen.

Terms You Should Know ...

	EOF	EOF (end-of-file) is a #define symbolic constant --. EOF is defined in the stdio.h include file.

Reading a String from the Keyboard with Less Overhead gets( )

A series of characters can be read from the keyboard by using the *gets( ) function*. This function requires that the name of the character array that will be assigned the string be passed as an argument to the function.

The gets( ) function reads all the characters in the keyboard buffer up to the *new line character*, which is created when the Enter key is pressed. Each character is assigned sequentially to each element of the character array that is passed to the function. The gets( ) function automatically replaces the new line character with a null character therefore creating a string.

A null pointer is returned if the gets( ) function encounters an error or an end-of-file condition.

The technique for using the gets( ) function is illustrated on the opposite page. Here, a character array called name is declared as having 20 elements. Next, the user is prompted to enter a name at the keyboard. The gets( ) function is called and the name of the character array is passed to the function.

The gets( ) function reads the keyboard buffer and assigns each of the characters from the keyboard buffer to each element of the character array called name. The last character is a null enabling any string function to utilize the information that is entered from the keyboard.

A word of caution! Be sure that the character array declared in the program is large enough to hold the information that is entered at the keyboard. The gets( ) function does not limit the number of characters read from the keyboard to the size of the array.

The gets( ) function reads characters from the keyboard until the Enter key is pressed. Those characters are copied to the character array referenced in the argument passed to the gets( ) function. A null character is automatically added to the character array to create a string.

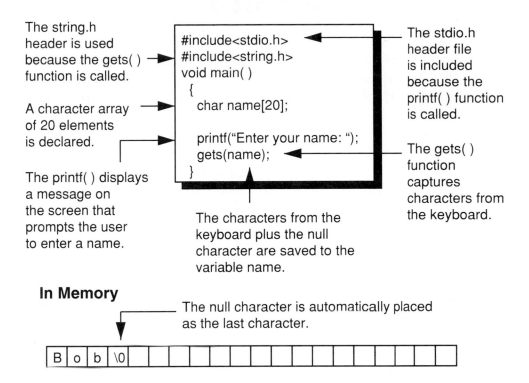

The string.h header is used because the gets( ) function is called.

A character array of 20 elements is declared.

The printf( ) displays a message on the screen that prompts the user to enter a name.

```
#include<stdio.h>
#include<string.h>
void main( )
  {
    char name[20];

    printf("Enter your name: ");
    gets(name);
  }
```

The stdio.h header file is included because the printf( ) function is called.

The gets( ) function captures characters from the keyboard.

The characters from the keyboard plus the null character are saved to the variable name.

In Memory

The null character is automatically placed as the last character.

| B | o | b | \0 | | | | | | | | | | | | | | | | |

Reading a String from the Keyboard with Greater Control scanf( )

Multiple data types can be read from the keyboard by using the *scanf( ) function*. This function requires two or more arguments. The actual number of arguments depends on the number of variables that are used to store the data that is read from the keyboard.

The first argument is a string that contains format specifiers. A *format specifier* is a symbol that is a place-holder for a variable. Variables are used as subsequent arguments to this function. There must be a format specifier within the first argument for each variable used with the scanf( ) function.

The table on the next page contains a list of format specifiers for the scanf( ) function. Each data type has a corresponding format specifier.

A format specifier instructs the scanf( ) function to read and convert characters read from the keyboard to values of the specified data type. This value is automatically assigned to the corresponding variable in the argument list. That is, when the first format specifier is read, the value of the first field from the keyboard buffer is converted to the corresponding data type and stored at the location in memory specified by the first argument. This sequence continues until all the specifiers in the format string are read.

The scanf( ) function considers an input field as characters up to the first white-space character, which is a space, table, or newline character. That is, a user can separate data items by entering a space between each data at the keyboard.

Although this discussion about the scanf( ) function assumes that the input is coming from the keyboard, this function reads input from standard-in, which is normally the keyboard but can be redirected to another source.

The scanf( ) function is used to read characters from the keyboard and copy those characters to variables of different data types. For example, characters that are numbers can automatically be converted into the proper numeric data type by using the scanf( ) function. Likewise, characters that comprise a string can be read directly into a character array. The scanf( ) function automatically places a null character as the last character value in the array.

The scanf( ) function requires two arguments. The first argument contains the format specifier within quotations. The second argument contains a reference to the address of the variable that will receive the value read by the scanf( ) function.

Format Specifiers for the scanf( ) Function	
Format Specifier	Description
%c	Read One Character
%d	Read a Decimal Value
%i	Read an Integer Value
%e	Read a Floating-Point Value
%f	Read a Floating-Point Value
%h	Read a Short Integer Value
%o	Read an Octal Value
%s	Read a String
%p	Read a Pointer
%x	Read a Hexadecimal Value

Reading a String
scanf( )

The example on the opposite page illustrates how to use the scanf( ) function in an application. Here, a character array called name is declared as having 20 elements. Next, the user is prompted to enter the name at the keyboard.

The scanf() function reads the keyboard buffer and converts the data from the buffer into characters, which are then assigned to elements in the character array name.

Notice that the string format specifier is used (%s) in the format string, which is the first argument of the scanf( ) function. This function reads each format specifier in the format string from left to right. When the first format specifier is encountered, the scanf( ) function beings reading the keyboard buffer until a white space character is read. All the data that is read is converted to the corresponding data type and stored in the related variable argument. The scanf() function then proceeds to the next format specifier in the format string and repeats the action.

In the case of a string, the scanf( ) function converts the white space character into a null character and stores it as the last character in the character array. In this example, the new line character that is placed in the keyboard buffer by the Enter key is converted into the null character.

Data entered from the keyboard can be separated into two or more variables by using multiple format specifiers, as shown below. Here, the user enters the salary amount, then a space, followed by the bonus amount. The scanf( ) function automatically copies the salary amount into the address of the first argument and the bonus amount into the address of the second argument. Notice that the ampersand operator is used to reference the address of these variables.

scanf(" %f %f",&salary, &bonus);

The printf( ) function displays a message on the screen that prompts the user to enter a name.

The sprintf( ) function captures characters from the keyboard.

The characters from the keyboard plus the null character are saved to the variable name.

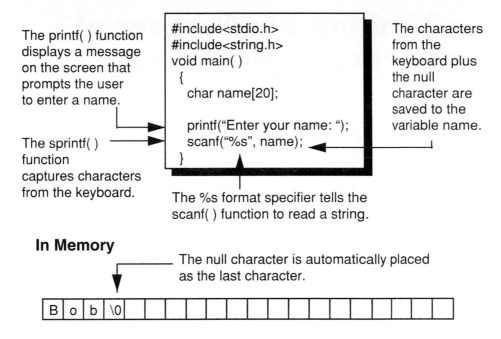

```
#include<stdio.h>
#include<string.h>
void main( )
  {
    char name[20];

    printf("Enter your name: ");
    scanf("%s", name);
  }
```

The %s format specifier tells the scanf( ) function to read a string.

In Memory

The null character is automatically placed as the last character.

B	o	b	\0																

Did You Know ...

All variables used in the scanf( ) function must be preceded by the ampersand operator except when a string is being read from the keyboard. Specifying the name of the character array without an index reference points to the address of the first element in the character array.

Limiting the Number of Characters Read from the Keyboard

One of the problems with reading data from the keyboard is that the amount of data may exceed the space that is reserved in memory for it. This is especially true when reading a string from the keyboard. For example, the program prompts the user to enter a name; however, there isn't any control on the number of characters that is used for the name.

The number of characters can be specified by using the scanf( ) function. This technique is illustrated in the top example on the opposite page. Here, the program reserves space in memory for 20 characters, which includes the null character. Next, the program prompts the user to enter a name.

Notice that when the scanf( ) function is called, there is an integer value between the percentage symbol and the s in the format specifier. This value instructs the scanf( ) function to read no more than 18 characters from the keyboard buffer. Fewer than 18 characters can be read.

The bottom example illustrates the method that is used to read an integer from the keyboard using the scanf( ) function. The integer format specifier instructs the scanf( ) function to convert the data read from the keyboard into an integer, then store this data into the address of integer variable age.

Remember, the scanf( ) function expects to receive a format string and an address as arguments. In the first example, the name of the character array is used. The name of an array causes the compiler to reference the address of the first element of the array. This is the same as if the program used the following syntax. The ampersand operator used in the second example explicitly instructs the compiler to use the address of the variable.

&name[0];

A programmer can limit the number of characters that the scanf() function reads by placing a maximum field modifier between the percentage sign and the format specifier.

```
#include<stdio.h>
#include<string.h>
void main( )
  {
    char name[20];

    printf("Enter your name: ");
    scanf("%18s", name);
  }
```

Here, only 18 characters will be read from the keyboard by the scanf() function.

scanf( ) Reading an Integer

The %i format specifier is used to tell the scanf() function that an integer is to be read from the keyboard.

```
#include<stdio.h>
#include<string.h>
void main( )
  {
    int age;

    printf("Enter your age: ");
    scanf("%i", &age);
  }
```

Notice that the ampersand operator must be used since the scanf( ) function expects to receive the address of the integer variable age.

In Memory

age

2000

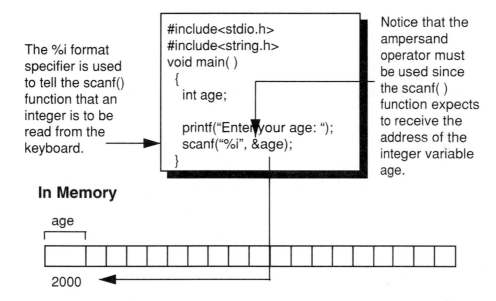

Receiving More than One Value at the Same Time

Multiple values can be read from the keyboard using the scanf( ) function by using multiple format specifiers and multiple arguments. This is shown in the top example on the next page. Here, the scanf( ) function is instructed to read two integers from the keyboard buffer.

The scanf( ) function reads bytes up to the first white space character, then converts these values to an integer and stores the integer in the age1 integer variable. The scanf( ) then returns to the next byte in the keyboard buffer and repeats this process, storing the results in the age2 integer variable.

In this example, the user enters the first age, then presses the space bar, and enters the second age. The space bar places a space character in the keyboard buffer. A space character is a white space character and is used as a field separator for the scanf( ) function.

Creating Your Own Separator

Any character can be used to separate fields other than a white space character. This is shown in the example at the bottom of the next page. Here, the scanf( ) format string contains format specifiers for integers and characters. The integers are the values that are stored in memory. The characters are discarded.

Notice that an asterisk is placed between the percentage symbol and the c in the format specifier for the characters. The asterisk instructs the scanf( ) to disregard the character. This allows the user to enter data, such as a telephone number, using hyphens as separators between fields of the telephone number. The scanf() uses those separators as field separators to assign the components of the telephone number to the proper integer variables.

Receiving More than One Value at the Same Time

The scanf() function can be told to read more than one value by passing the function additional format specifiers and variable addresses.

```
#include<stdio.h>
#include<string.h>
void main( )
  {
    int age1, age2;

    printf("Enter your age and your child's age: ");
    scanf("%i%i", &age1, &age2);
  }
```

The user must separate each data item with a space, tab, or new line. Commas, semicolons and other commonly used separators are not permited.

Creating Your Own Separator

A programmer can have the scanf() read a character but not assign the value to a variable by placing an asterisk between the % sign and the format code.

```
#include<stdio.h>
#include<string.h>
void main( )
  {
    int area, exchange, number;

    printf("Enter your telephone number \n ");
    printf(" ex. xxx-xxx-xxxx ");
    scanf("%i%*c%i%*c%i", &area, &exchange, &number);
  }
```

Here, the hyphens between the numbers are read as characters then discarded.

Another Way to Create Your Own Separator

In the example on the previous page, asterisks are used between the % symbol and the c in the format string to instruct the scanf( ) function to disregard the character that appears in this position in the keyboard buffer. This technique discards any character.

However, another approach to achieve similar results is to specify the character within the format string. This technique is illustrated on the opposite page.

Notice that each of the format specifiers in the format string is separated by a hyphen. The scanf( ) function looks for a hyphen in the keyboard to signify the end of the field. The hyphen will be discarded by the scanf( ) function.

A word of caution! The scanf( ) function attempts to match the character specified in the format string with the characters in the keyboard buffer. If characters do not match, then the scanf( ) continues to store the character as part of the current field. This function does not validate the format of the data entered by the user. That is, if the user failed to enter a hyphen, then there will not be a valid field separator entered in the keyboard buffer.

Although the hyphen character is used in this example, a combination of characters could also be used. The following statement illustrates this point. Characters used in this example would not make like choices for field separators but they could be used with the scanf( ) function.

scanf("%i$%i^%i",&area, &exhange, &number);

Another word of caution! Field separators defined in the scanf( ) format string do not appear on the screen. The program must rely on the user to properly enter the separator character.

A programmer can incorporate the separator character directly in the first argument to the scanf( ) function. →

```
#include<stdio.h>
#include<string.h>
void main( )
 {
  int area, exchange, number;

  printf("Enter your telephone number \n ");
  printf(" ex. xxx-xxx-xxxx ");

  scanf("%i-%i-%i", &area, &exchange, &number);
 }
```

The scanf( ) function is told to discard characters that are read from the keyboard that match those found within the format argument. In this example, the scanf() function is told to discard the hyphens.

A Word of Caution ...

Be careful when constructing the format argument of the scanf(). Characters within this argument that are not format specifiers will be matched and discarded when read from the keyboard. A poorly constructed format argument could cause your program to discard data.

Displaying a String on the Screen with Less Overhead puts( )

An efficient method for displaying a string on the screen is to call the *puts( ) function*. The puts( ) function is limited to displaying a string; therefore, the overhead that is necessary to handle other data types is not built into this function.

The puts( ) function requires one argument, which is the reference to the string that is to be displayed on the screen. Although the screen is the target of the puts( ) function in most applications, the puts( ) function sends the string to standard out. By default the screen is standard-out, however, standard-out can be redirected by the program or by using operating system commands.

In the example on the opposite page, the program declares a character array called name that contains 20 elements. Next, the printf( ) function is used to display a string that prompts the user to enter a name at the keyboard. The gets() function is called to read data from the keyboard and convert the data into character values, then those values are assigned to elements of the character array name.

Remember, the gets( ) function automatically converts the new line character, which is placed in the keyboard buffer when the user presses the enter key, to a null character thus creating a string from a series of characters.

Finally, the puts( ) function is called and passed the name of the character array. The string is then displayed on the screen.

Although this example passes the name of a character array to the puts( ) function, a literal string can also be passed to this function. For example, puts("Enter your name: "); has the same effect as the printf( ) statement that is shown on the opposite page.

The puts( ) function displays the string referenced in the argument to the screen. This function takes up less program memory and runs faster than the printf( ) function. The puts( ) function can only display a string. The printf( ) function displays strings and variables of other data types.

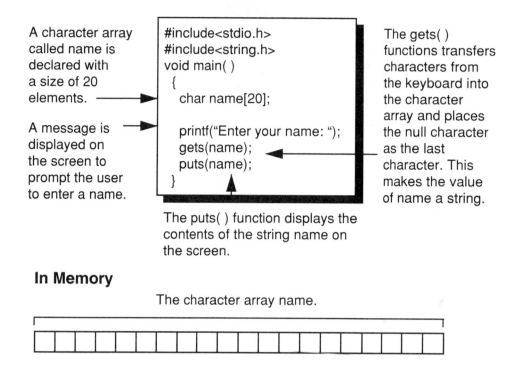

A character array called name is declared with a size of 20 elements.

A message is displayed on the screen to prompt the user to enter a name.

```
#include<stdio.h>
#include<string.h>
void main( )
  {
    char name[20];

    printf("Enter your name: ");
    gets(name);
    puts(name);
  }
```

The gets( ) functions transfers characters from the keyboard into the character array and places the null character as the last character. This makes the value of name a string.

The puts( ) function displays the contents of the string name on the screen.

In Memory

The character array name.

Displaying a String on the Screen with Greater Control printf( )

So far in this chapter, we've discussed techniques for displaying a character and a string to the screen. Obviously, there is a way to display an assortment of data types to the screen using the same function. This is possible by calling the printf( ) function.

The *printf( ) function* is used in many examples throughout this book, so by now you have an idea of how to display data using this function. However, nearly all of the examples used the printf( ) function to display a literal string. That is, a string of characters that is enclosed within double quotation marks.

As can be imagined, the printf( ) function can display more than literal strings. It can display a combination of literal strings and data of all types.

The printf( ) function is similar to the syntax used for the scanf( ) function in that the first argument is a format string and subsequent arguments are references to data that is to be displayed on the screen. The format string contains characters that are to be literally displayed on the screen and format specifiers that are place-holders for data. The table on the opposite page contains a listing of format specifiers for each data type.

In the example shown below, the printf( ) function displays both a literal string and a float data type. The %f is the format specifier that holds the place for the salary variable. That is, the variable salary replaces the % symbol in the string. Data and literal characters can be combined anywhere in the format string.

```
printf(" Your salary is: %f", salary);
```

The printf( ) function is used to display values to the standard-out, which is usually the screen. This function requires one argument and can use more than one argument if data is to be displayed. The first argument contains the literal string that is to be displayed. The literal string also contains format specifiers if data is to be displayed. A format specifier takes the position of the data within the literal string. Variables that represent the data become the remaining arguments to the function.

Format Specifiers for the printf( ) Function	
Format Specifier	Description
%c	One Character
%d	Decimal
%i	Integer
%e	Scientific Notation
%f	Floating Point
%g	Use The Shorter Of Either %e Or %f
%o	Octal
%s	String
%u	Unsigned Decimal
%x	Hexadecimal
%%	Display a percentage sign
%p	Pointer

Displaying a String
printf ( )

The example on the top of the opposite page illustrates the technique for displaying a string using the printf( ) function. First, the program declares a character array called name that has 80 elements. Next, the printf( ) function is used to display a literal string that prompts to the user to enter a name.

The program then calls the gets( ) function to read data from the keyboard buffer and converts that data into characters storing them in the character array name. This function also places a null as the last character in the array.

Finally, the printf( ) function is called again. This time the format string contains literal characters and the format specifier for a string. Reference to the string is contained in the second argument to the printf( ) function. In this case, the name of the character array that contains the string is used as the argument value.

Displaying an Integer
printf( )

The example at the bottom of the next page shows how to display an integer using the printf( ) function. In this program, an integer called age is declared then assigned the value 30. The printf( ) function is then called to display the combination of the literal characters Age: with the value of the integer variable age. The integer value replaces the % symbol in the format string when the string is displayed on the screen.

A word of caution! The printf( ) function displays the format string at the current cursor position on the screen. Some programmers use the space character, the tab character, and the new line character to position the cursor to a desired location before displaying the information. Although this technique is successful, many compilers have built-in library functions that move the screen cursor more efficiently.

Displaying a String
printf( )

The prinf( ) function displays the string literal " Hello", and the value of the string that is referenced in the second argument.

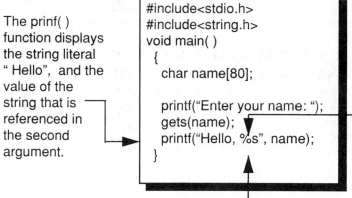

```
#include<stdio.h>
#include<string.h>
void main( )
  {
    char name[80];

    printf("Enter your name: ");
    gets(name);
    printf("Hello, %s", name);
  }
```

The printf( ) specifier %s is used as a place-holder for the value of the string name.

The first character of the string name replaces the '%' character in the literal string. The last character of the string name replaces the 's' in the literal string.

Displaying an Integer
printf( )

The %i format specifier is used to represent the integer variable passed as the second argument to the printf( ) function.

```
#include<stdio.h>
void main( )
  {
    int age;

    age = 30;
    printf("Age: %i", age);
  }
```

Padding the Data with Spaces

The width of data that is displayed on the screen using the printf( ) function can be fixed by specifying the maximum width within the format specifier. This technique is shown in the example at the top of the next page.

In this example, a character array called ENum is declared as having six elements. The program then copies a literal string to the character array by using the strncpy( ) function. Notice that this number (1234) is flush left. That is, the first character appears in the first position.

Since the contents of the character array will vary in length, the integer 6 is placed between the % symbol and the s in the format specifier. This instructs the printf( ) function that the width of the contents of the character array must be at least 6 characters.

Therefore, when the printf( ) function displays the character array, the printf( ) function will automatically add two space characters to the first two positions on the screen before displaying the string.

Specifying the Minimum and Maximum Width of Data

The example on the bottom of the next page determines both a maximum and minimum width for the data. Here, the program copies a string of seven characters to the ENum character array.

The format specifier instructs the printf( ) function that the data must be not less than three characters wide and no more than 6 characters wide. Notice that the minimum and maximum values for the widths are separated by a dot operator. Since the size of the contents of the character array is one character more than the maximum width, the printf( ) function displays only the first six characters of the string.

Padding the Data with Spaces

```
#include<stdio.h>
#include<string.h>
void main( )
  {
    char ENum[6];

    strncpy(ENum, "1234",4);
    printf("%6s", ENum);
  }
```

The prinf( ) function automatically adds the necessary spaces to fill the width identified in format specifier.

Output

1234

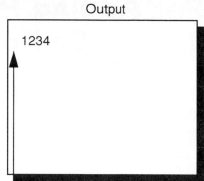

The printf() function is told that the width of the ENum variable should be no less than six characters. Two spaces are added to the beginning of the displayed data resulting in "1234" being shown on the screen.

Specifying the Minimum and Maximum Width of Data

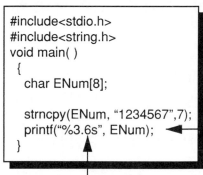

```
#include<stdio.h>
#include<string.h>
void main( )
  {
    char ENum[8];

    strncpy(ENum, "1234567",7);
    printf("%3.6s", ENum);
  }
```

The printf( ) function is told that the data must be at least three characters wide and not more than six characters.

Output

123456

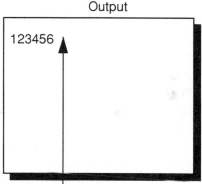

If the length of the data is less than three characters, the printf( ) will automatically add more characters to the beginning of the data on the screen. Characters beyond the sixth character are truncated.

Adding Padding at the End of the Data

In the previous section, Characters were added to the beginning of data so that the data filled a minimum width on the screen. Remember, these additional characters only affect the way the data appears on the screen. The actual value of the data in memory is not affected.

These additional characters are always added to the front of the data by default. However, by placing a minus sign in front of the minimum width value, the printf() function adds the characters to the end of the data.

This technique is illustrated in the example at the top of the opposite page. Here, a character array called ENum is declared as having six elements. The strncpy() function is then called to copy the four-character string to the character array.

Next, the printf( ) function is called. Notice that a minus sign is placed between the % symbol and the value of the minimum width in the format specifier. Now the output shows that the string is displayed flush left. The next data displayed on the screen appears two spaces beyond the last character in the string.

Specifying the Number of Decimal Places

The printf( ) function can be instructed to display a specific number of decimal places by an appropriate value within the format specifier. This is shown in the example at the bottom of the next page. Here, a float called salary is declared that is then assigned the value of 34123.345.

However, the program displays eight of these digits with two decimals places by specifying the value 8.2 in the format specifier. The last digit following the decimal is not displayed on the screen.

Adding Padding at the End of the Data

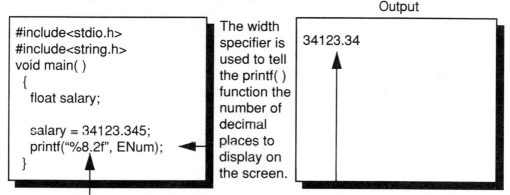

```
#include<stdio.h>
#include<string.h>
void main( )
  {
    char ENum[6];

    strncpy(ENum, "1234",4);
    printf("%-6s", ENum);
  }
```

A minus sign between the % and the number adds the padding to the end of the data on the screen.

Output

1234

The printf() function is told that the width of the ENum variable should be no less than six characters. Two spaces are added to the end of the displayed data resulting in "1234" shown on the screen.

Specifying the Number of Decimal Places

Output

```
#include<stdio.h>
#include<string.h>
void main( )
  {
    float salary;

    salary = 34123.345;
    printf("%8.2f", ENum);
  }
```

The width specifier is used to tell the printf( ) function the number of decimal places to display on the screen.

34123.34

The number to the left of the decimal specifies the maximum number of characters that are to be displayed including the decimal. The number to the right of the decimal indicates the number of decimal places. Characters beyond the specified maximum number of characters are truncated on the screen.

Displaying a String
Constant in C++
cout <<

Throughout this chapter, I have presented functions that read data from the keyboard and display data to the screen. Remember, these are the default settings for standard-in and standard-out. Standard-in and standard-out can be redirected to sources other than the keyboard and the screen.

These functions are available in C++ because they are part of the C language. However, C++ offers additional techniques for reading and writing data that will be covered in the remaining pages of this chapter.

The first of these methods is to use the combination of *cout* and the *insertion operator* (<<). cout is an identifier for the out-stream. This is equivalent to standard-out. The insertion operator accepts the data to the right of the insertion operator and sends the data to the object to the left of the insertion operator.

An example of this technique is shown on the opposite page. There is only one statement in the program. This statement instructs the insertion operator to take the string "Hello,world," and send it to standard-out, which is identified by the cout identifier.

Notice that there are no format specifiers used in this statement. The printf( ) function required format specifiers to allow the function to handle the data properly. In contrast, the insertion operator knows how to identify the data type of the data and therefore does not require a format specifier.

Any type of data can be used in the example on the next page without the need to inform the cout identifier the data type of the data. This is a major improvement that C++ provides over the printf( ) function.

All the input and output techniques illustrated previously can be used in C and C++. However, C++ has another way of displaying information on the screen. This is by using the cout identifier. The cout identifier is actually referred to as an object that was previously defined as the standard-out stream. The cout identifier uses the insertion operation (<<) to send the string to the cout identifier.

The cout identifier is used to send the string constant to the standard-out stream.

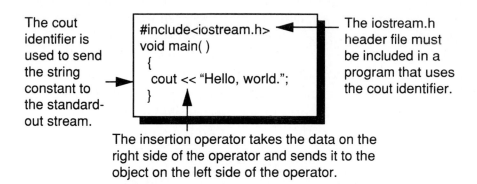

The iostream.h header file must be included in a program that uses the cout identifier.

The insertion operator takes the data on the right side of the operator and sends it to the object on the left side of the operator.

Terms You Should Know ...

○	Object	An object is a unit that combines both data and the functions that operate on that data.
○	Stream	A stream refers to the concept of a flow of data. The standard-out stream refers to a stream of data flowing to the screen. The standard-in stream refers to a flow of data received from the keyboard.

Displaying a String Variable Using cout

The cout identifier is data type-independent. That is, any data type can be used with cout without having to prep the cout identifier. The next few examples illustrate this flexibility.

In the example at the top of the next page, the program uses the cout identifier to display the contents of a string. Here, the program declares a character array called greeting that has 20 elements. Next, the literal string "Hello" is copied to the character array using the strncpy( ) function.

Finally, the name of the character array is used in the display statement. Here, the insertion operator is instructed to take the characters beginning at the address referenced by the character array greeting and send them to the cout indentifer.

Displaying a Non-String Variable Using cout

The next example on the opposite page illustrates displaying an integer using the cout identifier. This program declares an integer variable called age then assigns the value 30 to the variable.

Next, the insertion operator is instructed to take the value of the age variable and send the value to the cout identifier, which in turn displays the value of the integer variable on the screen.

The same technique that is illustrated in this example can be used with any data type that is available in C++. The data type of the variable to be displayed become irrelevant to the programmer when the cout identifier is used in place of using the printf( ) function.

Displaying a String Variable Using cout

Here, the string constant is copied to the character array greeting.

```
#include<iostream.h>
#include<string.h>
void main( )
  {
    char greeting[20];
    strncpy(greeting,"Hello.",6);
    cout << greeting;
  }
```

The insertion operator sends the contents of the variable to the cout identifier, which sends the characters to the standard out-stream (the screen).

Displaying a Non-String Variable Using cout

The cout identifier doesn't require the use of any format specifiers to display data of various data types. The insertion operator knows how to recognize the data type of the data that appears to the right of the insertion operator.

The cout identifier is used to send the integer variable to the standard out-stream.

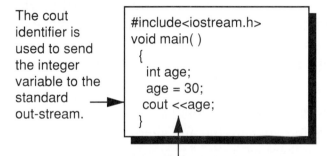

```
#include<iostream.h>
void main( )
  {
    int age;
    age = 30;
    cout <<age;
  }
```

The insertion operator knows that the variable age is an integer. It then makes the necessary arrangements to have the integer variable properly displayed on the screen.

Displaying Strings and Non-Strings Together Using cout

More than one value can be displayed with a single statement by *cascading* the insertion operator. Cascading the insertion operator means that the output from an insertion operator is joined together with input value of the next insertion operator. By combining insertion operations, multiple data can be displayed on the screen using a single statement.

This technique is shown on the next page. In this example, the program declares a character array called greeting that has 20 elements. The program also declares an integer called EmpNum and assigns the value 5 to this variable.

Next, the strncpy( ) function is called to copy the literal string "Hello," to the character array greeting. The display statement executes from right to left. First, the right most insertion operator takes the value of the EmpNum variable and joins this value with the value of the character array greeting.

The insertion operator takes the combined value of the greeting character array and EmpNum integer variable and sends them to the cout identifier. The cout identifier displays each of these data consecutively on the screen. Any number of data can be joined together on the screen by cascading insertion operators.

Here is a hint. A display statement that cascades insertion operators into a single cout identifier can extend beyond a single line. Remember, the compiler ignores the white space characters, such as the new line character. Therefore, the display statement can be carried over to multiple lines.

A word of caution! There are two requirements that must be met for a statement to extend to more than one line. First, only the last line in the statement can end with a semicolon, and second, a literal string can be broken into another line if the line ends with a backslash (\ ) or if the strings ends with a double quote and the first nonblank character on the next line is also a double quote.

The insertion operation can be cascaded to display more than one data type at the same time without having to use multiple statements. The cascade effect requires that multiple insertion operators be used to the right of the cout identifier.

Two variables are declared: a character array called greeting and an integer called EmpNum.

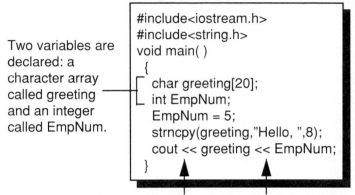

```
#include<iostream.h>
#include<string.h>
void main( )
{
    char greeting[20];
    int EmpNum;
    EmpNum = 5;
    strncpy(greeting,"Hello, ",8);
    cout << greeting << EmpNum;
}
```

Two insertion operators are used. The first insertion operator cascades the integer value to the string value. Both variables are then sent to the standard out-stream.

Did You Know ...

The insertion operator is the same symbol that is used for the bit-wise operator. The C++ compiler doesn't become confused because the C++ language allows for overloading operators. Overloading changes the functionality of an operator depending on how the operator is used in the statement. In the above illustration, the compiler knows that a bitwise operation isn't to be performed.

Reading a String from the Keyboard Using C++
cin >>

Data can be read from standard-in, which is usually the keyboard, by using the combination of the *cin identifier* and the *extraction operator* (>>). The cin identifier identifies standard-in. The extraction operator takes data from the stream on the left of the extraction operator and places the data to the object on the right of the insertion operator.

This method is illustrated on the opposite page. In this program, a character array called greeting is declared as having 80 elements. Next, the display statement is executed. Here, the literal string that prompts the user to enter data using the keyboard is sent to the cout identifier. The cout identifier displays the string on the screen.

Next, the read statement is executed. This statement uses the extraction operator to receive data from standard-in and assign the data to the character array greeting. Finally, a display statement is used to welcome the person with a personal message on the screen.

Notice that the cin identifier and the extraction operator function similarly to the cout identifier and the insertion operator except the direction of data flow is reversed. Also notice that neither requires a data type identifier.

The insertion operator automatically converts the incoming data to the appropriate data type before storing the data in the designated memory location. The programmer need not write code to handle this conversion.

Avoid confusion! Remember, statements that use the insertion operator execute right to left. That is, the object on the right of the insertion operator is passed to the object on the left of the insertion operator. The reverse is true when working the extraction operator.

Data can be read from the keyboard by using the C++ cin identifier. The cin identifier is also a C++ object that actually refers to the standard-in stream, which is usually the keyboard. The cin identifier uses the extraction operator (>>). The extraction operator takes input from the stream specified to the left of the operator and places the data in the variable specified to the right of the operator.

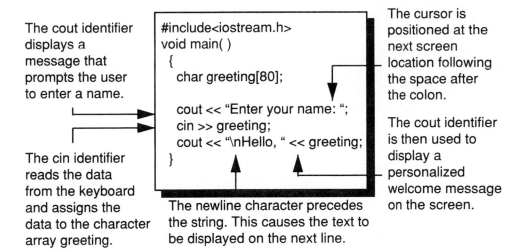

The cout identifier displays a message that prompts the user to enter a name.

```
#include<iostream.h>
void main( )
  {
    char greeting[80];

    cout << "Enter your name: ";
    cin >> greeting;
    cout << "\nHello, " << greeting;
  }
```

The cin identifier reads the data from the keyboard and assigns the data to the character array greeting.

The newline character precedes the string. This causes the text to be displayed on the next line.

The cursor is positioned at the next screen location following the space after the colon.

The cout identifier is then used to display a personalized welcome message on the screen.

Did You Know ...

The extraction operator can be cascaded using the same technique that is used for the insertion operator. However, this is rarely done because each reading of the keyboard is usually preceded by a prompt.

Manipulators

There are two *manipulators* that enable the program to modify how the output of the data is displayed on the screen using the cout identifier and the insertion operator. These are the *endl* and *setw( )* *manipulators*.

The endl manipulator, which is shown in the top example on the opposite page, places a new line in the output stream. This has the same effect as placing the \n characters in a printf( ) function format string. Data following the endl manipulator is displayed at the beginning of the next line.

In this example, the program declares a character array called greeting that contains 80 elements. Next, the cout identifier and the insertion operator are used to display a prompt for the user to enter a string into the keyboard. The cin identifier combined with the extraction operator receives the input from the keyboard and assigns the value to the character array.

Finally, the endl manipulator is placed at the beginning of the output stream. This causes the data that follows to be displayed on a new line.

The setw manipulator is illustrated in the bottom example on the next page. The setw manipulator establishes the minimum width of the next data in the output stream. In this example, the setw manipulator contains a width of 10 characters. This means that the width of the contents of the fname character array must be displayed as having no less that 10 characters.

If the content of the character array is less than 10 characters, then the setw manipulator automatically adds spaces to the beginning of the character array to pad the width of the data.

A manipulator is an operator that modifies the way data is displayed using the insertion operator. Here are two manipulators: endl and setw. The endl manipulator places a linefeed into the stream. The setw manipulator determines the width of the data that is to be displayed on the screen.

The endl manipulator moves the cursor to the next line on the screen before the welcome message is displayed.

```
#include <iomanip.h>
void main( )
  {
    char greeting[80];

    cout << "Enter your name: ";
    cin >> greeting;
    cout << endl << "Hello, " << greeting;
  }
```

The first setw manipulator will add spaces at the end of the fname string if the string is less than 10 characters. The second setw will assure that the lname string will display 20 characters.

```
#include<iomanip.h>
void main( )
  {
    char fname[10], lname[20];
    cout << "Enter your first name: ";
    cin >> fname;
    out << "Enter your last name: ";
    cin >> lname;
    cout << setw(10)<< fname << setw(20) << lname;
  }
```

Working with Files and Streams

- File Input–Output
- Mode Specifiers
- Closing a File
- Writing a Character to a File
- Reading a Character from a File
- Tricks of the Trade
- Writing a String to a File
- Reading a String from a File
- Writing an Integer to a File
- Reading an Integer from a File
- Writing a Block of Data to a File
- Reading a Block of Data from a File
- Creating a Database File
- Reading a Record
- Writing Various Data Types to a File
- Using the fprint() Function
- Reading Various Data Types from a File
- Using the fscanf() Function
- Moving to Specific Locations in a File
- Returning to the Beginning of the File
- Deleting a File
- Using a File in C++
- Writing Information to a File Using C++
- Reading a String from a File Using C++
- Writing a Single Character to a File Using C++
- Reading a Single Character from a File Using C++
- Writing an Object to a File
- Reading an Object from a file
- Specify the File Mode in C++

File Input–Output

C++ offers several methods to save and retrieve information from a file. Since C++ is a superset of the C programming language, all of the file input and output functions that are avaiable in C are also avaiable in C++. In addition to these routines, C++ has additional class libraries that are designed for this purpose.

Before discussing the C++ file input and output classes, let's explore the C language library functions that handle file I/O. The first of these is the *fopen( ) function*. The fopen( ) function opens a file stream in a specific file access mode. A *file stream* is a series of data that flows from a file. The last data in a file stream is the *end of file marker*. The *access mode* determines how the file will be accessed. Access modes include read, write and append, among other modes.

The fopen( ) function requires two arguments. The first argument is the name of the file that is to be opened by the function. The file name can also include the drive specifier and the path name. The second argument is the symbol that is used to describe the access mode. Both arguments must be enclosed in double quotation marks.

After the fopen( ) function completes the task, this function returns a file pointer. If the file could not be opened, then the function returns a null file pointer, otherwise the pointer references the file.

A word of caution! Always check the file pointer returned by the fopen( ) function to determine if there is trouble opening the file. If so, then the program can abort with a message, as is illustrated on the opposite page.

Once a valid file pointer is received from the fopen( ) function, the pointer is used with other input and output functions to manipulate the opened file. The file pointer is actually a pointer to a structure that contains information about the file stream. The tag name of this structure is FILE and the declaration statement for a file pointer is shown on the first line of the main( ) function.

Most programs that you'll create require that data be saved to and retrieved from a file. This process is called file input-output. There are several functions that are used to manage file operations. Each of these is discussed in this section. The key that allows these functions to work with a file is a file pointer. A file pointer identifies the file to each of these functions.

Opening A File
fopen( )

The fopen( ) function is used to open a file. Two arguments are required. The first argument specifies the name of the file and must be enclosed within quotation marks. The second argument is the mode that defines how the file is to be opened. A pointer to the file is returned by the function if the file was opened. A null is returned if the file couldn't be opened.

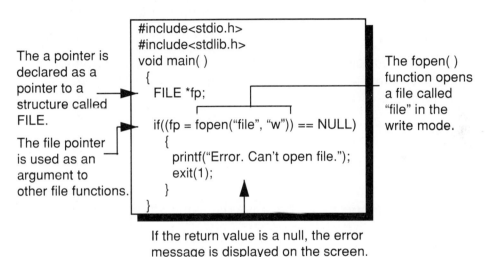

The a pointer is declared as a pointer to a structure called FILE.

The file pointer is used as an argument to other file functions.

```
#include<stdio.h>
#include<stdlib.h>
void main( )
  {
    FILE *fp;

    if((fp = fopen("file", "w")) == NULL)
      {
        printf("Error. Can't open file.");
        exit(1);
      }
  }
```

The fopen( ) function opens a file called "file" in the write mode.

If the return value is a null, the error message is displayed on the screen.

Mode Specifiers for the fopen( ) Function

The fopen( ) function offers a diverse selection of file access specifiers. This function can open both text and binary files (DOS OS/2 only). Text and binary files differ in the way an end of line is marked. In a *text file*, a carriage return line feed character is stored in the file to indicate the end of a line. On some computers a new line character signals the end of a line.

There is no end-of-line indicator in a binary file. A *binary file* is treated as a continuous stream of data without any delimitor except for an end-of-file marker.

Each of these file types have their own set of file access mode specifiers. The "w," "r," and "a" file access mode specifiers are used for text files and instruct the fopen( ) function to open the file stream for write, read and append respectively. The "w" file access mode specifier causes the first character of the stream to be written starting with the beginning of the file. In contrast, the "a" file access mode specifier starts writing data to the end of the file.

These file access mode specifiers have the same effect on a binary file by placing a "b" as the last character in the specifier. For example, "wb," "rb", and "ab" write, read and append to a binary file.

Placing a plus sign at the end of mode causes the fopen( ) function to open the file in both modes. For example, "w+," "r+," and "a+" open the file for both read and write mode for a text file. The same is true with the "wb+," "rb+" and "ab+" open a binary file in read-write mode.

A word of caution! In most cases, avoid using the *write file access mode specifier*. This specifier always rewrites the file causing all data in the existing file to be lost. A better method is to use the append file access mode specifier. The *append specifier* always writes at the end of the file and therefore insures, the integrity of the existing data in the file. If the file does not exist, then the append specifier automatically causes the fopen( ) function to create the file.

Mode Specifiers for the fopen( ) Function

Mode Specifier	Description
"w"	Create and write to a text file.
"r"	Open and read a text file.
"a"	Open and append to a text file.
"wb"	Create and write to a binary file.
"rb"	Open and read a binary file.
"ab"	Open and append to a binary file.
"w+"	Create a text file for writing and reading.
"r+"	Open a text file for writing and reading.
"a+"	Open a text file for writing and reading.
"wb+"	Create a binary file for writing and reading.
"rb+"	Open a binary file for writing and reading.
"ab+"	Open a binary file for writing and reading.

Terms You Should Know ...

File Pointer	A file pointer actually points to a structure that contains the name of the file, the status of the file and the location of the file.
Text File	The bytes in a text file are interpreted as ACSII values and contain carriage return-line feed (on a pc) at the end of a line.
Binary File	The bytes of a binary file can be interpreted various ways depending on the format of the file. There is no end-of-line character in a binary file.

Closing a File
fclose( )

Every file stream that is opened using the fopen( ) function in a C++ program must be closed by using the *fclose( ) function*. The fclose( ) function does not require an argument although an argument that contains the file pointer to the stream that is to be closed can be used with the fclose( ) function.

If an argument is omitted, the fclose( ) function closes all file streams that were opened with the fopen( ) function. However, specific file streams can be closed by specifying the file pointer to that stream as an argument to the fclose( ) function. Only the file stream that is specified in the argument will be closed. All other file streams remain opened.

At the bottom of the next page is an example that also calls the fclose( ) function. However in this example, the fp file pointer is passed to the fclose( ) function. Only this file stream is closed—although this is the only file stream that is opened in the program. This technique explicitly closes a specific file stream.

A word of caution! Be alert to where the fclose( ) function is called in a program. Only call this function upon exiting the file access routine of the application or right before the application terminates. Failure to follow this guideline could cause unexpected errors in the application.

For example, the application might use the file pointer in a function call without realizing that the file stream is closed at that point in the application. This is especially true in complex applications that consist of many source code files.

The fclose( ) function is used to close files that have been opened by the program. The fclose( ) function closes all the files. You can close a specific file by passing the file pointer as an argument to the fclose( ) function. The fclose( ) returns a zero value upon closing the file. A non zero value is returned if the fclose( ) function cannot close the file.

```c
#include<stdio.h>
void main( )
  {
    FILE *fp;

    if((fp = fopen("file", "w")) == NULL)
      {
        printf("Error. Can't open file.");
        exit(1);
      }
    fclose();
  }
```

Closing a Specific File

Here, the fclose( ) is told to close the file that is pointed to by the file pointer fp. Any other file will remain open. Only the "file" will be closed.

Closing All Files

The fclose( ) function is called without specifying which file to close. Any file that was opened by the program including the file pointed to by the fp file pointer is closed.

```c
#include<stdio.h>
void main( )
  {
    FILE *fp;

    if((fp = fopen("file", "w")) == NULL)
      {
        printf("Error. Can't open file.");
        exit(1);
      }
    fclose(fp);
  }
```

Writing a Character to a File
putc( )

Individual characters can be written to an opened file stream by using the *putc( ) function*. This function requires two arguments. The first argument consists of the character that is to be written to the file. The second argument is the pointer to the file stream.

After the putc( ) function executes, the function returns a character that contains one of two values. If the character is successfully written to the file, then the function returns the character to the calling statement. However, an end-of-file (EOF) character is returned if there is a problem during the execution of the function.

The example on the opposite page shows the proper use of the putc( ) function. Here, a character variable letter is declared then assigned the value 'A.' The name of this variable and the pointer to the file stream are passed to the putc( ) function.

Notice that the putc( ) function call is made within a compound statement. Besides calling the putc( ) function, the statement also evaluates the return value from the function. If the return value is the end-of-file character, then the code block beneath the if statement is executed, which displays an error message on the screen. However, this code block is ignored if the end-of-file character is not returned signifying a successful execution of the function.

This program uses the EOF symbolic constant in place of the end-of-file character. The definition of the EOF symbolic constant is created using the #define preprocessor command in the stdio.h header file.

A word of caution! Always evaluate the return value from the putc( ) function. Don't assume that the character will be successfully written to the file. The disk might be full or not accessible.

The putc( ) function is used to write a single character to a file. Two arguments are required for the putc( ) function. The first argument contains the character that is to be written to the file. The second argument is the pointer to the file. The file must be opened prior to using the putc( ) function. The character is returned by the function after the character is written to the file. If there is an error, the function returns an EOF, which is defined in the stdio.h header file.

Here, the putc( ) function writes the character 'A' to the opened file.

Remember, EOF is a #define identifier that is replaced with a value by the compiler.

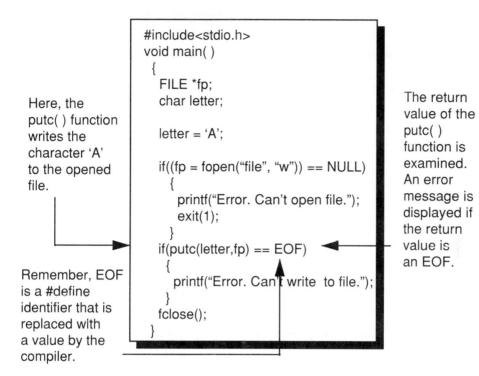

```c
#include<stdio.h>
void main( )
  {
    FILE *fp;
    char letter;

    letter = 'A';

    if((fp = fopen("file", "w")) == NULL)
      {
        printf("Error. Can't open file.");
        exit(1);
      }
    if(putc(letter,fp) == EOF)
      {
        printf("Error. Can't write  to file.");
      }
    fclose();
  }
```

The return value of the putc( ) function is examined. An error message is displayed if the return value is an EOF.

Reading a Character from a File
getc( )

A single character can be read from an open file stream by calling the *getc( ) function*. This function requires a single argument, which is the pointer to the file stream that contains the character. The getc( ) function returns the next character in the file stream to the calling statement.

It is important to understand the location of the internal file pointer. The *internal file pointer* points to the current location within the file stream. For example, the internal file pointer points to the first byte of the file stream when the fopen( ) function opens the file stream.

Each time the getc( ) function is called, the internal file pointer moves one byte further into the file until the end of file character is reached. Subsequent calls to the getc( ) function will no longer move the internal file pointer. However, the end-of-file character is returned to the calling statement.

In the example on the opposite page, a character variable called letter is declared. After the file is opened, a call is made to the getc( ) function and the file pointer that is returned by the fopen( ) function is passed to the getc( ) function.

Notice that the return value from the getc( ) function is assigned to the letter variable. Next, the program evaluates the value of the letter function. An error message contained within the code block beneath the if statement is executed if the end-of-file character is returned by the getc( ) function.

Alternatively, the call of the getc( ) function and the evaluation of the return value can be combined in a compound expression as part of the if statement. This technique is illustrated on the previous page. However, the return value must still be assigned to the character variable otherwise the character cannot be used within the program.

The getc( ) function reads a single character from the opened file. This function requires one argument, which is the pointer to the file. The getc( ) returns the next character read from the file. An EOF is returned if no more characters are available.

The getc( ) function is called to read the next character from the file and assign that character to the character variable letter.

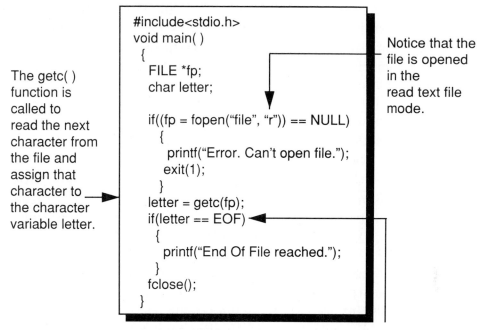

Notice that the file is opened in the read text file mode.

```
#include<stdio.h>
void main( )
  {
    FILE *fp;
    char letter;

    if((fp = fopen("file", "r")) == NULL)
      {
        printf("Error. Can't open file.");
        exit(1);
      }
    letter = getc(fp);
    if(letter == EOF)
      {
        printf("End Of File reached.");
      }
    fclose();
  }
```

The program determines if the value of the character variable letter is equal to EOF. If so, then a message is displayed on the screen.

Tricks of the Trade

Functions presented on the previous page that read and write functions to a file stream return an end of file to the calling statement if the function is unsuccessful. Code is then written in the program to evaluate the return value from the function. If an end-of-file character is returned, then the program displays an appropriate error message on the screen.

This technique is acceptable when working with text file streams. However, the results of the evaluation of the return value can be misleading if the function is working with a binary file stream. Although a binary file stream does have an end-of-file character at the end of the file, the file stream could also have data within the file stream that has equal value to the EOF macro definition. Remember, the program is actually comparing the return value of the function to a value that is represented by the EOF macro that is defined in the stdio.h header file.

Therefore, a safer technique to use to determine if the file stream is at the end of file is to call the *feof( ) function*. This function requires a single argument, which is the file pointer to the file stream. However, unlike the file stream functions discussed in this chapter previously, no character is returned by this function. Instead, a C++ true or false value is returned. Remember, a true in C++ is represented by a nonzero value while a false is a zero. In the example shown on the opposite page, the feof( ) function is called as part of the if statement.

Notice that the NOT operator (!) is used in this expression. The statement within the code block is executed only if the expression in the if statement evaluates true. The value of this expression is the return value of the feof( ) function, which is true only if the end of the file stream is reached. However, it is illogical to read from the end of a file stream. Therefore, the NOT operator is used to reverse the logic. If the return value is zero, then make it a true so that the code block is executed. The getc( ) function reads the next character from the file stream and passes that value to the putch( ) function, which displays the character on the screen. The feof( ) function can be used with both binary and text files.

The EOF #define identifier is not a good way to determine if the program has reached the end of the file if you are reading a binary file. A binary file can have values within the file that are equal to the value of EOF. This will result in a false indication that the end of the file has been reached. A better method is to use the feof( ) function to test for the end of file.

This program reads each character from the file and displays them on the screen.

The feof( ) function returns a true value (non zero) if the end of file is detected. The NOT operator (!) tests if the return value is not true.

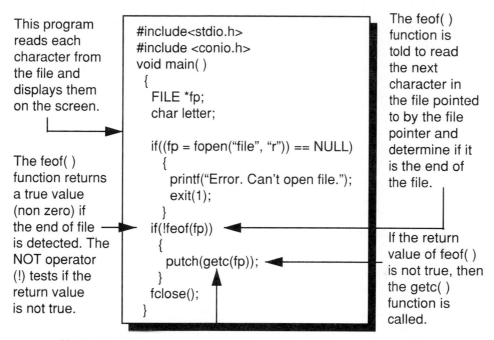

```c
#include<stdio.h>
#include <conio.h>
void main( )
  {
    FILE *fp;
    char letter;

    if((fp = fopen("file", "r")) == NULL)
      {
        printf("Error. Can't open file.");
        exit(1);
      }
    if(!feof(fp))
      {
        putch(getc(fp));
      }
    fclose();
  }
```

The feof( ) function is told to read the next character in the file pointed to by the file pointer and determine if it is the end of the file.

If the return value of feof( ) is not true, then the getc( ) function is called.

Notice that the getc( ) function is used as the argument to the putch( ) function. Actually, the return value of the getc( ) function is passed to the putch( ) function is display the character on the screen.

Writing a String to a File
fputs( )

Most applications require that a series of characters be written to a file stream. One method to accomplish this task is to execute several putc( ) function calls within a loop. However, a more efficient way is to call the *fputs( ) function*. The puts( ) function writes a string of characters to a file stream.

Remember, a string is a character array where the last character in the array is a null character. The fputs( ) function requires that the series of characters be a formal string whereas executing several putc( ) functions does not require that the characters that are being written to a file be in a string.

The fputs( ) function requires two arguments. The first argument is the name of the string, which is the name of the character array without any square brackets. Remember, C++ treats the name of the array as the pointer to the first element in the array. The second argument is the file pointer to the file stream. The fputs( ) function returns a nonnegative value if the string is successfully written to the file otherwise an end of file is returned.

In the example on the opposite page, a character array called msg is declared then assigned the string "Hello." Once the file stream is opened using the fopen() function, the fputs( ) function is called within the if statement. The code block within the if statement will only execute if the fputs( ) function returns an end of file. If an EOF is returned, an error message is displayed on the screen and the program exits using the exit( ) function.

Notice that the string.h header file is included in this program. This must appear in the program since the strncpy( ) function is used. The prototype for the strncpy( ) function is contained in the string.h header file. A compiler error occurs if this header file is missing from the program.

The fputs( ) function writes a string of characters to a previously opened file. This function requires two arguments. The first argument contains a pointer to the string that will be written to the file. The second argument contains the pointer to the file. A nonnegative value is returned if the function successfully writes the string to the file. An EOF value is returned if an error has occurred.

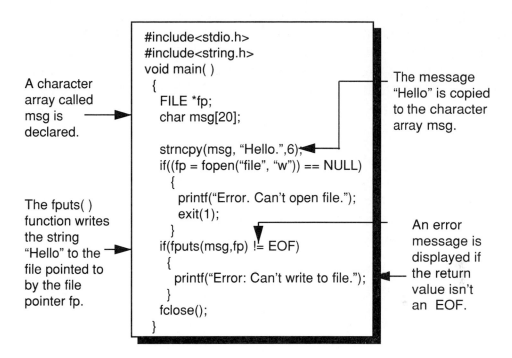

A character array called msg is declared.

The message "Hello" is copied to the character array msg.

```
#include<stdio.h>
#include<string.h>
void main( )
   {
     FILE *fp;
     char msg[20];

     strncpy(msg, "Hello.",6);
     if((fp = fopen("file", "w")) == NULL)
        {
          printf("Error. Can't open file.");
          exit(1);
        }
     if(fputs(msg,fp) != EOF)
        {
          printf("Error: Can't write to file.");
        }
     fclose();
   }
```

The fputs( ) function writes the string "Hello" to the file pointed to by the file pointer fp.

An error message is displayed if the return value isn't an EOF.

Reading a String from a File
fgets( )

Reading a series of a characters from a file can be accomplished by calling the getc( ) function several times. However, a more efficient method is to call the *fgets( ) function*. There are three arguments that are required, the first of which is the name of the array that will receive the characters. Next is an integer that specifies the number of characters that are to be read from the file stream. And the last argument is the file pointer to the file stream.

The null character, which identifies the character array as a string to C++ functions, is not in the file stream itself. Therefore, the fgets( ) function does not continue reading characters from the file stream until the first null character is read, which is the technique with other C++ functions that work with strings.

Instead, the fgets( ) function reads characters from the file stream until one of three conditions exists. The first condition is to specify the number of characters to be read. The next condition is to specify if a new line character is read. Once a new line character is read, the fgets( ) function stops even if the second argument specifies that more characters are to be read. The final condition that halts the operation of the fgets( ) function is if an end-of-file character is read.

The fgets( ) function returns a null character if no characters are available to be read from the file stream or the specified number of characters. The first character is automatically placed at the address of the first element in the character array. Subsequent characters are placed at succeeding addresses.

Although the null character is not read from the file stream, the fgets( ) function automatically places a null character as the last character in the specified character array. Therefore, if no characters are read from the file stream, the fgets( ) function places a null character at the first address in the specified array otherwise the null character is placed at the next address in the array. A word of caution! Make sure that sufficient space is reserved to hold the null character.

The fgets( ) function reads a string of characters from an open file. This function requires three arguments. The first argument is the pointer to the previously defined character array that will hold the string value. The second argument contains the number of characters that are to be read from the file. Don't include the null character in the count. The third argument points to the opened file. The fgets( ) stops reading characters when a new line character is read, the end of file has been reached, or the specified number of characters have been read. This function returns the address of the string or a null pointer. It is recommended that the feof( ) function or the ferror( ) function be used to test the results of the fgets( ) function.

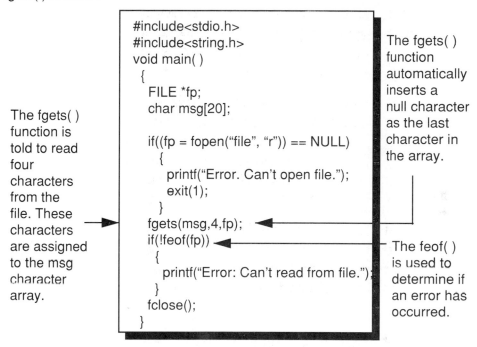

The fgets( ) function is told to read four characters from the file. These characters are assigned to the msg character array.

```
#include<stdio.h>
#include<string.h>
void main( )
  {
    FILE *fp;
    char msg[20];

    if((fp = fopen("file", "r")) == NULL)
      {
        printf("Error. Can't open file.");
        exit(1);
      }
    fgets(msg,4,fp);
    if(!feof(fp))
      {
        printf("Error: Can't read from file.");
      }
    fclose();
  }
```

The fgets( ) function automatically inserts a null character as the last character in the array.

The feof( ) is used to determine if an error has occurred.

Writing an Integer to a File
putw( )

An integer value is written to a file stream by using the *putw( ) function*. Two arguments are required for this function. The first argument contains the integer value that is to be written to the file stream and the other argument is the file pointer to the file stream.

The putw( ) function returns the integer that is written to the file to the calling statement in the program. However, if an error occurs during the execution of the putw( ) function, the return value is an end-of-file character.

In the example on the opposite page, an integer variable called a is declared then assigned the value 10. A file stream is opened using the fopen( ) function, then the putw( ) function is called from within the if statement. The first argument to this function is the integer variable a. The second argument is fp, which is the file pointer to the file stream.

The putw( ) function is part of a compound expression where the return value from this function is automatically evaluated. If the return value is an end-of-file character, then an error message is displayed on the screen and the program exits using the exit( ) function otherwise the program continues. Although the next statement in the program closes the file stream and ends the program, most applications that use the putw( ) function proceed to more meaningful statements.

A word of caution! The end-of-file character is a legitimate integer; therefore a more prudent way to determine if the end of file is encountered by the putw( ) function is to use the *ferror( ) function*. Call the ferror( ) function immediately before calling the putw( ) function. This technique is illustrated below.

```
if (!ferror(fp))
    putw(a,fp);
```

The putw( ) function writes an integer to an open file. Two arguments are required. The first argument contains the integer value that is to be written to the file. The second argument contains the pointer to the file. The putw( ) function returns the integer that was written to the file if the function executed successfully. An EOF is returned if the function was unable to write the integer to the file.

Here, the putw( ) function writes the value of integer variable a to the opened file.

Remember, EOF is a #define symbolic constant that is replaced with a value by the compiler.

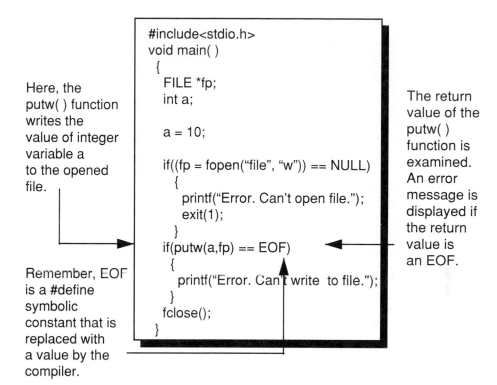

```
#include<stdio.h>
void main( )
  {
   FILE *fp;
   int a;

   a = 10;

   if((fp = fopen("file", "w")) == NULL)
     {
       printf("Error. Can't open file.");
       exit(1);
     }
   if(putw(a,fp) == EOF)
     {
       printf("Error. Can't write to file.");
     }
   fclose();
  }
```

The return value of the putw( ) function is examined. An error message is displayed if the return value is an EOF.

Reading an Integer from a File
getw( )

Call the *getw( ) function* whenever an integer must be read from a file stream. The getw( ) function requires that the file pointer be passed to it as an argument. This function returns the integer or an end-of-file character that must be assigned to a variable so the integer can be used within the program.

A word of caution! The end-of-file character is a valid integer. Remember, characters are stored in a file stream using their ASCII equivalent values, which are integers. Therefore, the integer being read from the file could have the same value as the integer that is used to represent the end-of-file character.

There are two methods that can be used to avoid this confusion. Prior to calling the getw( ) function, call either the feof( ) function or the ferror( ) function. Both functions have the same effect on the program. Each of these functions requires that the file pointer to the file stream be passed as an argument.

These functions then interrogate the file stream to determine if the end of file is reached or if some other error exists with the file. Both functions return a true (non-zero) value or a false (zero) value to the calling statement. The program should test the return value before calling the getw( ) function.

One of these techniques is illustrated in the example shown on the opposite page. Here, the feof( ) function is called with the fp file pointer passed to the function. If the file stream is not at the end of file, then the feof( ) function returns a zero. However, the code block beneath the if statement is executed only if the expression in the if statement evaluates true. Therefore, the NOT operator (!) is used to reverse the logic. That is, if the return value from the feof( ) function is zero, the NOT operator logically reverses that value to nonzero. If the return value is non-zero, then the NOT operator logically reverses that value to zero so that the proper evaluation is made for the if statement.

The getw( ) function reads an integer from an open file. Only one argument is required. This argument contains the pointer to the file that will be read by the getw( ) function. The function returns either the integer or an EOF if the current position is the end of the file.

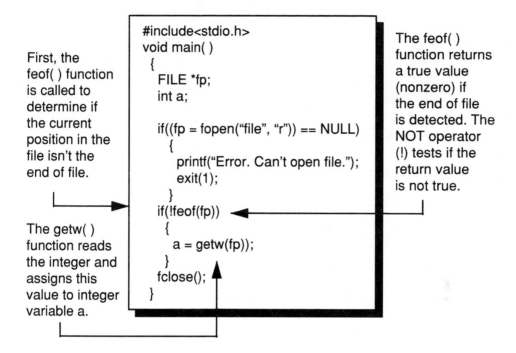

First, the feof( ) function is called to determine if the current position in the file isn't the end of file.

The getw( ) function reads the integer and assigns this value to integer variable a.

```
#include<stdio.h>
void main( )
  {
   FILE *fp;
   int a;

   if((fp = fopen("file", "r")) == NULL)
     {
       printf("Error. Can't open file.");
       exit(1);
     }
   if(!feof(fp))
     {
       a = getw(fp));
     }
   fclose();
  }
```

The feof( ) function returns a true value (nonzero) if the end of file is detected. The NOT operator (!) tests if the return value is not true.

Writing a Block of Data
to a File
fwrite( )

An efficient way to write data to a file stream is to write an entire block of data at the same time. A block of data consists of data that is stored in sequential memory addresses. For example, a typical block of data is an array or a structure. An array contains a series of data of the same data type that is stored along side each other in memory. Likewise, a structure consists of a series of data of the same or different data type stored sequentially in memory.

A block of data is written to a file stream by using the *fwrite( ) function*. This function requires four arguments, the first of which is the address of the starting data in the block. The next argument is an integer that determines the number of bytes that are to be written to the file stream. The third argument is the number of sets that are to be written. The last argument is the file pointer to the file stream.

In the example on the opposite page, a block of data the size of one variable is written to the file. Here, a float called salary is declared and the value 30500 is assigned to the variable. Next, a binary file is opened for read access and the fwrite( ) function is called.

Notice that the ampersand operator (&) is used in the first argument. Remember, the fwrite( ) function is expecting the address of the beginning of the block. The variable name salary references the value at the address and not the address itself. The ampersand references the address of the variable rather than the value.

The second argument uses the sizeof( ) operator. Always use this operator instead of entering the number of bytes of the block. Remember, the byte size of a variable is dependent on the computer. The sizeof( ) operator adjusts for this difference. There is only one set of the block that is to be written, therefore the integer 1 is passed as the third argument. Finally, the fp file pointer variable is passed as the fourth argument to the fwrite( ) function.

The fwrite( ) function writes a block of data of a specific size to the file. Any type of data can be written to a file using the fwrite( ) function as long as the file is opened as a binary file. The fwrite( ) function requires four arguments. The first argument is a pointer to the buffer that contains the data that is to be written to the file. The second argument specifies the number of bytes that are contained in the buffer. The third argument is the number of items of the specified size that are to be written to the file. And the last argument is the pointer to the file. A true value (1) is returned if the data has been successfully written to the file otherwise a non true value is returned.

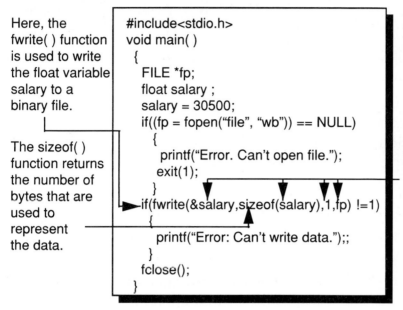

Here, the fwrite( ) function is used to write the float variable salary to a binary file.

The sizeof( ) function returns the number of bytes that are used to represent the data.

```
#include<stdio.h>
void main( )
{
    FILE *fp;
    float salary ;
    salary = 30500;
    if((fp = fopen("file", "wb")) == NULL)
    {
        printf("Error. Can't open file.");
        exit(1);
    }
    if(fwrite(&salary,sizeof(salary),1,fp) !=1)
    {
        printf("Error: Can't write data.");;
    }
    fclose();
}
```

The address of salary is used as the first argument. The return value from the sizeof( ) function sets the number of bytes that are to be written to the file. The third argument tells the compiler that one item of salary is to be written. The file pointer is the last argument.

Reading a Block of Data
from a File
fread( )

The counterpart to the fwrite( ) function that is presented on the previous page is the *fread( ) function*. This function reads a block of data from a file stream. The syntax for the fread( ) function is nearly identical to that of the syntax used for the fwrite( ) function. Actually, the only difference is that the name of the function changes. The argument list remains that same.

This is an important fact to keep in mind when writing code to write and read blocks of data to and from a file stream. First, create the code that writes to the file stream using the fwrite( ) function, then copy this function to the read segment of program and change the function name to fread( ).

Of course, the functionality of the fread( ) function differs from that of the fwrite( ) function, so the appropriate variables must be used in the fread( ). An example of this is shown on the next page.

Here, a float called salary is declared just as it is in the example of the fwrite( ) function on the previous page. However, no value is assigned to this variable until after the fread( ) function is called. Notice that the ampersand operator still precedes the name of the variable in the fread( ) argument list. The fread( ) function requires the starting address in memory where the block is to be stored.

In this example, the address of the variable salary is the location in memory where the fread( ) will place the block of data read from the file stream. The sizeof( ) operator is also used in the fread( ) function to identify the number of bytes that is to be read from the file stream.

A word of caution! The data type used to store the block of data must be the same data type that was used to store the written data to the file. A mismatch of data types could cause the wrong number of bytes to be read from the file stream.

The fread( ) function reads a block of data of a specific size from a file. Any type of data can be read from a file using the fread( ) function as long as the file is opened as a binary file. The fread( ) function requires four arguments. The first argument is a pointer to the buffer that will be assigned the data that is read from the file. The second argument specifies the number of bytes that are to be read from the file. The third argument is the number of items of the specified size that are to be read from the file. And the last argument is the pointer to the file. A true value (1) is returned if the data has been successfully read from the file otherwise a non true value is returned.

Here, the fread( ) function is used to read the float variable salary from a binary file.

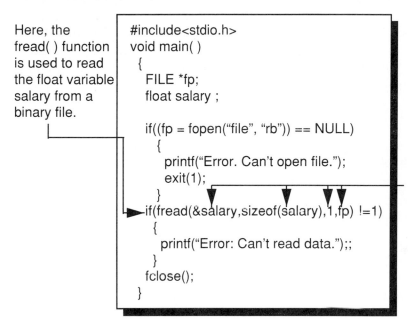

```
#include<stdio.h>
void main( )
{
    FILE *fp;
    float salary ;

    if((fp = fopen("file", "rb")) == NULL)
    {
        printf("Error. Can't open file.");
        exit(1);
    }
    if(fread(&salary,sizeof(salary),1,fp) !=1)
    {
        printf("Error: Can't read data.");;
    }
    fclose();
}
```

The address of salary is used as the first argument. The return value from the sizeof( ) function sets the number of bytes that are to be read from the file. The third argument tells the compiler that one item of salary is to be read. The file pointer is the last argument.

Creating a Database File

Most applications associate variables with other variables into a logical unit, then treat the logical unit as a single entity. Typically, a logical unit is a collection of variables stored as an instance of a structure. Once a structure is defined and an instance declared, the programmer can use C++ syntax to reference elements of the structure or the structure itself.

When data is stored in an organized collection in a file stream, the collection is commonly refered to as a database. A *database* consists of columns and rows also known as *fields* and *records*, respectively. Each element in an instance of a structure directly relates to columns of a database. Likewise, each instance of a structure directly relates to a record of the database.

A combination of a structure with the fwrite( ) and fread( ) functions enables a program to create a simple database application using C++. There is another method to create a database using C++ that is discussed later in this chapter.

An example of writing a record to this simple database application is illustrated on the opposite page. The fread( ) function is used to read the record from the file stream. First, the structure called comp is defined and an instance of that structure called emp1 is declared. Remember, space is reserved in memory for the structure only when an instance of the structure is declared and not when a structure is defined. After the file pointer is declared, values are assigned to elements of the structure. Notice that the name of the instance followed by the dot operator is used to reference each element of the structure.

Next, the file is opened and the fwrite( ) function is called and the address of the emp1 instance of the structure is passed to the fwrite( ) function. Remember, this is the address of the empnum element. All the other elements in the structure are stored consecutively in memory. The sizeof( ) is then used to determine the size of the structure. The size of the block of data that is to be written to the file stream is the total size of all the elements in the structure.

By combining a structure with the fwrite( ) and fread( ) functions, you can quickly create a database. Each copy of the structure is a record of the database. Each element of the structure is a field of the record. The fwrite( ) function writes one or more records to the database file while the fread( ) function reads records from the database.

Write a Record

The structure called comp is defined and one instance of the structure is declared.

Notice that the address of the data block is the address of the emp1 instance of the structure.

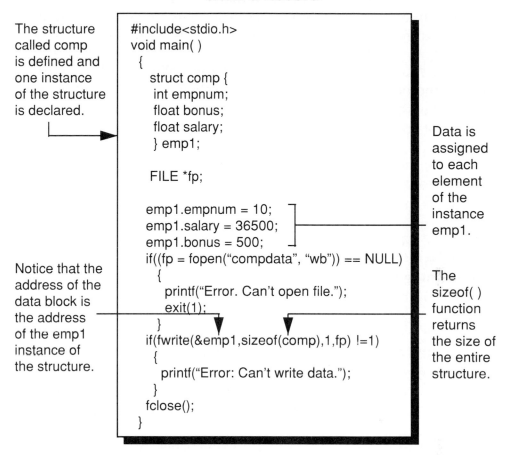

```
#include<stdio.h>
void main( )
  {
    struct comp {
    int empnum;
    float bonus;
    float salary;
    } emp1;

    FILE *fp;

    emp1.empnum = 10;
    emp1.salary = 36500;
    emp1.bonus = 500;
    if((fp = fopen("compdata", "wb")) == NULL)
      {
        printf("Error. Can't open file.");
        exit(1);
      }
    if(fwrite(&emp1,sizeof(comp),1,fp) !=1)
      {
        printf("Error: Can't write data.");
      }
    fclose();
  }
```

Data is assigned to each element of the instance emp1.

The sizeof( ) function returns the size of the entire structure.

Reading a Record

A record can be read from this simple database by using the fread( ) function. This technique is illustrated in the example on the opposite page. The program begins by defining the structure in the image of the record, then an instance of the structure called emp1 is declared.

A word of caution! Always be sure that the definition of the structure matches the description of the record, otherwise there could be a misalignment of the data. That is, the fread( ) function does not validate data assignments to elements of a structure.

Remember, the fread( ) function only copies a block of bytes from a file stream to a memory location. It is the structure definition that gives meaning to that data.

The fread( ) function, as is shown on the next page, reads a single record into the block of the memory. This is because the third argument contains the integer 1. If the value of this argument is changed to 2, for example, then two blocks of data the size of the structure are read from the file stream.

Another word of caution! Be sure to allocate sufficient space in memory for all of the records that are to be read from the file stream. The fread( ) function places the entire block of data in consecutive locations in memory beginning with the address specified in the first argument.

If a single instance of the structure is declared, such as is the case on the next page where the fread( ) statement is instructed to read two records from the file stream, then the program will not be able to easily access the second record. A better approach is to declare instances of the structure for each block of data that is to be read. Each record can then be accessed by referencing each instance of the structure.

The fread( ) function automatically reads a data block in the size of the structure from the file and assigns the data to the appropriate element of the structure.

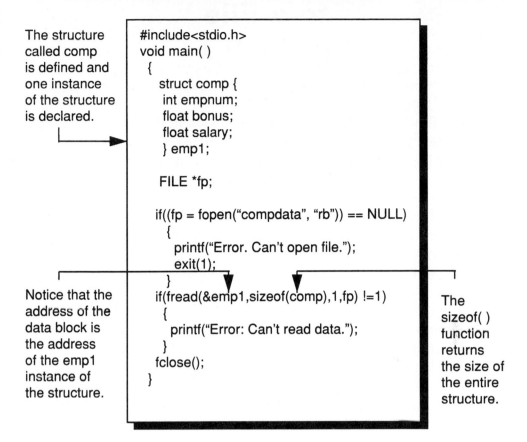

The structure called comp is defined and one instance of the structure is declared.

```
#include<stdio.h>
void main( )
   {
      struct comp {
      int empnum;
      float bonus;
      float salary;
      } emp1;

      FILE *fp;

      if((fp = fopen("compdata", "rb")) == NULL)
         {
         printf("Error. Can't open file.");
         exit(1);
         }
      if(fread(&emp1,sizeof(comp),1,fp) !=1)
         {
         printf("Error: Can't read data.");
         }
      fclose();
   }
```

Notice that the address of the data block is the address of the emp1 instance of the structure.

The sizeof( ) function returns the size of the entire structure.

Writing Various Data Types to a File
fprintf( )

In previous chapters, information is displayed on the screen by calling the printf() function. The same function with slight modifications is used to write information to a file stream. The unique feature of the fprintf( ) function is that data is written to a file in a specified format.

The *fprintf( ) function* requires at least two, but sometimes more, arguments. The first argument is the file pointer to the file stream. The second argument is the string that is to be written to the file. The string can be a constant. That is, the characters that are contained within the double quotation marks are literally written to the file stream.

The string can also contain format specifiers. A format specifier is a place-holder within the string where data of a specific data type is placed when the string is written to the file stream. A list of format specifiers is on the opposite page. If a format specifier is used in the string, then an argument containing the reference to the data that will replace that format specifier must be passed to the fprintf( ) function. For each format specifier in a string, the fprintf( ) function must be passed a reference to a data source.

Below is the syntax used for the fprintf( ) function. This statement causes the contents of the string within the double quotations to be written to the file stream pointed to by the fp file pointer. Notice that the format specifier %s is used to position the data within the string. The actual data is contained in the third argument of the character array fname, which is a string. The first element of the string fname replaces the %s symbol in the string. The remaining elements follow sequentially. Additional data can be included in the string by inserting the appropriate format specifier then using the comma operator to separate the additional arguments.

```
fprintf(fp,"Hello, %s",fname);
```

The fprintf( ) function writes assorted data types to a file using a similar technique as is used with the printf( ) function. The fprintf( ) function requires at least three arguments. The first argument is the pointer to the file. The second argument is the string that contains the format specifiers for each data. The last argument(s) contains the data that is to be written to the file. The data is written to the file in the same format (text) as the data is printed on the screen using the printf( ) function. The fprintf( ) function returns the number of characters that was printed. A negative number is returned if there is an error.

Format Specifiers for the fprintf( ) Function

Format Specifier	Description
%c	One Character.
%d	Decimal.
%i	Integer.
%e	Scientific Notation.
%f	Floating Point.
%g	Use the Shorter of Either %e or %f.
%o	Octal.
%s	String.
%u	Unsigned Decimal.
%x	Hexadecimal.
%%	Display a percentage sign.
%p	Pointer.

Using the fprintf( ) Function

The top example on the opposite page illustrates the technique for writing multiple data elements to a file stream using the fprintf( ) function. First, the fp file pointer is passed to the fprintf( ) function to identify the file stream. Next is the string that is written to the file.

Notice that the string only contains format specifiers. That is, only data that is stored outside of the string itself is to be written to the file. The place-holders for the data are the format specifiers %i and %f. These tell the fprintf( ) function that an integer and two floats will be included in the string at the location of the format specifiers.

The data itself is referenced outside of the quotation marks in three additional arguments that are passed to the fprintf( ) function. These are empnum, bonus and salary. The fprintf( ) function replaces each format specifier in order. That is, the first format specifier is replaced by the first argument that follows the quotation marks, the second format specifier is replaced by the second argument, and so on.

A word of caution! Be sure that the number of format specifiers equals the number of arguments otherwise the compiler will signal an error.

In contrast, no data is used in the example at the bottom of the opposite page. Here, a string constant is written to the file stream. Only two arguments are required for the fprintf( ) function. These are the fp file pointer, which points to the file stream, and the string that that will be written to the file stream.

No format specifiers are necessary in this example because no data elements are to be written to the file stream. All the information that is stored in the file is contained within the quotation marks.

Writing Data

Reference to the data that will be written to the file.

Format specifiers.

The file pointer.

The fprintf( ) function writes both integer and float data to the file.

```c
#include<stdio.h>
void main( )
  {
    FILE *fp;
    int empnum;
    float bonus = 500
    float salary;
    empnum = 101;
    salary = 35500'

    if((fp = fopen("compdata", "w")) == NULL)
      {
        printf("Error. Can't open file.");
      }
    fprintf(fp,"%i%f%f",empnum,bonus,salary);
    fclose();
  }
```

```c
#include<stdio.h>
void main( )
  {
    FILE *fp;
    if((fp = fopen("compdata", "w")) == NULL)
      {
        printf("Error. Can't open file.");
      }
    fprintf(fp,"This is a test");
    fclose();
  }
```

Writing a String Constant

A string of characters can be written to the file by enclosing the characters within quotations in the second argument to the function.

Working with Files and Streams

Reading Various Data Types from a File
fscanf( )

Information that is stored in a specific format in a file stream can easily be retrieved by using the *fscanf( ) function*. This function is similar to the fprintf( ) function. Both functions use format specifiers to transfer data between memory and a file stream.

Below is the syntax for the fscanf( ) function. Further discussion about using the fscanf( ) function is contained in the next section. The fscanf( ) function requires at least three arguments. The first argument is the file pointer to the file stream. In the example below, fp is the file pointer. Next is the string that will receive the data from the file stream. This string must contain format specifiers for each data element that is read from the file stream. A table of format specifiers for the fscantf( ) function is contained on the next page. Only the %s format specifier is used in this example.

And finally, the remaining arguments reference the memory locations where the data will be stored after it is read from the file stream. In this example, fname is a character array. The fscanf( ) reads characters from the file stream and stores them sequentially in memory beginning at the address of the first element of the fname array. The fscanf( ) function moves to the next format specifier (if any exists) when a null character is read from the file stream.

fscanf(fp, "%s",fname);

Similar to the fprintf( ) function, multiple memory locations can be specified by using an appropriate set of format specifiers and arguments.

A word of caution! Be sure that the data types of the format specifier, of the variable and of the data read from the file stream and are the same; otherwise data integrity could be in jeopardy.

The fscanf( ) function can read an assortment of data from a text file. Three arguments are required. The first argument is the pointer to the file. The second argument contains format specifiers for each data element that is to be read from the file. Format specifiers must be enclosed within quotations. The last argument contains reference to the variables where the data will be stored. The fscanf( ) function returns the number of values that were assigned to a variable or an EOF.

Format Specifiers for the fscanf( ) Function	
Format Specifier	Description
%c	Read One Character.
%d	Read a Decimal Value.
%i	Read an Integer Value.
%e	Read a Floating-Point Value.
%f	Read a Floating-Point Value.
%h	Read a Short Integer Value.
%o	Read an Octal Value.
%s	Read a String.
%p	Read a Pointer.
%x	Read a Hexadecimal Value.

Using the fscanf( ) Function

The fscanf( ) function reads data from a file stream and assigns the data to variables. This is illustrated in the two examples on the opposite page. In the top example, three data items are read from the file stream pointed to by the fp file pointer.

The first data item is an integer, as indicated by the format specifier %i in the string argument of the fscanf( ) function. This format specifier correlates to the data type of the first data argument in the function, which is the variable empnum. That is, the fscanf( ) function reads the first data from the file stream, then assigns the data to the empnum variable.

The next data item is a float. The %f format specifier inserted within the string argument identifies the data type of the next data item. The fscanf( ) function then assigns the next data item to the variable bonus. The same process occurs for the last data item.

Actually, fscanf( ) reads bytes of information from the file stream. The number of bytes that is read for each data item is determined by the format specifier. For example, a %c indicates that data the size of a character is to be read from the file stream. On most computers, a character is a byte. Therefore, the function reads one byte, stops reading from the file stream, assigns the byte to the next variable on the argument list, then reads the next format specifier.

Likewise, a %i indicates that data the size of an integer is to be read from the file stream. An integer is two bytes on many computers. The fscanf( ) then reads the next two bytes from the file stream and assigns them to next variable.

The example at the bottom of the opposite page checks the return value from the fscanf( ) function to determine if the end of file is reached. The fscanf( ) function returns the number of fields that were successfully stored and an EOF value if the end of file is read.

Reference to the data that will hold the values read from the file.

Format specifiers.

The file pointer.

The fscanf( ) function reads both integer and float data from the file.

```c
#include<stdio.h>
void main( )
  {
    FILE *fp;
    int empnum;
    float bonus;
    float salary;

    if((fp = fopen("compdata", "r")) == NULL)
      {
        printf("Error. Can't open file.");
        exit(1);
      }
    fscanf(fp,"%i%f%f",&empnum,&bonus,&salary);
    fclose();
  }
```

```c
#include<stdio.h>
void main( )
  {
    FILE *fp;
    int empnum;
    float bonus, salary;
    if((fp = fopen("compdata", "r")) == NULL)
      {
        printf("Error. Can't open file.");
        exit(1);
      }
    if(fscanf(fp,"%i%f%f",&empnum,&bonus,&salary) == EOF)
      printf("Error: End of file detected");
    fclose();
  }
```

This program reads the return value. A message is displayed if the end of file has been detected.

Moving to Specific Locations in a File
fseek( )

Conceptually, a file stream resembles a long roll of tape. The beginning and end of the tape is the beginning and end of the file stream. Data is stored consecutively on the tape starting at the beginning of the tape. Every file stream has an *internal file pointer*. An internal file pointer is a mechanism that records the current position in the file.

When the file stream is initially opened, the internal file pointer is positioned at the beginning of the file. As each byte is read from the file stream, the internal file pointer moves to the next byte along the stream. For example, after the first byte is read by the program, the internal file pointer moves to the second byte.

However, if a block of data is read from the file stream, then the internal file pointer moves to the byte that begins the next block of data. For example, when the fread( ) function reads a block of data the size of 20 bytes, the internal file pointer is positioned at byte 21 after the fread( ) function has executed.

The program can move the file pointer to any location in a file stream by using the *fseek( ) function*. This function requires three arguments. The first argument is the pointer to the file stream. In the example on the opposite page, the file pointer is named fp.

The second argument is the number of bytes to move the internal file pointer. In this example, the internal file pointer is moved to the 128th byte. The last argument determines the starting position of the internal pointer. A zero value instructs the fseek( ) function to start at the beginning of the file. A 1 value starts at the current position, and a 2 value starts at the end of the file. In this example, the fscanf( ) function is instructed to move to the 128th byte from the current position. Once the internal file pointer is repositioned, the other file stream function can be called to manipulate the data stored in the file stream at this new location.

354

The fseek( ) function enables you to move to a specific location in the file. This function requires three arguments. The first argument is the pointer to the file. The second argument is the offset value, which is a long integer. This is the number of bytes that are to be skipped from the origin. The origin is the third argument. The value of the origin can be 0 is used to start at the beginning of the file, 1 is used to start at the current file position, or 2 is used to start at the end of the file. A zero is returned if the fseek( ) function successfully repositions the file. A nonzero value is returned if there is an error. The fseek( ) should only be used on binary files since character translations of a text file can cause position errors to occur.

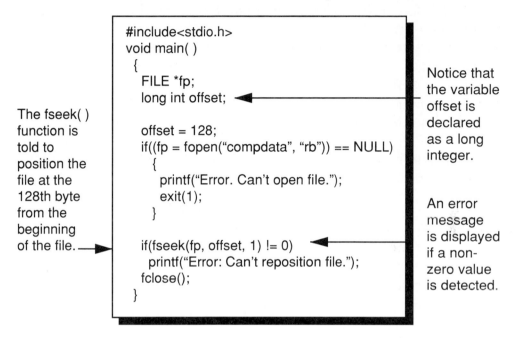

The fseek( ) function is told to position the file at the 128th byte from the beginning of the file.

```
#include<stdio.h>
void main( )
  {
    FILE *fp;
    long int offset;

    offset = 128;
    if((fp = fopen("compdata", "rb")) == NULL)
      {
        printf("Error. Can't open file.");
        exit(1);
      }

    if(fseek(fp, offset, 1) != 0)
      printf("Error: Can't reposition file.");
    fclose();
  }
```

Notice that the variable offset is declared as a long integer.

An error message is displayed if a non-zero value is detected.

Returning to the Beginning of a File rewind( )

The fseek( ) function, presented in the previous section, enables the program to move about the file stream with little restraint. However, the program needs to keep track of both the number of the byte that is to be read and the position of the internal file pointer.

C++ offers another function that is called to reset the position of the internal file pointer to the beginning of the file stream. This function is called *rewind*( ). The rewind( ) function accepts a single argument, which is the file pointer to the file stream. Once this function is called, the internal file pointer of the file stream is moved to the beginning of the file.

This technique is illustrated in the example at the top of the opposite page. Here, the fp file pointer is passed to the rewind() function.

Deleting a File unlink( )

A file stream can be removed from the media (disk) by using the *unlink*( ) *function*. This function has an effect similar to using the operating command to delete a file.

The bottom example on the next page shows how the unlink( ) function is used. Here, a character array is declared then the string that contains the file name is copied to the character array. The name of the character array is then passed to the unlink( ) function. Notice that the name of the file is used and not a file pointer to the file stream. The file pointer is assigned a value only when the file stream is opened. An opened file stream cannot be deleted.

Returning to the Beginning of the File
rewind( )

The rewind( ) function moves the position to the beginning of the file. The pointer to the file is the only argument for this function.

The rewind( ) function is called to move to the beginning of the file.

```
#include<stdio.h>
void main( )
  {
    FILE *fp;
    if((fp = fopen("compdata", "rb")) == NULL)
      {
        printf("Error. Can't open file.");
        exit(1);
      }
    rewind(fp);
    fclose();
  }
```

Deleting a File
unlink( )

The unlink( ) function removes a file from the disk. This function requires one argument, which is a pointer to the string that contains the name of the file that is to be deleted. A zero value is returned if the file is deleted; otherwise a nonzero value is returned.

The unlink() function is used to delete the test.txt file from the disk.

```
#include<stdio.h>
#include<string.h>
void main( )
  {
    char file[12];
    strncpy(file,"test.txt",8);
    unlink(file);
  }
```

Using a File in C++

Throughout this chapter we have explored techniques for saving and retrieving information to and from a file stream. These methods can be used in C++ and in C. Beginning with this section of the chapter, let's explore ways of achieving similar results by using C++ constructs. That is, these techniques cannot be used in the C language.

Previously in this chapter, we discussed programs called stand-alone library functions to manipulate a file string. However, C++ contains classes that manage file input and output. These classes have data members and function members that can be called from within a C++ program to save and retrieve data from a file stream.

A flow chart on the opposite page illustrates the relationship of these classes and their function members. There are two central classes that are used for file stream manipulation. These are the *istream class* and the *ostream class*. The istream class contains function members and receives information from a file stream. Likewise, the ostream class has function members that send information to a file stream.

The istream class, as shown on the next page, has four main ways of reading information from a file stream. These are the *get( )*, *getline( )* and *read( ) function members* and the *extraction operator (>>)*.

The ostream class has three ways of writing to a file stream. These are the *put()*, and *write() function members* and the *insertion operator (<<)*.

Characteristics of both classes are inherited by the derived class iostream. The istream, ostream, and iostream classes are library classes. That is, they are predefined and supplied with the compiler. A programmer needs only to use the appropriate include file in the source code, then reference function members of the class. The following pages show how these function members are used in a program.

Information is written to and read from a file in C++ by using streams. A *stream* is a flow of data. There are various streams and each stream is associated with a particular class. Each class has function member that knows how to process information for a particular kind of stream.

The chart that is shown below illustrates the relationships among the stream classes. The istream class and the ostream class are used to receive information from a file and to write information to a file.

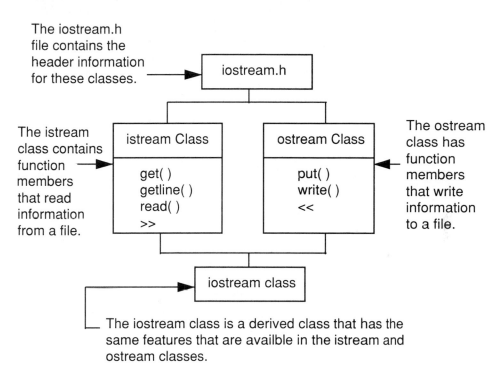

The iostream.h file contains the header information for these classes.

iostream.h

The istream class contains function members that read information from a file.

istream Class

get( )
getline( )
read( )
>>

The ostream class has function members that write information to a file.

ostream Class

put( )
write( )
<<

iostream class

The iostream class is a derived class that has the same features that are availble in the istream and ostream classes.

Writing Information to a File Using C++

Whenever information is to be written to or read from a file, the program must initially open the file. This is done by declaring an instance of the *ofstream class* as is illustrated in the example on the opposite page. Notice that this technique does not use file pointers. Instead, an instance of an appropriate class is declared.

On the first line of the main( ) function, outfile is declared as the name of an instance of the ofstream class. Any name can be given to the instance. The string containing the name of the file that is to be opened is passed to the constructor of the instance.

Once the file stream is opened, the program references the file stream by using the name of the instance. In this example, the insertion operator is used to write information to the opened file.

The insertion operator writes information to the screen. The functionality is the same regardless of whether the insertion operator is in a statement that writes to the screen or to a file. Remember, the insertion operator takes the data from the right of the insertion operator and passes the data to the object on the left of the insertion operator.

In this example, the string is passed by the insertion operator to the outfile object. Remember, an instance of a class is called an object. The outfile object "knows" how to manipulate the data so that the data is stored in the appropriate file stream.

The ofstream class is derived from the ostream class, which is described on the previous page. This class requires that the program contain the fstream.h include file.

You must create an object of the ostream class to open a file using C++. The string that contains the name of the file that is to be opened is placed within parentheses to the right of the object. The insertion operator is used to place the data that appears to the right of the insertion operator into the stream that appears to the left of the insertion operator.

The fstream.h file must be included in every program that reads or writes to a file.

Here, outfile is declared as an object of the ofstream class.

The string that contains the name of the file is placed within parentheses.

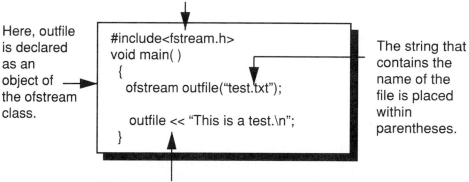

```
#include<fstream.h>
void main( )
    {
        ofstream outfile("test.txt");

        outfile << "This is a test.\n";
    }
```

The insertion operator inserts the string into the outfile stream, which is the file itself.

Did You Know ...

The string that contains the name of the file is actually passed as an argument to the constructor of the object. The insertion operator can write information to a file because the insertion operator is overloaded with the file-writing feature.

Reading a String from a File Using C++

A string of data can be read from a file stream by using an instance of the *ifstream class*. This class is derived from the istream class. This technique is illustrated on the opposite page.

First, the file stream must be opened for reading. This is accomplished automatically by creating an instance of the ifstream class. In this example, the name of the instance is infile, however, any name can be given to the instance as long as the name does not use any C++ reserved words.

Similar to the instance of the ofstream class that is discussed on the previous page, the name of the file stream, contained within double quotation marks, is passed to the constructor of the infile instance. The constructor then opens the file stream in the appropriate mode.

Next, a character array called data is declared that reserves enough memory to hold 80 characters. The program enters a while loop. The while loop statement is the name of the instance of the ifstream class. This instance returns a true value to the while loop until the end of the file stream is reached at which time a false value is returned and the program exits the loop.

Within the code block of the loop is a single statement. This statement calls the getline( ) function member of the instance infile. Notice the proper syntax for calling this function. The name of the instance is followed by the dot operator, then the name of the function member.

The *getline( ) function member* requires two arguments. The first argument is the name of the array that will be assigned the value of the character read from the file stream. The second argument is an integer that specifies the number of characters that are to be read by the getline( ) function member.

Reading a file requires that you declare an object of the ifstream class. The ifstream class contains the getline( ) member function, which reads a string from the file. The getline( ) member function requires two arguments. The first argument is the character array that will be assigned the string. The second argument is the maximum number of characters that will be read from the file. The function will read the file until either the limit is reached or a newline character is read.

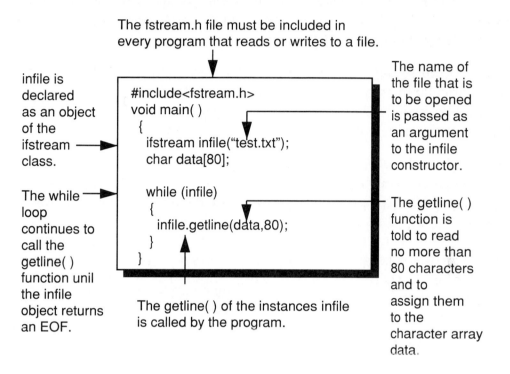

The fstream.h file must be included in every program that reads or writes to a file.

infile is declared as an object of the ifstream class.

```
#include<fstream.h>
void main( )
{
    ifstream infile("test.txt");
    char data[80];

    while (infile)
    {
        infile.getline(data,80);
    }
}
```

The name of the file that is to be opened is passed as an argument to the infile constructor.

The while loop continues to call the getline( ) function unil the infile object returns an EOF.

The getline( ) of the instances infile is called by the program.

The getline( ) function is told to read no more than 80 characters and to assign them to the character array data.

Writing a Single Character to a file Using C++

A string of characters can be written to a file using the technique shown on the previous pages. However, individual characters can also be written to a file by using the *put( ) function member* of the ofstream class.

In the top example on the opposite page, an instance of the ofstream class is declared as outfile. The string that contains the name of the file stream is passed to the constructor of the outfile instance, which opens the file in the write mode.

Next, a character array is declared and initialized with the string "This is a test." Instead of using the insertion operator to place the string to the file, the program calls the put( ) function member of the outfile instance of the ofstream class. Actually, multiple calls are made to this function member, one call for each character in the string. The for loop statement manages this process.

The put( ) function member requires a single argument, which is the reference to the character that is to be written to the file stream. In this example, each element of the character array is individually written to the file stream. The outfile object already knows the location of the file stream.

Reading a Single Character from a File Using C++

Individual characters can be read from a file by using the *get( ) function member* of the ifstream class. This technique is illustrated in the bottom example on the opposite page.

First, an instance of the ifstream class called infile is declared with the name of the file stream passed as a string to the constructor of the instance. The get( ) function member is called in the while loop. Notice that the variable that will be assigned the value from the file stream is passed as an argument to the get( ) function member.

Writing a Single Character to a File Using C++

The put( ) member function of the ofstream class is used to write a single character to an open file. This function requires an argument, which is the name of the variable that contains the character that is to be written to the file.

The put( ) member function of the ofstream class object "outfile" is used to write each element of the character array "data" to the file. ➤

```
#include<fstream.h>
#include<string.h>  ◄
void main( )
  {
    ofstream outfile("test.txt");
    char data[] = "This is a test";

    for (int x = 0; x < strlen(data); x++)
      outfile.put(data[x]);
  }
```

Notice that the string.h file is included in the program since the strlen( ) function is called by the program.

Reading a Single Character from a File Using C++

The get( ) member function of the ifstream class is used to read a single character from an open file. This function requires an argument, which is the name of the variable that will be assigned the character that is read from the file.

The get( ) member function of the ifstream class object "infile" is used to read a character from the file to the ➤ character variable "data."

```
#include<fstream.h>
void main( )
  {
    ifstream infile("test.txt");
    char data;
    while (infile)
      {
        outfile.get(data);
      }
  }
```

Writing an Object to a File

Most C++ applications treat data as an element of a larger group. Structures are used previously in the chapter to group data into a related data block. A preferred method to use in C++ is to group data into a class. That is, data becomes data members of a class definition.

Remember, an instance of the class is called an *object* and it is only when an instance is declared that memory is actually reserved for the data members of the class. Programs can write an object to a file stream by using the *write( ) function member* of the ofstream class.

This technique is illustrated in the example on the opposite page. First, the class employee is defined. An instance of that class called emp1 is then declared as the first line in the main( ) function.

The program calls the getdata( ) function member, which prompts the user to enter values for data members of the instances at the keyboard. Once data is collected, the object emp1 is written to a file stream.

An instance called outfile of the ofstream class is declared. The file stream name test.txt is passed to the constructor of the outfile instance. Next, the write( ) function member of the outfile instance is called.

The write( ) function member requires two arguments. The first argument is a character pointer that contains the address of the object that is being written to the file stream. The second argument is the size of the object in bytes.

Notice that a temporary character pointer is created (char *) then assigned the address of the emp1 object. This is called *casting a pointer*. Also notice that the sizeof( ) operator is used to determine the size of the object in bytes. Only the data members of the object are written to the file stream—not the function members.

The data portion of an object is written to a file using the write( ) member function of the ofstream class. This function requires two arguments. The first argument is a character pointer to the object. The second argument is the number of bytes that are to be written to the file.

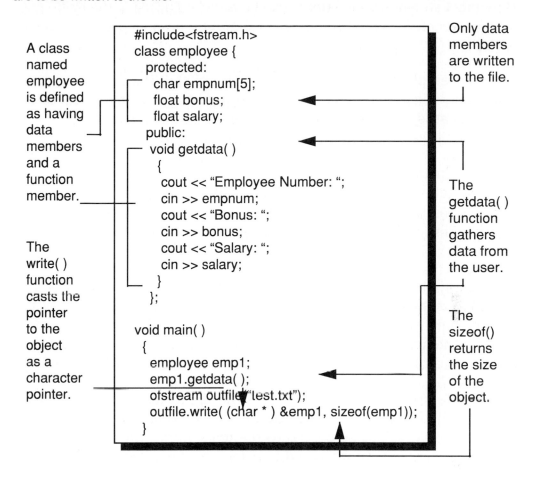

A class named employee is defined as having data members and a function member.

The write( ) function casts the pointer to the object as a character pointer.

```
#include<fstream.h>
class employee {
  protected:
    char empnum[5];
    float bonus;
    float salary;
  public:
    void getdata( )
      {
      cout << "Employee Number: ";
      cin >> empnum;
      cout << "Bonus: ";
      cin >> bonus;
      cout << "Salary: ";
      cin >> salary;
      }
};

void main( )
  {
  employee emp1;
  emp1.getdata( );
  ofstream outfile("test.txt");
  outfile.write( (char * ) &emp1, sizeof(emp1));
  }
```

Only data members are written to the file.

The getdata( ) function gathers data from the user.

The sizeof() returns the size of the object.

Reading an Object from a File

An object stored in a file stream can be retrieved by using the *read( ) function member* of the ifstream class as is shown in the example on the opposite page.

In this example, a class called employee is defined. The data members of the class must conform to the definition of the data members of the object that is going to be read from the file stream. Data integrity is in jeopardy if these definitions are not identical.

Next, an instance called emp1 of the employee class is declared. The following statement declares an instance called infile of the ifstream class and passes the name of the file stream to the constructor of the infile object. This is the object that will receive the data stored in the file stream.

The read( ) function member of the infile object is then called. Notice that the read( ) function member is structured similarly to that of the write( ) function member. The read( ) function member requires two arguments. The first argument is a character pointer that contains the address of the object that will receive the data from the file stream.

In this example, emp1 is the object. However, a character pointer must be cast in the argument. This creates a temporary character pointer (which is expected to be passed to the read( ) function member). Next, the ampersand operator is used to reference the address of the object emp1, which is assigned to the temporary character pointer.

The final argument to the read( ) function member is the number of bytes that are to be read from the file stream. It is wise to use the sizeof( ) operator to determine the size of the object emp1. Remember, only the data members of the class are read from the file stream. Once the data is assigned to the data members of the class, the program calls the show-data( ) function member to display the data on the screen.

The data portion of an object is read from a file using the read( ) member function of the ifstream class. This function requires two arguments. The first argument is a character pointer to the object. The second argument is the number of bytes that are to be read from the file.

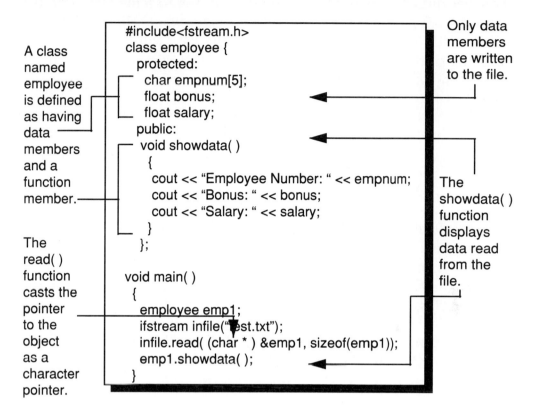

A class named employee is defined as having data members and a function member.

The read( ) function casts the pointer to the object as a character pointer.

```
#include<fstream.h>
class employee {
    protected:
        char empnum[5];
        float bonus;
        float salary;
    public:
        void showdata( )
        {
            cout << "Employee Number: " << empnum;
            cout << "Bonus: " << bonus;
            cout << "Salary: " << salary;
        }
};

void main( )
{
    employee emp1;
    ifstream infile("Test.txt");
    infile.read( (char * ) &emp1, sizeof(emp1));
    emp1.showdata( );
}
```

Only data members are written to the file.

The showdata( ) function displays data read from the file.

Specify the File Mode in C++

Whenever data members of an object are written to a file stream in the previous examples, the program never specifies where the data is to be placed within the file. It is assumed that the data will be stored at the beginning of the file. Of course in doing so, the existing data, if any, is overwritten by the new data.

A program can explicitly instruct the compiler where to write data members of an instance to a file stream by using the appropriate file mode specifier. The file mode specifier is passed as an argument to the constructor of the instance of the ofstream class. Actually, the file mode specifier is a static variable that is defined in the base class called *ios*.

The example at the top of the opposite page illustrates how to utilize the file mode specifier in an application. This example is an enhancement of the same example used to describe the write( ) function member previously in this chapter. It is assumed that the class definition for the employee class is contained in a header file.

First, an instance of the employee class called emp1 is declared, then the getdata( ) function member of this class is called to receive data from the user.

Next, an instance of the ofstream class called outfile is declared. Two arguments are passed to the constructor of the outfile object. The first argument is the name of the file stream and the second argument is the file mode specifier. The constructor is instructed to open the file stream in the append mode. That is, write the data members of the object to the end of the file stream. No existing data will be overwritten.

Notice that the ios base class name is followed by the scope resolution operator and then by the file mode specifier. The table at the bottom of the next page contains a list of other file mode specifiers. Each is passed to the constructor in the same fashion as the *ios::app file mode specifier* is passed in this example.

This program declares an object of the employee class that was previously defined.

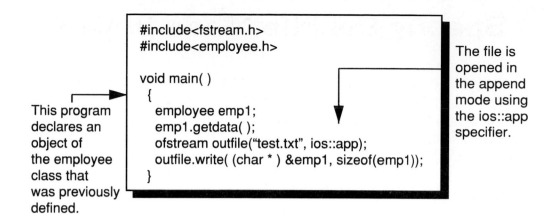

```
#include<fstream.h>
#include<employee.h>

void main( )
  {
    employee emp1;
    emp1.getdata( );
    ofstream outfile("test.txt", ios::app);
    outfile.write( (char * ) &emp1, sizeof(emp1));
  }
```

The file is opened in the append mode using the ios::app specifier.

A Closer Look

The scope resolution operator.

ios is the base class. → ios::app ← app is the static variable that is defined in the base class.

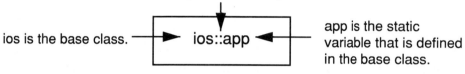

File Mode Specifiers For C++	
Mode Specifier	**Description**
ios::in	Open for reading (default for ifstream class).
ios::out	Open for writing (default for ofstream class).
ios::app	Append, add to the end of the file.
ios::ate	Erase the file before reading or writing.
ios::binary	Open in binary mode.

Chapter Fourteen

Working with Memory Management

Computer Memory

Memory is divided into two sections: *stack memory* and *heap memory*. Stack memory is memory used for running a program. The stack memory is divided into segments. Each segment contains a specific type of information. For example, there is a *code segment* that contains the instructions of the program. There is also a *global name segment* that is reserved for global variables. Likewise, there is a *local name segment* for local variables. And then there is the *register segment*, which contains reference values to the current instruction, the current position of the stack and other such values.

Each segment of the stack is a fixed size. Therefore, there is a limited amount of memory that is reserved by the compiler for program instructions and data. In addition, each memory location that is reserved for data is named. That is, the programmer assigns an alias called a variable name for reserved memory in the data segment. The data segment consists of both the global and local named segments.

As each function is called, data values declared within the function are *pushed* onto the local name segment of the stack memory. When a function terminates, those data values are purged from the stack. This is calling *popping data* from the stack.

In comparison, heap memory is *unnamed memory*. That is, reserved memory on the heap is not given a variable name. Instead, the function that reserves a portion of heap memory returns a pointer to the first byte in the block of the reserved heap memory.

Although the size of stack memory is fixed at compile time, the size of the heap memory is limited only by the amount of memory that is available in the computer. This allows the programmer more flexibility working with data than is available from using stack memory.

Computer memory is divided into two major areas: the stack and the heap. The stack is organized memory that contains the program and the data that the program manipulates. In comparison, the heap memory is the remaining memory that is available in the computer.

Stack Memory

Code Segment.

Global Named Segment.

Local Named Segment.

Register Segment.

Heap Memory

Terms You Should Know ...

	Code Segment	The place in stack memory where the program resides.
○	Global Named Segment	The place in stack memory where global variables reside.
	Local Named Segment	The place in stack memory where local variables reside.
○	Register Segment	The place in stack memory where the program pointer resides.

Storing Data on the Stack

Without much thought programmers save values to stack memory by declaring named memory within the program. *Named memory* is the data segment of stack memory that is reserved by the program when a variable is declared in the program.

The term named memory stems from the technique that uses a reference to the memory location by using an alias for the address rather than the memory address itself. Remember, the alias for an address in memory is the name of a variable.

The data segment in stack memory is divided into two segments. These are the *global name segment* and the *local name segment*. The global name segment contains global variables whose scope extends for the full life of the program. The local name segment contains local variables whose scope extends for the life of the code block that is declared the variable.

In the example illustrated on the opposite page, the variable max is declared outside any code block. This statement reserves memory the size of the integer in the global name segment of the data segment of stack memory.

Within the main( ) function, two other integers called min and diff are declared. Since these variables are declared within the code block of the main( ) function, space the size of two integers is reserved in the local name segment of the data segment of stack memory.

The program itself is loaded into the code segment of the stack. Each instruction is then executed in sequence. The *instruction pointer*, which holds the address of the current instruction, is contained in the register segment of the stack memory.

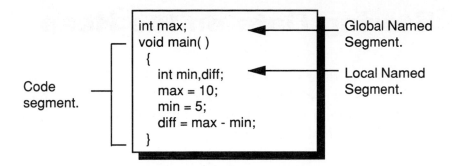

```
                          int max;                    ──►  Global Named
                          void main( )                      Segment.
                            {
                              int min,diff;          ──►  Local Named
Code                         max = 10;                      Segment.
segment.                     min = 5;
                              diff = max - min;
                            }
```

Problems with Stack Memory
⭘ The amount of stack memory that is required for global and local variables is fixed when the program is compiled.
⭘ The programmer must know in advance how much stack storage is needed by the program.
Once stack memory is allocated, stack memory cannot be freed and reused by the programmer when the program is running.

Storing Data on the Heap

A method of storing data within heap memory is by using the *malloc( ) function*. This function can be used both in C++ and in C. malloc( ) requires the programmer to specify the number of bytes to be reserved as a parameter to the malloc( ) function.

An attempt is then made to allocate the requested block of memory from the heap. If malloc( ) is successful, a character pointer to the first address of the block is returned to the statement that is called malloc( ). However, a null is returned if memory could not be reserved. This is usually caused by a lack of sufficient memory to meet the request of the program.

The example shown on the next page illustrates the proper technique for calling malloc( ). First, the program declares a character pointer called str that will eventually contain the address of the first byte of the allocated block of memory.

Next, malloc( ) is called. Notice that the integer value 10 is passed to malloc( ). This means that the program is requesting the allocation of 10 bytes of heap memory. The returned value is then stored in the pointer str. The value of the pointer is examined to determine if the pointer contains a null. That is, to determine if malloc( ) successfully allocated heap memory.

If the pointer is null, the program informs the user that there is insufficient memory to complete the task. However, if the pointer contains an address, then the program reads a string from the keyboard and assigns the string to the pointer str. The string pointed to by variable str is then displayed on the screen using the printf( ) function.

The last statement in the program calls the *free( ) function*. This function releases previously allocated memory. The free( ) function requires one parameter, which is the pointer to the block of heap memory that was reserved by either the malloc() function or the calloc( ) function, which is discussed in the next section.

The malloc( ) function is passed the number of bytes to be allocated as a parameter to the function. malloc( ) returns a character pointer to the first block of allocated heap memory. A null pointer is returned if heap memory cannot be allocated.

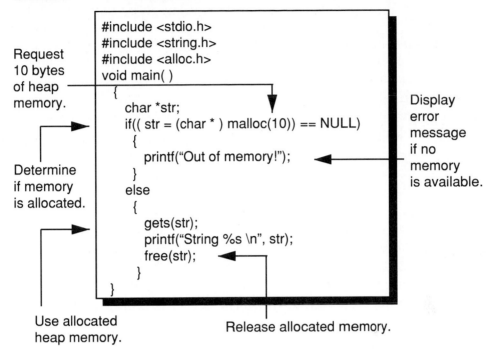

Request 10 bytes of heap memory.

Determine if memory is allocated.

Use allocated heap memory.

Display error message if no memory is available.

Release allocated memory.

```c
#include <stdio.h>
#include <string.h>
#include <alloc.h>
void main( )
{
    char *str;
    if(( str = (char * ) malloc(10)) == NULL)
    {
        printf("Out of memory!");
    }
    else
    {
        gets(str);
        printf("String %s \n", str);
        free(str);
    }
}
```

Heap Memory

*str

0 1 2 3 4 5 6 7 8 9

Storing an Array of Objects on the Heap

The *calloc( ) function* performs a task similar to that of the malloc( ) function. That is, calloc( ) also reserves memory on the heap. The difference is that calloc( ) allocates an array of objects rather than a single object as is allocated by the malloc( ) function.

The calloc( ) function requires that the programmer pass it two parameters. The first parameter consists of an integer value that represents the number of objects that will be placed into the allocated heap memory. The second parameter is the size of one of these objects.

This technique is illustrated on the opposite page. The first parameter that is passed to the calloc( ) function is the integer value 15, which asks calloc( ) to reserve heap memory for 15 objects. The next parameter uses the return value from the sizeof( ) operator to tell calloc( ) the size of one of the objects in bytes. Reference to the object is passed to the sizeof( ) operator. In this example, the object is a char. Therefore, calloc( ) is asked to allocate heap memory in the size of 15 bytes.

Like the malloc( ) function, the calloc( ) function returns a character pointer to the first byte of the allocated heap memory. A null value is returned if the calloc( ) function is unsuccessful in reserving memory. Notice that the program on the opposite page examines the return value of the calloc( ) function and displays an error message on the screen if a null pointer is returned by calloc( ).

The program then proceeds to use the allocated memory by reading a string from the keyboard, then displaying the string on the screen. Once the information contained in the heap memory is utilized, the program releases the allocated heap memory so that the memory can be reused. This is made possible by calling the free( ) function. This function can only be used to release heap memory and not stack memory.

The calloc( ) function requires two parameters. The first parameter specifies the number of objects. The second parameter is the size of one object. calloc() returns a character pointer to the first byte in the allocated memory block. A null is returned if heap memory cannot be allocated.

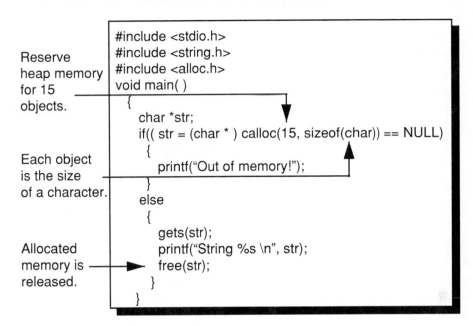

Reserve heap memory for 15 objects.

Each object is the size of a character.

Allocated memory is released.

```
#include <stdio.h>
#include <string.h>
#include <alloc.h>
void main( )
    {
        char *str;
        if(( str = (char * ) calloc(15, sizeof(char)) == NULL)
            {
                printf("Out of memory!");
            }
        else
            {
                gets(str);
                printf("String %s \n", str);
                free(str);
            }
    }
```

Heap Memory

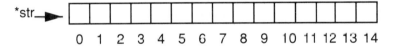

*str

0 1 2 3 4 5 6 7 8 9 10 11 12 13 14

Reallocating Heap Memory

Once heap memory is allocated using either malloc( ) or calloc( ), this portion of memory can be made available again by using the *free( ) function*. This technique is illustrated on the previous pages and in the example shown on the next page.

However, if the space is going to be reclaimed immediately after the allocation is released, then reallocating the memory is a more efficient method to use rather than releasing the allocation then using malloc( ) or calloc( ) again to reclaim the space in heap memory.

Reallocation of currently allocated heap memory is achieved by calling the *realloc( ) function*. This technique is illustrated on the next page. The realloc( ) function adjusts the previous allocation as required. Two parameters are required by the realloc( ) function. The first parameter is the pointer to the block of heap memory that is to be reallocated. The second parameter is an integer value that represents the size in bytes of the reallocated memory.

Notice that in the program on the next page, the malloc( ) function is called to allocate 10 bytes of heap memory. The address of the first byte of this block of memory is returned and assigned to the str pointer. The program then stores a string at this memory location and displays the string on the screen.

Instead of releasing this block of memory, the program calls the realloc( ) function. This function is passed to the str pointer, which points to the allocated block of memory. Also passed in is the integer value 15, which tells the realloc( ) function to increase the size of the previously allocated block by five bytes.

A null pointer is returned if there is insufficient memory; otherwise, the address of the adjusted block is returned and assigned to the str pointer.

The realloc( ) function changes the size of a previously allocated memory that is reserved by malloc( ) or calloc( ). realloc( ) requires two parameters. The first parameter is the pointer to the block of allocated memory. The second parameter is the number of bytes to be allocated.

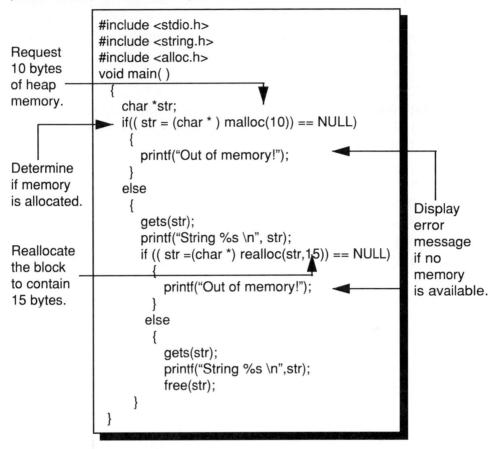

Request 10 bytes of heap memory.

Determine if memory is allocated.

Reallocate the block to contain 15 bytes.

```
#include <stdio.h>
#include <string.h>
#include <alloc.h>
void main( )
{
    char *str;
    if(( str = (char * ) malloc(10)) == NULL)
    {
        printf("Out of memory!");
    }
    else
    {
        gets(str);
        printf("String %s \n", str);
        if (( str =(char *) realloc(str,15)) == NULL)
        {
            printf("Out of memory!");
        }
        else
        {
            gets(str);
            printf("String %s \n",str);
            free(str);
        }
    }
}
```

Display error message if no memory is available.

Another Way of Storing Data on the Heap

The techniques illustrated so far in this chapter can be used both in C++ and C. C++ also offers another method for allocating space in heap memory. This is by using the new operator.

The *new operator* requires that the data type of the data that will be stored in the heap memory be provided to the right of the new operator. This is shown in the example on the opposite page. This statement reserves the number of bytes in heap memory that is required to store an integer.

Notice that the new operator does not require that the programmer specify the number of bytes that should be allocated in memory. The new operator already knows the data type that is specified in the statement and can determine for itself the number of bytes to reserve in heap memory.

In the example on the opposite page, the new operator returns either a pointer to the block of allocated memory or a zero if memory cannot be allocated.

Also notice that the program examines the return value. However, there is a twist when the expression is evaluated. The new operator is called as part of the if statement. Remember, the code block of an if statement executes only if the expression in the if statement evaluates to a true. A true value is any value except a zero.

The dilemma is that the new operator returns a zero if there is a problem allocating memory. This value will not trigger the if statement. However, look closely and notice the not operator (!), which tells the compiler to execute the if code block if the expression evaluates to a not true value—a false value, which is a zero.

Memory allocated by the new operator is released by using the delete operator as shown on the next page.

The new operator is used to reserve heap memory. The new operator requires that the programmer specify the data type of the memory that is to be allocated. The new operator determines the actual number of bytes that are required by the object.

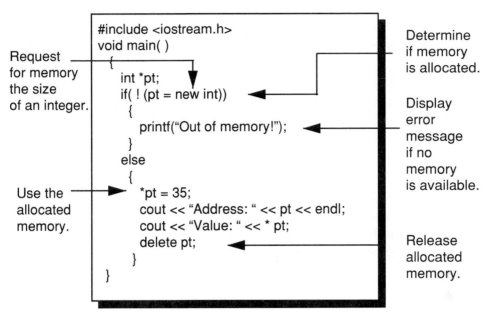

Request for memory the size of an integer.

Use the allocated memory.

```
#include <iostream.h>
void main( )
{
    int *pt;
    if( ! (pt = new int))
    {
        printf("Out of memory!");
    }
    else
    {
        *pt = 35;
        cout << "Address: " << pt << endl;
        cout << "Value: " << * pt;
        delete pt;
    }
}
```

Determine if memory is allocated.

Display error message if no memory is available.

Release allocated memory.

Heap Memory

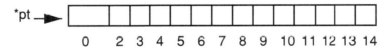

*pt

0   2 3 4 5 6 7 8 9 10 11 12 13 14

Using a Dynamic Array

On the previous page, the new operator is used to allocate a single object in heap memory, which is an integer. There is another technique using the new operator to allocate a larger amount of memory by declaring a *dynamic array*. A dynamic array is an array that resides in heap memory.

The method of allocating a dynamic array is similar to the way a single object is allocated using the new operator. The new operator is followed by the data type of the object. In the case of a dynamic array, the data type is followed by the number of elements of the array enclosed in square brackets.

The program on the opposite page shows how to allocate a dynamic array. In this example, the new operator is asked to allocate space for 10 integers on the heap. Remember, the integer value represents the number of elements of the dynamic array and not the number of bytes that are to be reserved in memory. The new operator determines the actual number of bytes that are reserved.

Programs that use the new operator must also check the value of the pointer returned by the new operator. A zero value—which is a null pointer—means that memory is not allocated. Using unallocated memory can cause the program to crash. Remember, the compiler will not catch this type of error since the amount of available heap memory is unknown until the program is running.

Each element of the dynamic array can be accessed in the same manner as any array element is accessed. In this case, the name of the pointer is used as the name of the array. This is shown in the example on the next page where pt is used to represent the dynamic array.

Also notice that the delete operator is called to release the allocated memory.

A dynamic array is a series of consecutive bytes that is reserved in heap memory. The dynamic array is allocated by using the new operator and by identifying the number of array elements that are needed by the program.

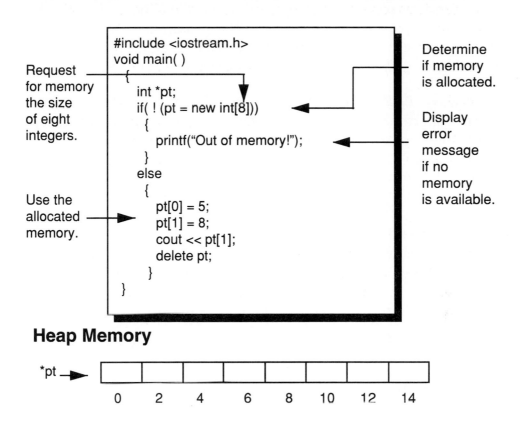

Request for memory the size of eight integers.

Use the allocated memory.

```
#include <iostream.h>
void main( )
{
    int *pt;
    if( ! (pt = new int[8]))
    {
        printf("Out of memory!");
    }
    else
    {
        pt[0] = 5;
        pt[1] = 8;
        cout << pt[1];
        delete pt;
    }
}
```

Determine if memory is allocated.

Display error message if no memory is available.

Heap Memory

*pt →

0   2   4   6   8   10   12   14

Working with
Sorting and Searching Data

- The Bubble Sort
- Inside the Bubble Sort
- The Linear Search
- The Binary Search
- A Close Look at the Binary Search Routine

The Bubble Sort

Information can be placed in either alphabetical or numerical order by creating a *bubble sort* routine. This routine places the smaller values at the top of the list and the higher values towards the bottom of the list. The list itself is a single or multidimensional array.

Before creating a Bubble Sort routine, load data into an array as is illustrated on the opposite page. Here, 10 integers are randomly assigned to the elements of the array called dat. Next, the program steps through each element by using two for loops.

The routine compares the value of the current array element with the value of the next array element. If the value of the current array element is greater than the value of the next array element, then the values are switched. This process continues until each of the elements of the array is evaluated.

Although the example on the next page illustrates ordering numerical data, the same technique can be used for sorting characters. The only change that needs to be made is to assign character values to the array. This will cause the compiler to use the ASCII value of the character as the key to the sort.

When an integer data type is assigned a character value, the compiler uses the ASCII value of the character. This technique is shown below. The value of integer variable dat is the same. The character 'A' has the ASCII value of 65. The character 'B' has the ASCII value of 66. Therefore, the Bubble Sort reorders the array based upon numeric values although the programmer is sorting characters.

```
int dat = 'A';
int dat = 65;
```

A sort is the task of placing data into a logical order, such as numerical or alphabetical. A simple technique for sorting data is using the bubble sort, which is also referred to as the *sinking sort*. The smaller values bubble to the top of the pile while the larger values sink to the bottom of the pile.

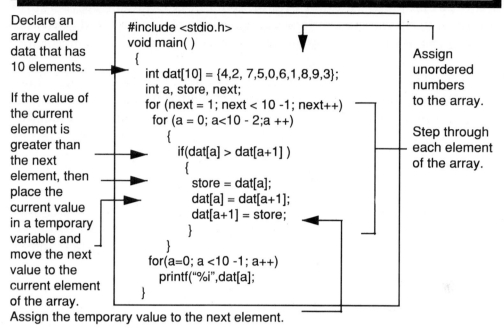

Declare an array called data that has 10 elements.

If the value of the current element is greater than the next element, then place the current value in a temporary variable and move the next value to the current element of the array. Assign the temporary value to the next element.

```
#include <stdio.h>
void main( )
{
    int dat[10] = {4,2, 7,5,0,6,1,8,9,3};
    int a, store, next;
    for (next = 1; next < 10 -1; next++)
      for (a = 0; a<10 - 2;a ++)
      {
          if(dat[a] > dat[a+1] )
          {
            store = dat[a];
            dat[a] = dat[a+1];
            dat[a+1] = store;
          }
      }
      for(a=0; a <10 -1; a++)
        printf("%i",dat[a];
}
```

Assign unordered numbers to the array.

Step through each element of the array.

In Memory

dat[0]	dat[1]	dat[2]	dat[3]	dat[4]	dat[5]	dat[6]	dat[7]	dat[8]	dat[9]
4	2	7	5	0	6	1	8	9	3

Inside the Bubble Sort

The example on the opposite page takes a closer look at the operations of the Bubble Sort. The first line of memory illustrates how each array element might appear in memory. The element is identified above the box and the value placed into that memory location is contained within the box.

The first statement within the if code block (shown below) places a copy of the value of the first array element into a temporary memory location, which is identified with the variable name store. After the first statement executes, memory should appear like the second line of memory.

store = dat[0];

Next, the program calls the second statement (shown below) within the if code block. This statement assigns the value of the next array element to the current array element.

dat[0] = store;

Finally, the value placed in the temporary variable store is then assigned to the next array element. This statement is also illustrated below. This process continues until all of the elements are placed in the proper numeric order.

dat[1] = store;

Although the example shows the Bubble Sort routine in the main( ) function of the program, a better method is to place the Bubble Sort into a function. Pass the function the pointer to the array, which is the name of the array without referencing square brackets. After the sort is completed, the function returns the pointer to the array back to the calling statement.

The First Pass

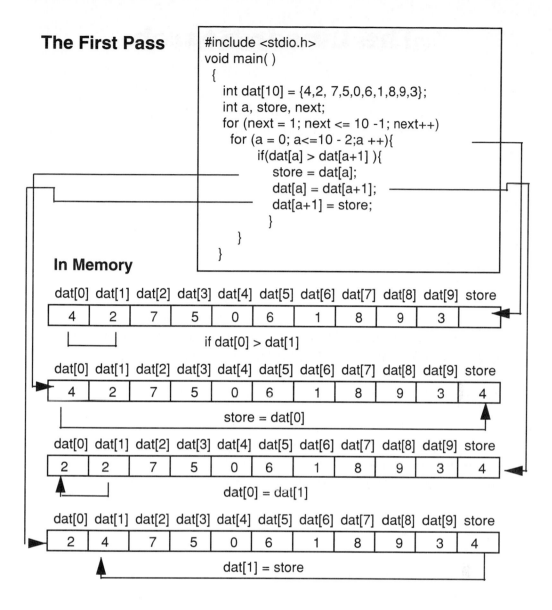

```
#include <stdio.h>
void main( )
 {
    int dat[10] = {4,2, 7,5,0,6,1,8,9,3};
    int a, store, next;
    for (next = 1; next <= 10 -1; next++)
     for (a = 0; a<=10 - 2;a ++){
         if(dat[a] > dat[a+1] ){
            store = dat[a];
            dat[a] = dat[a+1];
            dat[a+1] = store;
            }
          }
      }
```

In Memory

dat[0]	dat[1]	dat[2]	dat[3]	dat[4]	dat[5]	dat[6]	dat[7]	dat[8]	dat[9]	store
4	2	7	5	0	6	1	8	9	3	

if dat[0] > dat[1]

dat[0]	dat[1]	dat[2]	dat[3]	dat[4]	dat[5]	dat[6]	dat[7]	dat[8]	dat[9]	store
4	2	7	5	0	6	1	8	9	3	4

store = dat[0]

dat[0]	dat[1]	dat[2]	dat[3]	dat[4]	dat[5]	dat[6]	dat[7]	dat[8]	dat[9]	store
2	2	7	5	0	6	1	8	9	3	4

dat[0] = dat[1]

dat[0]	dat[1]	dat[2]	dat[3]	dat[4]	dat[5]	dat[6]	dat[7]	dat[8]	dat[9]	store
2	4	7	5	0	6	1	8	9	3	4

dat[1] = store

The Linear Search

Besides placing data in a particular order, programs frequently have a need to search for values. One method of conducting this search is to examine each piece of data and compare it to the search criteria. *Searchkey* is the term that refers to the search criteria.

When the program executes a routine that searches through each data element, the program is said to be using a *Linear Search* technique. A Linear Search is useful when searching through small amounts of data. For large data sources, a Binary Search is appropriate. A *Binary Search* is presented in the next section.

An example of the Linear Search technique is shown on the opposite page. First, a series of integer values are assigned randomly to an array. Next, an integer variable called searchkey is declared and is assigned the integer value six. This statement is shown below.

```
if (dat[a] == searchkey)
```

The program then steps through each element of the array. The searchkey is then compared with the value of the current array element. If they match, then a message is displayed on the screen. Otherwise, the routine moves on to the next element of the array.

A Linear Search is a simple routine to write; however, in many cases this is not the most efficient method of search data. The problem stems from the fact that a Linear Search must read through each array element. This can be a time-consuming task if the array is a moderate size. In comparison, a Binary Search of data dramatically shortens the time the application requires to search data. This is because a Binary Search eliminates half the remaining data elements on each pass.

A Linear Search is a technique used for finding a particular value that is assigned to an array. Typically, the array has a small number of elements and the values are not sorted. For large arrays, the Binary Search method is preferred, which is discussed later in this chapter.

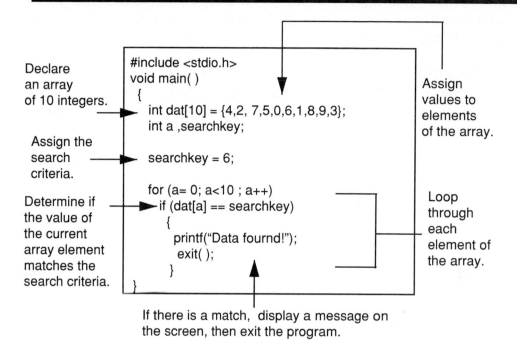

Declare an array of 10 integers.

Assign the search criteria.

Determine if the value of the current array element matches the search criteria.

```
#include <stdio.h>
void main( )
  {
    int dat[10] = {4,2, 7,5,0,6,1,8,9,3};
    int a ,searchkey;

    searchkey = 6;

    for (a= 0; a<10 ; a++)
      if (dat[a] == searchkey)
        {
          printf("Data fournd!");
          exit( );
        }
  }
```

Assign values to elements of the array.

Loop through each element of the array.

If there is a match, display a message on the screen, then exit the program.

The Binary Search

The *Binary Search* is a fast way to locate information in an array. The first requirement is that data is stored in an array in sort order. The Binary Search requires that data be in alphabetical or numerical order before initiating a Binary Search.

Notice that the example on the opposite page contains an array of 20 elements. This is a small amount of data and could have been searched using the Linear Search technique. However, this array can be used to illustrate the Binary Search technique.

The program creates and assigns integer variables that hold the minimum (min) index value of the array, the maximum (max) index value of the array, and the search criteria in the variable searchkey.

Next, the program steps through the array. Each time the program calculates the center index number of the array. Remember, when two integers are divided and the result is assigned to another integer, only the integer portion of the number is transferred.

Therefore, if the variable min equals zero and the variable max equals 19 the sum is 19 and the center is 8 and not 8.5 since the variable center only accepts the integer value of the results. The .5 is discarded.

With each pass of the loop, the Binary Search routine adjusts the minimum and maximum index value of the array elements and the center element of the array.

Since the Binary Search routine only works with half the array, fewer executions of the loop are necessary. In this example, there are only three loops necessary. That is, the searchkey is found on the third pass of the loop. A more detailed review of the inner workings of this review is illustrated in the next section.

A Binary Search is used when large amounts of sorted data need to be searched. A Binary Search divides the number of elements to be searched in half after each comparison is made to the search critieria. Therefore, this technique is more efficient and finds data faster than a Linear Search.

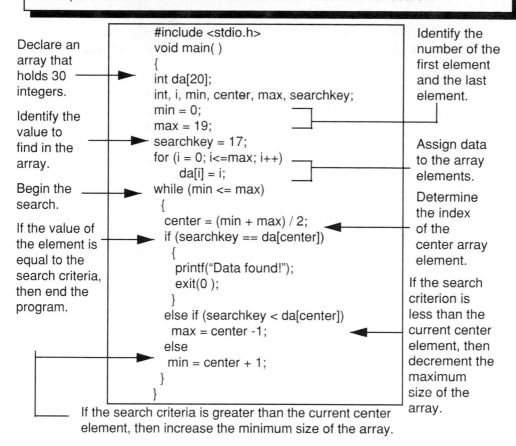

Declare an array that holds 30 integers.

Identify the value to find in the array.

Begin the search.

If the value of the element is equal to the search criteria, then end the program.

```
#include <stdio.h>
void main( )
{
    int da[20];
    int, i, min, center, max, searchkey;
    min = 0;
    max = 19;
    searchkey = 17;
    for (i = 0; i<=max; i++)
        da[i] = i;
    while (min <= max)
    {
        center = (min + max) / 2;
        if (searchkey == da[center])
        {
            printf("Data found!");
            exit(0 );
        }
        else if (searchkey < da[center])
            max = center -1;
        else
            min = center + 1;
    }
}
```

Identify the number of the first element and the last element.

Assign data to the array elements.

Determine the index of the center array element.

If the search criterion is less than the current center element, then decrement the maximum size of the array.

If the search criteria is greater than the current center element, then increase the minimum size of the array.

A Close Look at the Binary Search Routine

The illustration on the next page depicts how the array used in the previous section appears in memory. The array contains 20 elements each assigned sequential values beginning with zero. Each block on the opposite page represents a memory location the size of an integer and the corresponding value that is stored at that location.

Notice that at the beginning of the first pass of the loop, the variable min has a value of zero and the variable max is assigned the value 19. The variable center is assigned the value 9.

The routine then determines if the value of the center array element is equal to, greater than, or less than the searchkey. In this case, the center array element (da[9]) has a value (9) that is less than the searchkey (17).

The array is divided into half. Next, the value of min is 10, which is one more than the previous value. The value of the max variable remains the same. A new center array element is calculated. On the second pass, array element da[14] becomes the center.

Again, the Binary Search routine determines if the value of the center array element (da[14]) has a value (14) that is less than the searchkey (17).

The array is again divided into half. The next value of min is 14 and the max value is still 19. The recalculated center element is da[17], which has a value of 17.

The final comparison is made between the value of the center array element (17) and the searchkey (17). They match. The data is found. Notice that this technique only made three comparisons. If a Linear Search technique is used, 17 comparisons would have to be made before the match was found.

First Pass

center = 0 + 19 = 19 / 2 = 9.5

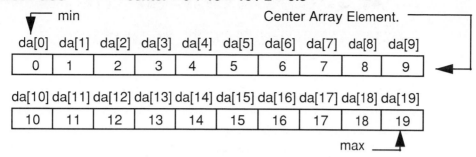

Second Pass

center = 10 + 19 = 29 / 2 = 14.5

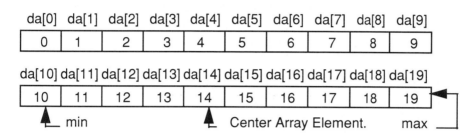

Third Pass

center = 15+ 19 = 34 / 2 = 17

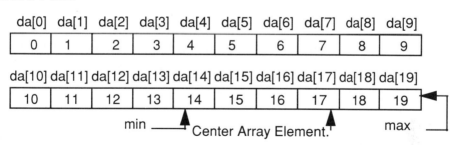

Chapter Sixteen

Working with Data Structures

- Linked Lists
- Adding a Node to a Linked List
- A Closer Look at Adding a Node
- Deleting a Node from a Linked List
- A Closer Look at Deleting a Node
- Stacks
- A Closer Look at the push() Function
- The pop() Function
- A Closer Look at the pop() Function
- Queues
- A Closer Look at the enterqueue() Function
- The exitqueue() Function
- A Closer Look at the exitqueue() Function

Linked Lists

Various techniques to group data are presented in this book. One of the most useful methods is to assign data to elements of an array. Each array element can then be referenced. However, there is a serious limitation to using an array in that the maximum number of elements must be declared when the program is written.

For example, suppose an array of 10 elements is declared in the program. Later, the program requires 11 elements. There isn't a technique that can increase the size of the array while the program is running. However, a different technique called a *linked list* overcomes this problem.

A linked list is a self-referential structure. Each instance of the structure can point to the next instance in the linked list. An instance of the structure is called a *node* on the linked list and the last node points to a null indicating that the list has ended.

In the illustration on the opposite page, a structure with a tag name called node is defined as having 2 members. The first member is an integer called val. This member contains that data. The second member is a pointer to a structure called nextnode. This member contains the address of the next node in the linked list.

Notice at the bottom of the next page is a view of two instances of the node structure as the data appears in memory. The first two blocks represent instance node A and the second set of blocks represents node B.

The first block in each set represents the val member of the structure. Node A has a val member value of 34 and node B has a val member value of 54. The second block in each set represents the address of the next node. Node A has the address 102, which is the address of node B. However, the second block in node B has no address. This is a null pointer and signals the end of the list.

A linked list is a collection of structures that references each other by using a pointer. Each instance of the structure is called a node and the pointer is called the pointer link. A linked list is used to organize data dynamically. The size of a linked list is determined by the availability of the computer's memory.

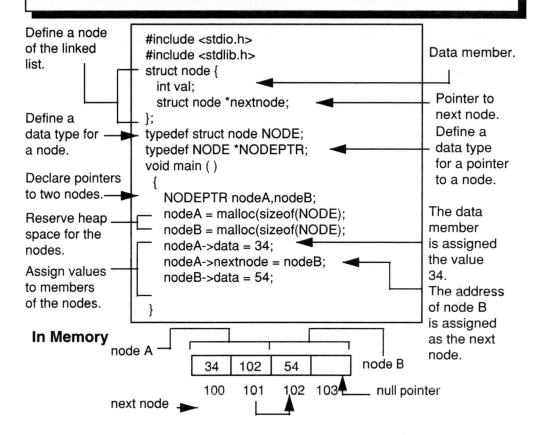

Define a node of the linked list.

Define a data type for a node.

Declare pointers to two nodes.

Reserve heap space for the nodes.

Assign values to members of the nodes.

```
#include <stdio.h>
#include <stdlib.h>
struct node {
    int val;
    struct node *nextnode;
};
typedef struct node NODE;
typedef NODE *NODEPTR;
void main ( )
{
    NODEPTR nodeA,nodeB;
    nodeA = malloc(sizeof(NODE);
    nodeB = malloc(sizeof(NODE);
    nodeA->data = 34;
    nodeA->nextnode = nodeB;
    nodeB->data = 54;
}
```

Data member.

Pointer to next node.

Define a data type for a pointer to a node.

The data member is assigned the value 34.

The address of node B is assigned as the next node.

In Memory

node A

34	102	54	

100   101   102   103   null pointer

node B

next node

Adding a Node to a Linked List

Nearly an endless number of nodes can be added to a linked list. The only constraint is the available heap memory that is on the computer. The technique for adding a node is illustrated on the opposite page. This example is actually a function definition. There isn't room enough on the page to show the main( ) function and other codes. Therefore, the additional code is shown below.

```
#include <stdio.h>
#include <stdlib.h>
struct node {
    int val;
    struct node *nextnode;
};
tpedef struct node NODE;
typedef struct node *NODEPTR;
void main( )
    {
       NODEPTR startnode = NULL;
      addnode(&startnode);
    }
```

The calling statement passes the addnode( ) function the value of the pointer to the startnode. From this information, the addnode( ) function reserves memory in the heap for the new node, then assigns data to the new node. Finally, the function adjusts the nextnode values to fit the new node into the linked list. A more detailed explanation of this process is shown in the next section.

Reserve heap space for a new node.

Declare pointers to nodes.

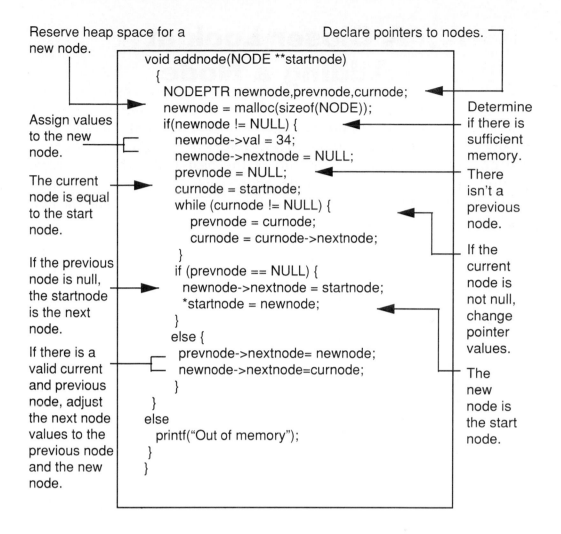

```
void addnode(NODE **startnode)
  {
    NODEPTR newnode,prevnode,curnode;
    newnode = malloc(sizeof(NODE));
    if(newnode != NULL) {
       newnode->val = 34;
       newnode->nextnode = NULL;
       prevnode = NULL;
       curnode = startnode;
       while (curnode != NULL) {
          prevnode = curnode;
          curnode = curnode->nextnode;
       }
       if (prevnode == NULL) {
          newnode->nextnode = startnode;
          *startnode = newnode;
       }
       else {
          prevnode->nextnode= newnode;
          newnode->nextnode=curnode;
       }
    }
    else
      printf("Out of memory");
  }
}
```

Assign values to the new node.

The current node is equal to the start node.

If the previous node is null, the startnode is the next node.

If there is a valid current and previous node, adjust the next node values to the previous node and the new node.

Determine if there is sufficient memory.

There isn't a previous node.

If the current node is not null, change pointer values.

The new node is the start node.

A Closer Look at Adding a Node

The illustration on the opposite page highlights the steps that are necessary to add a node to the linked list. Values of variables important to the program are shown at the top of the next page. The start node address is 102. The current node address is the same as the start node address. The previous node variable has a value of null and the new node has a value of 104.

These values directly relate to the current structure of the linked list, which is depicted in the "Before Adding a Node" memory diagram. Notice that the nextnode member of node B does not have a value. This is a null, which signals the end of the linked list. Node C doesn't have any values because the program is adding this node to the list.

The center blocks contain segments of the addnode( ) function. The first block of code (the while loop) assigns the current node address (102) to the previous node variable. The nextnode member (102) of the current node is assigned to the current node variable (null). The results of these operations are illustrated in the listing of variables to the left of the code boxes.

The bottom block of code assigns the address of the new node (104) to the nextnode member of the previous node (102). Finally, the nextnode member of the new node is assigned the value of the current node, which is null. This signals the end of the linked list.

The memory diagram shown at the bottom of the next page illustrates the heap memory after node C is added to the linked list. Now, node A points to node B, which in turn points to node C. Node C does not point to anything since node C is the last node on the linked list. Manipulating a linked list can be confusing. Read through this example carefully before moving onto the next section.

Add node C to the following linked list.

startnode = 102   prevnode = NULL

curnode = startnode   newnode = 104

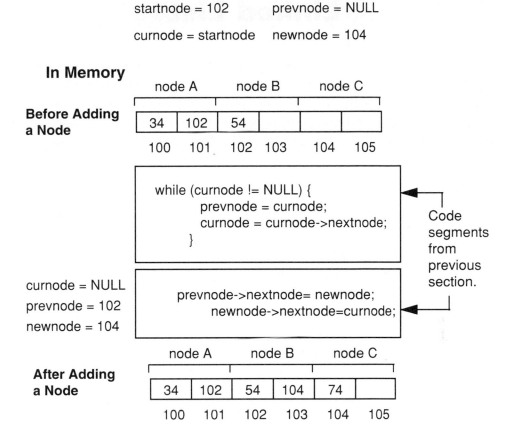

In Memory

	node A		node B		node C	

Before Adding a Node

34	102	54			
100	101	102	103	104	105

```
while (curnode != NULL) {
        prevnode = curnode;
        curnode = curnode->nextnode;
    }
```

Code segments from previous section.

curnode = NULL

prevnode = 102

newnode = 104

```
prevnode->nextnode= newnode;
    newnode->nextnode=curnode;
```

	node A		node B		node C	

After Adding a Node

34	102	54	104	74	
100	101	102	103	104	105

Deleting a Node from a Linked List

Any node on a linked list can easily be removed from the list by changing reference to the nextnode value of the appropriate nodes. The technique for deleting a node is made clear by utilizing the deletenode( ) function that is defined on the next page. There isn't room enough on the page to show the main( ) function and other code. Therefore, the additional code is shown below.

```
#include <stdio.h>
#include <stdlib.h>
struct node {
    int val;
    struct node *nextnode;
};
typedef struct node NODE;
typedef struct node *NODEPTR;
void main( )
  {
    NODEPTR startnode = NULL;
    addnode(&startnode);
  }
```

The calling statement passes the deletenode( ) function the value of the pointer to the startnode. From this information, the deletenode( ) function reassigns the nextnode address in the current node to the previous node. Finally, the function releases memory on the heap. A more detailed explanation of this process is shown in the next section.

Define a type of a node and
a pointer to a node.

Declare pointers to
nodes.

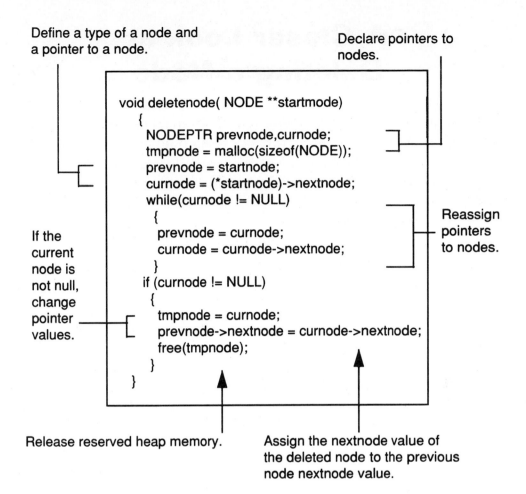

```
void deletenode( NODE **startmode)
   {
     NODEPTR prevnode,curnode;
     tmpnode = malloc(sizeof(NODE));
     prevnode = startnode;
     curnode = (*startnode)->nextnode;
     while(curnode != NULL)
       {
         prevnode = curnode;
         curnode = curnode->nextnode;
       }
     if (curnode != NULL)
       {
         tmpnode = curnode;
         prevnode->nextnode = curnode->nextnode;
         free(tmpnode);
       }
   }
```

If the
current
node is
not null,
change
pointer
values.

Reassign
pointers
to nodes.

Release reserved heap memory.

Assign the nextnode value of
the deleted node to the previous
node nextnode value.

A Closer Look at Deleting a Node

The example on the opposite page illustrates the technique for removing a node from a linked list. node B is the node that will be deleted. Near the top of the page is a list of important variables and their values. The startnode variable is set at 100, the curnode variable at 100, and the prevnode is a null pointer.

The top memory diagram shows the linked list in heap memory before node B is deleted. Remember, the first block in a set contains the value of the data for that node and the second block contains the address of the next node in the linked list.

This example shows two segments of the deletenode( ) function in the center blocks. The first block assigns the value of the start node (100) to the previous node variable. Next, the nextnode value of the start node (102) is assigned to the current node variable.

Since the current node isn't a null pointer, the program executes the while loop code block. The value of the current node (102) is assigned to the previous node and the value of the nextnode member of the current node (104) is assigned to the current node variable.

Again, the current node pointer is not null, so the program continues with the code block of the while loop. Here, the current node (102) is assigned to the temporary node. The value of the nextnode member of the current node (null) is assigned to the nextnode member of the previous node.

Notice the memory diagram at the bottom of the next page. This illustrates the linked list in heap memory after node B is deleted. Deleted? Node B is still in memory! This node has only be deleted from the linked list. Notice that node A skips node B and points to node C.

Delete node B on the following linked list.

startnode = 100   curnode = 100   prevnode = null

In Memory

	node A		node B		node C		tmpnode	
Before Deleting a Node	34	102	54	104	74			
	100	101	102	103	104	105	106	107

prevnode = 100
curnode = 102

prevnode = 100
curnode = 104

```
prevnode = startnode;
curnode = (*startnode)->nextnode;
while(curnode != NULL) {
    prevnode = curnode;
    curnode = curnode->nextnode;
}
```

Since the nextnode value of node A points to node C, node B is never called and is therefore deleted from the list.

```
if (curnode != NULL) {
    tmpnode = curnode;
    prevnode->nextnode = curnode->nextnode;
    free(tmpnode);
}
```

	node A		node B		node C		tmpnode	
After Deleting a Node	34	104	54	104	74		102	
	100	101	102	103	104	105	106	107

Stacks

A *stack* is a restricted linked list in that a node can be added to the list or deleted from the list only from the top of the list. This is referred to as the *last in-first out* arrangement. The last node that is added to the linked list is always at the top of the linked list and is always the next node to be removed from the stack.

Stacks maintain the order of sequence. For example, an instruction stack is used to assure that each instruction is performed in the proper order. The next instruction is always at the top of the stack.

A program requires two functions to manipulate the stack. These are the push( ) function and the pop( ) function. The push( ) function adds a node to the stack while the pop( ) function removes a node from the top of the stack. Both functions are discussed in detail in the next several sections.

A typical push( ) function is illustrated on the next page. Note that the function prototype has been removed due to space constraints. Here, a new node is added to the linked list. This node is a structure that has two members. The first member is an integer. The second member is a pointer to an instance of a structure, which is the next node.

The program must maintain the pointer to the top node on the stack. In this example, the address of the top of the stack is contained in the topnode variable. Presume that the topnode pointer variable already has a the address of the top node on the linked list from the last time the push( ) function was called.

Both the data and the address of the top node are parameters passed to the push() function. The push( ) function then reserves space in heap memory for the new node. The data value is assigned to the data member of the node structure and the nextnode member of the new node is assigned the address of the topnode variable. The topnode variable is then assigned the address of the new node, which becomes the top of the stack.

C++ Programmer's Notebook

A stack is a type of linked list that allows for nodes to be inserted and deleted from the top of the linked list. Two functions are used for manipulating the stack. These are the push( ) function and the pop( ) function. The push( ) function inserts a node onto the stack. The pop( ) function deletes a node from the top of the stack.

The push( ) Function

Define a node.

Declare a stack pointer.

Call the push( ) function.

Reserve heap memory for new node.

Assign the address of the current top of the stack to the next node.

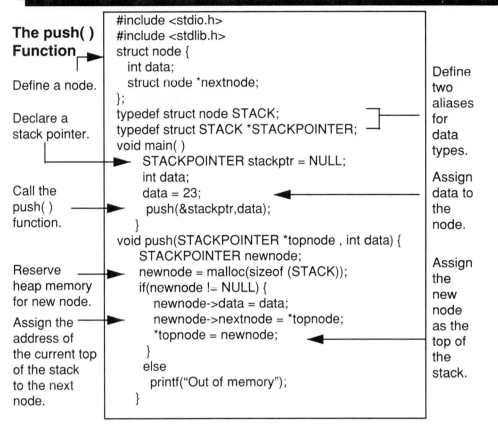

```c
#include <stdio.h>
#include <stdlib.h>
struct node {
    int data;
    struct node *nextnode;
};
typedef struct node STACK;
typedef struct STACK *STACKPOINTER;
void main( )
    STACKPOINTER stackptr = NULL;
    int data;
    data = 23;
    push(&stackptr,data);
}
void push(STACKPOINTER *topnode , int data) {
    STACKPOINTER newnode;
    newnode = malloc(sizeof (STACK));
    if(newnode != NULL) {
        newnode->data = data;
        newnode->nextnode = *topnode;
        *topnode = newnode;
    }
    else
        printf("Out of memory");
}
```

Define two aliases for data types.

Assign data to the node.

Assign the new node as the top of the stack.

A Closer Look at the push( ) Function

The concept of a stack can be confusing. The example on the next page should simplify your understanding of this concept. The example places a new node on the stack.

At the top of the page are three variables that are important to the push( ) function. The topnode variable contains the address of the top node on the stack. This address is assigned to the top node variable after the last node was placed on the stack. The data variable contains the integer value that will reside in the node. And the newnode variable holds the address of the new node. This address is returned by the malloc( ) function.

The memory diagram at the top of the page illustrates how the stack appears in heap memory. Each node consists of two sets of boxes. The contents of the first box in each set is the data member of the node. The second box contains the address of the next node down the stack.

In the center of the page is a segment of the push( ) function that is shown on the previous page. The if statement is used to determine if the newnode pointer variable points to null. This means that the malloc( ) function is unsuccessful and there isn't enough memory in the computer to accommodate the new node. An out of memory message is displayed on the screen.

Once heap memory is reserved, the data is assigned to the data member of the new node. Next, the address of the top node is assigned to the nextnode member of the node. Remember, the current top node is "pushed" down the stack. This node now becomes the second node on the list. The new node becomes the top node.

Finally, the topnode pointer variable is assigned the address of the new node. The results of this operation are depicted in the variables shown to the left of the code segment and by the updated memory diagram.

Add node C to the stack.

topnode = 102   data = 23

newnode = 104

In Memory

node A   node B

Before Calling push( )

34		54	100		
100	101	102	103	104	105

topnode = 104
nextnode = 102
newnode = 104

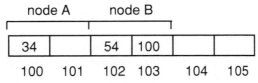

```
if(newnode != NULL) {
    newnode->data = data;
    newnode->nextnode = *topnode;
    *topnode = newnode;
```

Code segments from previous section.

node A   node B   node C

After Calling push( )

34		54	100	23	102
100	101	102	103	104	105

The pop( ) Function

A node is removed from the stack by calling the pop( ) function. An example of a pop( ) function is shown on the opposite page. Note that because of space limitations, the prototype for the pop( ) function is not included in the sample code.

In this example, the program is asked to retrieve data from the top of the stack. The data is actually the data member of the top node on the stack. The pop( ) function is called whenever data is retrieved from the stack. This function returns the data. A word of caution! Once the data is returned by the pop( ) function, the data and its node no longer reside on the stack.

The pop( ) function is passed a pointer variable that contains the address of the top node on the stack. A temporary node and an integer variable are declared within the pop( ) function. These will be used to hold the removed node and the return value respectively.

Next, the address of the top node is assigned to the temporary node and the data from the top node is assigned to the data variable. This is the value that is requested by the program.

Notice that the address contained in the nextnode member of the top node is assigned to the top node pointer variable. Remember, the next node is always the previous node on the stack. That is, the next lowest node on the stack. When the topnode pointer variable is assigned the address of the previous node, then the current top node is said to have "popped" off the stack.

Once another node rises to the top of the stack, the block of heap memory that is used by the former top node can be freed and made available to other parts of the program. Although the free( ) function is passed the temporary node, the former top node is released. Remember, the address of the former top node is the same address of the temporary node..

The pop( ) function is called to remove a node from a stack. Before the node is removed from the top of the stack, the data value is retained and is returned to the calling statement.

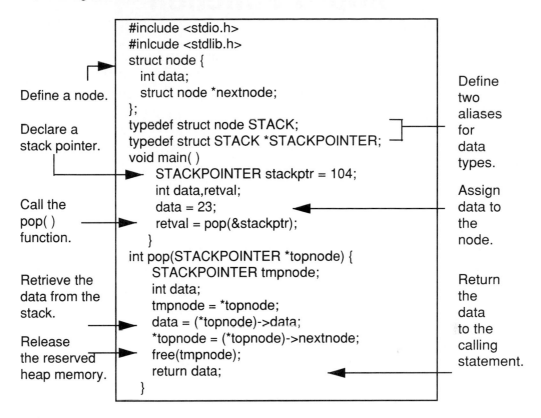

Define a node.

Declare a stack pointer.

Call the pop( ) function.

Retrieve the data from the stack.

Release the reserved heap memory.

Define two aliases for data types.

Assign data to the node.

Return the data to the calling statement.

```
#include <stdio.h>
#inlcude <stdlib.h>
struct node {
    int data;
    struct node *nextnode;
};
typedef struct node STACK;
typedef struct STACK *STACKPOINTER;
void main( )
    STACKPOINTER stackptr = 104;
    int data,retval;
    data = 23;
    retval = pop(&stackptr);
}
int pop(STACKPOINTER *topnode) {
    STACKPOINTER tmpnode;
    int data;
    tmpnode = *topnode;
    data = (*topnode)->data;
    *topnode = (*topnode)->nextnode;
    free(tmpnode);
    return data;
}
```

A Closer Look at the pop( ) Function

The objective of the example that is illustrated on the opposite page is to remove node C from the stack. Remember, node C is at the top of the stack so the program must make the next node down on the stack the top of the stack.

Two important variables for the pop( ) function are the topnode pointer variable and the integer data variable. The topnode pointer variable contains the address of the node that is currently at the top of the stack. The data variable is the integer assigned to the data member of the node that is at the top of the stack.

The contents of each of these variables before the pop() function is called are shown at the top of the next page. Notice that there isn't a value assigned to the data variable since the pop( ) function makes this assignment. Beneath these variables is a memory diagram that depicts the stack in heap memory.

The first memory block in a node is the data value and the second memory block is the address of the preceding node on the stack. Notice that there isn't a value for the nextnode member of node A. This is because node A is the last node on the stack. The nextnode member of the bottom node is a null pointer.

Code segments from the pop( ) are shown in the middle of the next page. After initializing a stack pointer and an integer, the program assigns the value of the topnode pointer variable (node C) to the temporary node. Next, the data member of the top node (node C) is assigned to the data variable that is returned to the calling statement.

Notice that the value of the nextnode member of the top node (node C) is assigned to the topnode pointer variable. This makes the previous node (node B) the new top node. Finally, memory reserved for the temporary node, which is really node C, is released using the free( ) function. The memory diagram at the bottom of the page shows the stack in heap memory after node C is removed.

C++ Programmer's Notebook

Remove node C from the stack.

topnode = 104   data = 23

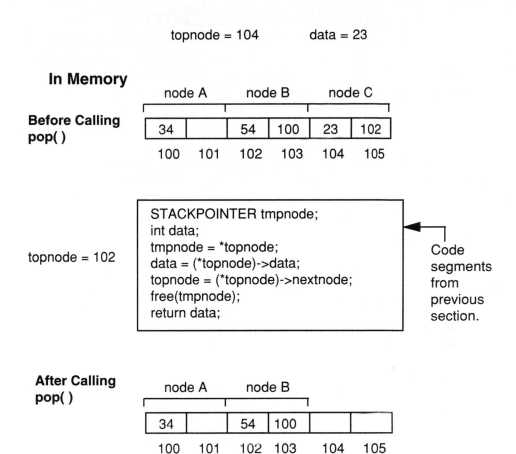

In Memory

Before Calling pop( )

node A   node B   node C

| 34 | | 54 | 100 | 23 | 102 |

100   101   102   103   104   105

topnode = 102

```
STACKPOINTER tmpnode;
int data;
tmpnode = *topnode;
data = (*topnode)->data;
topnode = (*topnode)->nextnode;
free(tmpnode);
return data;
```

Code segments from previous section.

After Calling pop( )

node A   node B

| 34 | | 54 | 100 | | |

100   101   102   103   104   105

Queues

A *queue* is a special type of linked list that restricts the addition and removal of nodes to the list. All nodes enter the queue at the bottom of the queue and are deleted from the queue from the top of the queue. This concept is commonly referred to as *first in-first out*.

For the sake of simplicity, two functions are created to facilitate the movement of nodes on the queue. These are the enterqueue( ) and exitqueue( ) functions. Any name can be used to identify these functions since these are user-defined functions.

The example illustrated on the opposite page contains the main( ) function and the enterqueue( ) function. This program places a new node onto the end of the queue.

The node contains two members: the data member, which is an integer, and the nextnode pointer variable. Remember, a node can have many members of different data types. The only requirement is that one of the members be a pointer variable to another node.

Three parameters are passed to the enterqueue( ) function. These are the addresses of the nodes that are at the top and bottom of the queue. The value of the data variable is also passed to the function.

The enterqueue( ) function creates a new node in memory then assigns the address of the new node to the nextnode member of the bottom node. Finally, the function assigns the address of the newnode to the bottom node pointer variable. The new node becomes the bottom node on the queue. Next in the queue is the node whose address is contained in the nextnode member of the bottom node (the new node). The example in the next section clarifies the technique for adding a node to a queue.

A queue is a linked list that adds nodes only to the bottom of the linked list and removes nodes only from the top of the linked list.

Add a Node to the Queue

Define a node.

Add a new node to the queue.

Reserve heap memory for the new node.

Assign values to members of the node.

Place the new node in the proper position in the queue.

```c
#include <stdio.h>
#include <stdlib.h>
struct node {
    int data;
    struct node *nextnode;
};
typedef struct node NODE;
typedef NODE *NODEDEPTR;
void main( ) {
     NODE headnode= NULL, tailnode=NULL;
     int data = 34;
     enterqueue(&headnode,&tailnode,data);
}
enterqueue(NODE *topnode,NODE *bottomnode, int val) {
    NODE newnode;
    newnode = malloc(sizeof(NODE));
    if (newnode != NULL ) {
      newnode->data = val;
      newnode->nextnode = NULL;
      if (topnode == NULL)
         *topnode = newnode;
      else
         (*bottomnode)->nextnode = newnode;
       *bottomnode = newnode;
    }
    else
      printf("Out of memory!");
}
```

A Closer Look at the enterqueue( ) Function

Placing a new node onto a queue can be a complex issue. Therefore, the diagram on the opposite page should help to make this technique clear. There are four important variables that must be known before a node can be added to a queue. These are described at the top of the page.

First, the function must know the location of the top and bottom nodes. The locations are heap memory addresses that are stored in the topnode and bottomnode pointer variables. Here, the top of the queue is located at memory address 100 while the bottom of the queue is at memory address 102. These are illustrated in the first memory diagram on the next page.

Remember, the actual numeric value of the address has no effect on the queue. The node at the top of the queue could be located at address 105 while the bottom node is located at address 100. A node's relative position in memory has no relationship to the node's position in the queue.

The new node in this example is located in heap memory 104. This address is returned by the malloc( ) function. The data variable has a value of 23.

The center block contains a segment of code from the enterqueue( ) function. This code places the new node onto the queue. First, the function determines if the value of the topnode pointer variable is null, that is, there isn't a node on the queue. If this is the case, the program assigns the address of the new node to the topnode pointer and to the bottomnode pointer variable. The new node, therefore, is the only node on the queue.

However, if there is a node on the queue, then the nextnode member of the bottom node is assigned the address of the new node. The address of the new node is also assigned to the bottomnode pointer variable.

Add node C to the queue.

topnode = 100   data = 23

bottomnode = 102   newnode = 104

In Memory

Before Calling enterqueue( )

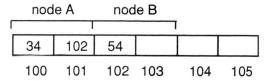

34	102	54			

100   101   102   103   104   105

topnode = 100

newnode = 104

```
if (topnode == NULL)
    *topnode = newnode;
else
    (*bottomnode)->nextnode = newnode;
*bottomnode = newnode;
```

Code segments from previous section.

After Calling enterqueue( )

node A   node B   node C

34	102	54	104	23	

100   101   102   103   104   105

The exitqueue( ) Function

A node can be removed from the queue only if the node is the next node at the top of the queue. Removing the node is performed by the exitqueue( ) function. This function requires two parameters, which are the addresses to the top node and the bottom node of the queue. Once the node is removed from the queue, the data member of the node is returned to the calling statement.

An example of an exitqueue( ) function is described on the next page. First, the function declares an integer called data, which will contain the value that is returned to the calling statement. A temporary node is created. This node is assigned the address of the top node.

Next, the value of the data member of the top node of the queue is assigned to the data variable. The second node on the queue is then moved to the top of the queue by assigning the address of the nextnode member of the top node (this is the address of the second node) to the topnode pointer variable.

The function then determines if there is a node remaining on the queue. If the topnode pointer variable is a null pointer, then there are no nodes on the queue and the function makes the bottomnode pointer variable a null pointer.

Finally, the function releases the address that is used by the temporary node. Remember, this address is the address of the former top node on the queue. Once this portion of heap memory is freed, memory can be reused by the program.

Notice that the program must maintain the pointer to the beginning and the end of the queue throughout the life of the program. The enter queue( ) and exitqueue( ) functions cannot operate successfully until these two addresses are known. A more detailed review of the exitqueue( ) function is presented in the next section.

The exitqueue( ) function removes a node from the beginning of the queue. Once the node is deleted, the next node in line becomes the top node on the queue and the heap memory that is used by the previous top node is released.

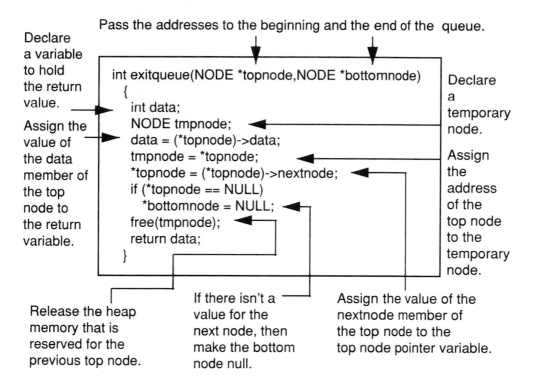

Pass the addresses to the beginning and the end of the queue.

Declare a variable to hold the return value.

Assign the value of the data member of the top node to the return variable.

```
int exitqueue(NODE *topnode,NODE *bottomnode)
   {
    int data;
    NODE tmpnode;
    data = (*topnode)->data;
    tmpnode = *topnode;
    *topnode = (*topnode)->nextnode;
    if (*topnode == NULL)
       *bottomnode = NULL;
    free(tmpnode);
    return data;
   }
```

Declare a temporary node.

Assign the address of the top node to the temporary node.

Release the heap memory that is reserved for the previous top node.

If there isn't a value for the next node, then make the bottom node null.

Assign the value of the nextnode member of the top node to the top node pointer variable.

A Closer Look at the exitqueue() Function

The diagram on the opposite page illustrates how a node is removed from the top of a queue. The objective of this exercise is to remove node A. Three variables are important to this process. These are the addresses of the top node and the bottom node of the queue and the variable that will return the data stored in the top node to the calling statement. The starting values of these variables are shown at the top of the page.

The top memory diagram depicts the queue in heap memory before the top node is removed from the queues. The first memory block in each set contains the value of the data member of the node. The second memory block contains the node that is next in line in the queue.

In the center of the page is the segement of code from the exitqueue( ) function. This segment removes the top node from the queue and repositions the next node in the queue. Two variables are declared. The integer variable data is used to store the value of the data member of the top node. This value is returned to the calling statement. A temporary pointer variable is declared. This is assigned the address of the top node so that memory used by that node can be released.

The function assigns the address of the top node (node A) to the temporary node. The value of the nextnode member (102) of the top node (node A) is assigned to the topnode pointer. This places node B at the top of the queue.

Next, the function determines if node A was the only node on the queue. That is, the topnode pointer variable is a null pointer. If so, the bottomnode pointer variable is made a null pointer.

Finally, the temporary node is removed from heap memory. Node A no longer exists. The memory diagram at the bottom of the page depicts the queue after node A is deleted from the queue.

Remove node A from the queue.

topnode = 100   data = 34

bottomnode = 104

In Memory

Before Calling exitqueue( )

node A   node B   node C

34	102	54	104	23	
100	101	102	103	104	105

topnode = 102

data = 34

```
int data;
NODE tmpnode;
data = (*topnode)->data;
tmpnode = *topnode;
*topnode = (*topnode)->nextnode;
if (*topnode == NULL)
    *bottomnode = NULL;
free(tmpnode);
return data;
```

Code segments from previous section.

After Calling exitqueue( )

node B   node C

		54	104	23	
100	101	102	103	104	105

Working with Templates

- Templates
- Templates with Multiple Parameters
- Class Template

Templates

Many C++ compilers offer a fast way to create multiple copies of related functions and classes with a minimum of code. This feature is called a *template*. A template enables the programmer to write a single segment of code and have the compiler generate related versions of the code.

Functions in C++ can be overloaded by changing the formal parameter list of each function. Each of these functions is related; however, each overloaded function requires its own function definition. If each of these functions has exactly the same code block and the only difference is the data type on the formal parameter list, then a template can be used to replace multiple definitions of the overloaded functions.

There are two kinds of templates: *template functions* and *template classes*. Both of these templates use a symbol to represent a valid data type. This symbol is replaced by a valid data type when the function is called or an instance of the template class is declared.

The example on the opposite page illustrates the technique for creating a template function. The *template header* consists of the keywords template and class. The symbol for the valid data type is enclosed within angled brackets. Beneath the template header is the function definition. Notice that the symbol P is used wherever the valid data type is normally used in the function.

The function is called twice in the program. The first time the function is called, an integer value is passed to the function. The second time that the function is called, a float value is a passed to the function. The compiler automatically uses the *template function* and makes the necessary data type substitutions. Overloaded functions that have the same code block are candidates for being converted to a template function.

A template is a feature of C++ that provides a short way of specifying a range of related functions and classes. There are two types of templates. A template function that is used for related functions and a template class used for related classes.

Template Functions

The compiler uses the template to overload the display( ) function when the functionality of the function remains the same but the data type of the parameter(s) to the function changes.

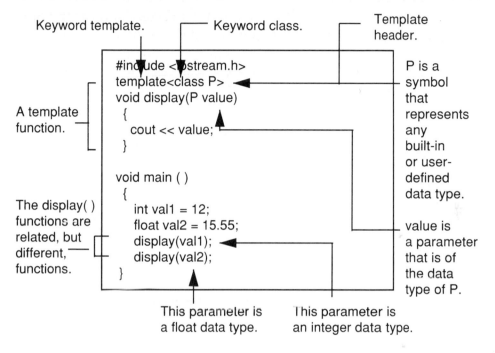

Keyword template.   Keyword class.   Template header.

```
#include <iostream.h>
template<class P>
void display(P value)
{
    cout << value;
}

void main ( )
{
    int val1 = 12;
    float val2 = 15.55;
    display(val1);
    display(val2);
}
```

A template function.

The display( ) functions are related, but different, functions.

P is a symbol that represents any built-in or user-defined data type.

value is a parameter that is of the data type of P.

This parameter is a float data type.

This parameter is an integer data type.

Templates with Multiple Parameters

Templates are similar to #define macros but are different. A drawback of using a #define macro is that the compiler does not perform data type checking. Remember, a #define macro is a preprocessor directive and has completed its operation prior to the execution of the compiler. However, templates offer the same capabilities that a #define macro provides plus the compiler performs data type checking.

A template can be defined as having one or more parameters. The formal parameters are declared within the parentheses of the function's header. Each parameter must be preceded by the data type of the parameter and be separated from other parameters on the list by using the comma operator.

There are two examples of this technique illustrated on the opposite page. The top example contains two parameters. The first parameter is of data type P. Remember, P is a symbol for any built-in or user-defined data type. The second parameter is an integer data type.

Each time the function is called in the program, two parameters must be passed to the function. The first parameter can be a different data type each time the function is called. However, the second data type must always be an integer data type.

The second example illustrates the same function. However, both parameters are of data type P. That is, a different pair of data types can be used whenever the program calls the function. The only requirement is that they are the same data type.

Data types on the formal parameter list of the template function are used within the function the same way as the data types are used in any function definition.

C++ Programmer's Notebook

More than one parameter can be used in a template function. Each parameter must be placed within the parentheses of the the template function and separated by the comma operator.

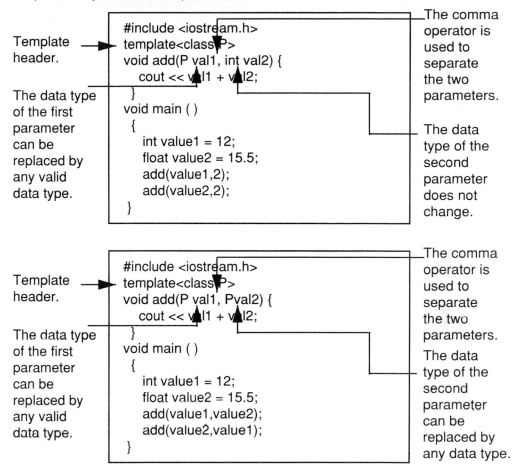

Template header.

The data type of the first parameter can be replaced by any valid data type.

```
#include <iostream.h>
template<class P>
void add(P val1, int val2) {
    cout << val1 + val2;
}
void main ( )
{
    int value1 = 12;
    float value2 = 15.5;
    add(value1,2);
    add(value2,2);
}
```

The comma operator is used to separate the two parameters.

The data type of the second parameter does not change.

Template header.

The data type of the first parameter can be replaced by any valid data type.

```
#include <iostream.h>
template<class P>
void add(P val1, Pval2) {
    cout << val1 + val2;
}
void main ( )
{
    int value1 = 12;
    float value2 = 15.5;
    add(value1,value2);
    add(value2,value1);
}
```

The comma operator is used to separate the two parameters.

The data type of the second parameter can be replaced by any data type.

Class Templates

A *class template* enables the creation of a class that is not type-specific but it can be customized to create a specific template class that is type-specific.

The example on the opposite page illustrates this technique. Here, a template class is created that uses data type P with the data member and the function member of the class. Remember, data type P is a symbol for any valid data type that is provided when an instance of the class is declared. The data type P is used throughout the class definition and the definition of function member just as if the data type is a valid data type.

An instance of the template class is created by using the name of the class followed by angled brackets that contain the class data type and the name of the instance of the class. This method is shown in the main( ) function at the bottom of the next page.

Notice that the first instance of class, called add, overwrites the data type P with an integer. The int keyword is placed within the angled brackets in the statement that declares the instances of the class. The second instance replaced the data type P with a float data type.

The restrictions on a template class are similar to the restrictions placed on using a template function. That is, instances of the class must remain identical except for the data type.

A template class has all the characteristics of a class in C++ in that it can be derived from a template class or a nontemplate class. Likewise, a non-template class can be derived from a class template. Also, a template class can have a friendship relationship with another template class or a nontemplate class.

A template class is used to define a general class where one or more types of parameters are changed to form a customized template of the class. Template classes are called *parameterized types.*

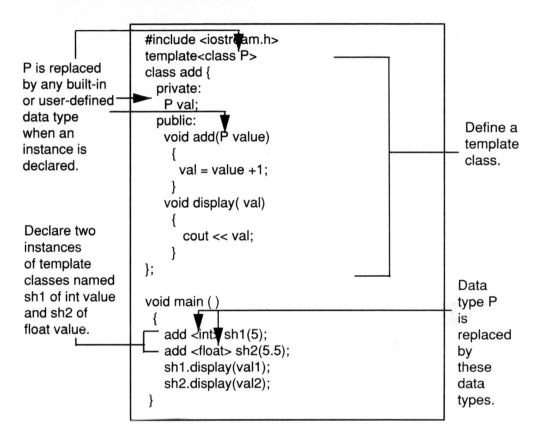

P is replaced by any built-in or user-defined data type when an instance is declared.

Declare two instances of template classes named sh1 of int value and sh2 of float value.

```
#include <iostream.h>
template<class P>
class add {
  private:
    P val;
  public:
    void add(P value)
      {
        val = value +1;
      }
    void display( val)
      {
        cout << val;
      }
};

void main ( )
  {
    add <int> sh1(5);
    add <float> sh2(5.5);
    sh1.display(val1);
    sh2.display(val2);
  }
```

Define a template class.

Data type P is replaced by these data types.

Programmer's Checklist

- General
- Keyword, Variables, Arrays, and Constants
- Expressions and Operators
- Program Control
- Functions
- Classes
- Input and Output

General

☐ Have you included the proper header file(s)?

Prototypes for many library functions and class definitions are contained in header files. Without including the proper header file in your program, a compiler error will occur. Consult your C++ compiler library manual for the specific header files for the functions and classes that you are using.

☐ Do you have the beginning and ending comment delimiters (/* */) properly positioned for each comment?

If you use the C convention comment delimiters in your program, make sure that there is both an opening and closing delimiter; otherwise segments of your program will not be recognized by the compiler.

☐ Are the characters used for the beginning and ending comment delimiters reversed (*/ /*)?

A common mistake is to transpose the C convention comment delimiters. The correct delimiters are /* */.

☐ Did you reserve memory using malloc() or a similar traditional C function then free that memory using delete?

Although the delete operator releases allocated heap memory, the operator will only release memory allocated by the new operator.

☐ Did you reserve memory using new, then free that memory using the free() function?

The free() function is used to release allocated heap memory that was reserved with one of the memory allocation functions, such as malloc(). The free() function does not have any effect on memory reserved with the new operator.

---

438   C++ Programmer's Notebook

Keywords, Variables, Arrays and Constants

☐ Is the name of any variable the same as a C++ keyword?

Keywords cannot be used to identify variables in your program. Be sure to review the naming convention that you use for variables to be sure that no variable is named the same as a keyword.

☐ Did you capitalize any keywords?

A common typographical error in a C++ program is to inadvertently capitalize a keyword. Remember, C++ is case-sensitive and all keywords are represented by lower case letters. The compiler will assume that a keyword that contains a capital letter is a name for a variable or other object and it will not be recognized as a keyword.

☐ Did you correctly specify the maximum number of array elements in an array definition?

Programmers can be confused by the index value of an array. When an array is declared, the total number of elements is specified within the square brackets. For example, int a[5]; declares an array of 5 elements where each element is an integer.

☐ Did you reference the first element of an array as 1 instead of 0?

Referencing an array element is also confusing. The first element of an array has an index number of zero—not one. Therefore, a[4] actually refers to the fifth element of the array and not the fourth array element.

☐ Is the array large enough to hold all the data that will be assigned to the array?

Special care must be taken when determining the size of an array that will be assigned the value of a string that is read from an input device, such as a file or keyboard. The array must be large enough to contain each letter of the string and the null character. The null character is always the last character of the array and transforms an array of characters to a string.

☐ Does the program reference an array element that exceeds the size of the array?

Although the program may correctly establish the size of an array, another part of the program could attempt to reference an element of an array that has not been declared. This is a common mistake when the programmer assumes that the first element of the array has an index number of one instead of two. Therefore, the program might try to access array element a[5], which does not exist.

☐ Did you use an integer data type to hold a fractional number?

Integer variables can only be assigned whole numbers even if the program attempts to assign a decimal value to the integer. The decimal value is truncated. You can change the data type of the variable to a float or cast a float data type.

☐ Did you use a data type to hold a value that is too large for the data type?

Be sensitive to the data type of variables. Data types and modifiers, such as unsigned, change the size of the number that can be assigned to the variable. Data can be lost if a number that is too large is assigned to a variable of a smaller data type.

☐ Did you convert a variable of a higher data type to a lower data type?

Converting the data type of a variable from a higher data type to a lower data type can provide misleading results. The value of the variable might change.

☐ Did you initialize all local variables?

Although the compiler automatically initializes all global variables, local variables remain uninitialized. An uninitialized variable is an open door for a bug. You can avoid this problem by immediately assigning a value to every variable at the time the variable is declared.

☐ Did you access a variable that is a local variable of another code block?

Local variables are variables that are declared within a code block (French braces). An attempt to access a local variable from outside the code block will cause a compiler error.

☐ Did you try to modify a const variable?

Although the value of variables is expected to change during the life of the variable, this is not the case when a variable is declared as a constant. The const modifier tells the compiler that the initial value of the variable will not change. Any attempt to change this value will cause a compiler error.

☐ Did you try to use a variable that is declared in another source code file without declaring the variable as extern?

Another common error is to reference a variable that is declared in a different source code file. Each source code file is compiled individually and joined together when the program is linked with library object files. Therefore, all of the variables used in a source code file are expected to be declared within the file. If the variable is declared in another file, then each source code file that uses this variable must redeclare the variable in the file using the extern modifier as shown here: extern int num.

☐ Are you properly using the asterisk operator and ampersand operator to access the value or the address of a variable?

The asterisk operator is used to declare a pointer. This rarely causes confusion. However, the asterisk operator is also used to reference a value contained at the address that is assigned to a pointer. For example, if pointer pt is assigned the address of integer variable int1 and variable int is assigned the value 5, then *pt reference, the value 5. The ampersand operator can also be confusing. The ampersand operator, when used with a variable, references the address of the variable. Let's continue with the previous example. Pointer pt can be assigned the address of variable int1 by using the following statement pt = &int1;

☐ Are all pointers immediately initialized?

When a pointer is declared, the pointer is given a random memory address that is replaced by a meaningful address when an address of a variable is assigned to the pointer. However, a program can produce unexpected results by referencing an uninitialized pointer, that is, a pointer that has not been assigned the address of a variable. Always initialize a pointer when the pointer is declared. This will prevent hard to find bugs from entering the program.

☐ Does each string end with a null character?

There isn't a data type called string in C++. A string is an array of characters, an array of char data type. However, certain library functions, such as string functions, can treat all the characters in an array as a string of characters when the last character in the array is a null character ("\0"). Without the null character, there isn't a string, just an array of characters.

☐ Did you use double quotations instead of single quotations when assigning a character ("A")?

Characters can be assigned to an element of a character array by specifying the character within single quotation marks in an assignment expression, such as letter = 'A.' If double quotation marks are used, however, the compiler assumes that the letter "A" is a string.

☐ Did you use single quotations instead of double quotations when assigning a string ('ABC')?

A string literal consists of a series of alphanumeric values that are enclosed within double quotation marks. When a string literal is passed to a string function, such as strcpy( ), which copies a string to another string, the function knows to places a null character as the last character of the string.

Expressions and Operators

☐ Do all statements end with a semicolon?

All statements in C++ must end with a semicolon. This is a requirement that can easily be missed if you are in a hurry writing or fixing a program. If you overlook placing a semicolon at the end of a statements, there will be a compiler error.

☐ Did you use the assignment operator (=) in place of the equal operator (==)?

Even the best programmer can inadvertently create an expression that divides a value by zero, which is not a valid calculation. If the potential problem is not discovered, a run-time error can occur.

☐ Did you place one or more spaces (= =, ! =, > =, < =) between each character of these operators ==, !=, >=, <=?

A common mistake occurs when using a compound operator, such as ==, !=, >=, <=. There is a natural tendency to place a space between each part of these operators. This is especially true since the C++ language ignores white space characters, such as the space character. However, this is one exception to that rule.

☐ Did you reverse the characters (=!, =<, =>) in the following operators !=, <=, >=?

Another common problem when working with compound operators is to reverse the order of each component of the operator. When you are quickly writing a program, the question nearly always comes to mind, "Is it less than or equal to or equal to or less than?" Answering this incorrectly results in a compiler error.

☐ Will the operators execute in the order that you expect in a complex expression?

Programmers who are new to using the C++ language almost always use an assignment operator in an expression that requires an equal operator. This is because some computer languages use the assignment operator for assignments and for equivalents.

☐ Is the modulus operator (%) being used with noninteger operands?

The modulus operator must be used with integer operands.

☐ Is there an expression that assigns a fractional number to an integer data type?

An integer data type should not be assigned a value that contains a fractional number. However, the compiler will not prevent you from making such an assignment. That is, there will not be any compiler, linker or run-time error reported. However, the fractional portion of the value will be truncated and only the integer portion of the number will be assigned to the integer.

☐ Is there an expression in the program that divides by zero?

One of the hardest bugs to locate in a program is caused by the misunderstanding of the order of operation of an expression. It is not uncommon for a programmer to assume particular order of operation that is contrary to the operator's precedence. When in doubt, always use parentheses to clarify an expression.

☐ Did you attempt to overload a nonoverloadable operator?

C++ enables you to add functionality to existing functions and operators. However, not all the operators in C++ can be enhanced by overloading the operator. Be sure to review all operator overloaded statements to ensure that the operator can be overloaded.

Program Control

☐ Are there matching French braces for all code blocks?

Ranking close to the number one bug in a C++ program is the problem of unmatched French braces. French braces define a code block. Since code blocks can be nested—one code block within another, it is easy for you to lose track of the closing French brace. A good programming technique is to immediately insert the closing French brace into the program whenever an opening French brace is inserted into the source code.

☐ Is there a semicolon at the end of an if statement? Remember, an if statement must not end with a semicolon.

The if statement heads the code block that will be executed if the statement evaluates true. However, there is a tendency for most C++ programmers to automatically place a semicolon at the end of each line since most statements are contained on a single line. An exception to this rule is with an if statement—along with other program control statements. The if statement does not end with a semicolon.

☐ Can all conditional statements evaluate to true?

A frustrating bug found in some programs stems from the misunderstanding of a conditional statement. A conditional statement —such as an if statement—executes a code block if the statement evaluates true. However, an improperly constructed conditional statement may never evaluate true and, therefore, the corresponding code block is never executed.

☐ Did you use a comma instead of a semicolon in the header of a for loop (for a=1, a<10, a++)?

When constructing a for loop statement, it is easy for a programmer to mistype a comma instead of a semicolon. This will cause a compiler error but can be prevented by carefully reviewing the source code before compilation.

☐ Are you sure that every loop can terminate?

It is not unusual for a programmer to create a runaway program. The program doesn't really run away but it does seem to run forever. The question that comes to mind while the program is running is, "Should it take this long to run the program or is there a bug in the program?" In the case of a bug, chances are the program has entered an endless loop. Examine each loop to make sure that the program has a way of breaking out of the loop.

Functions

☐ Did you include the data type of the return value in the function definition and function prototype?

Every function must specify the data type of the return value in the function prototype and in the function definition. If the function is not returning a value, then the return type of the function must be data type void. A compiler error will occur if the data type is not specified.

☐ Is every function returning the appropriate data type and value?

Every program in C++ requires a function prototype. This includes user-built functions and library functions. If the prototype is not contained in the source code itself, then the prototype should be contained in an appropriate header.

☐ Does each function have a corresponding function prototype?

The proper values must be assigned to the return value of a function otherwise unexpected errors might occur. This is true for any variable. For example, a value that contains a fractional number (decimal value) will lose the fractional value if it is assigned to a return value that is an int data type.

☐ Are there any function definitions that are located within the code block of another function definition?

A function definition must be created outside of a code block. Although this isn't a very common mistake, it can occur in programs that use large code blocks. In such a case, the programmer may not realize where the closed French brace of an existing function is located.

☐ Is there a semicolon at the end of any function definition?

Function definitions cannot end with a semicolon. Sometimes C++ programmers confuse a class definition with a function definition in that a class definition ends with a semicolon.

☐ Are you passing the proper number and data type of parameters to each function?

Make sure that all the parameters that are required by a function definition are passed to the function in a function call. This is especially important when the program contains overloaded functions where not passing a parameter can invoke a different function all together. If the parameters of the calling function don't match a defined function, then a compiler error will occur.

☐ Are there any functions that expect to be passed a pointer and you are passing a value?

It is easy for a new C++ programmer to be confused about pointers as they relate to passing data to a function. Double-check each function call to be sure that either the address of a variable or the value of the variable is correctly being passed to the function. Passing the value of the data when the function expects the address of the data sometimes can cause unpredictable results.

☐ Does the keyword class appear in the formal type parameter of function templates?

The concept of templates in C++ is new for many C++ programmers. Therefore, some confusion occurs when using a function template. The keyword class must appear in the formal type parameter of the function template.

Classes

☐ Do all class definitions end with a semicolon?

Confusion can occur between defining a class and defining a function. A class definition must end with a semicolon whereas a function definition does not end with a semicolon.

☐ Are data members of any class explicitly initialized in the class definition?

It is common to initialize a variable when the variable is declared. This assures that there will be at least a starting value for each variable. However, initialization cannot take place when declaring data members of a class.

☐ Is there a return type for any constructor?

Although a constructor is a function member of a class, a constructor cannot return a value to the program. However, a constructor can be passed a value from the program.

☐ Did you try to pass an argument to a destructor?

Some programmers become confused when dealing with destructors. In contrast to a constructor, a destructor cannot be passed a value.

☐ Is the program trying to call private or protected members of any class?

Only public data members and function members can be accessed directly by the program. Private members can be accessed either internally to the class or by a friend class. A protected member of a class can be accessed internally by the class or by a derived class.

☐ Did you try to create an instance of an abstract class?

An abstract class is a class that contains a pure virtual function. A pure virtual function does not have a code block associated with the function and is used as a place-holder for another function member of the class. Therefore, there cannot be an instance of an abstract class.

Input/Output

☐ Are you trying to write to an istream?

A file opened with istream is opened for read-only. Therefore, attempts to write to the file will fail.

☐ Are you trying to read from an ostream?

A file opened with ostream is opened for writing only. Therefore, attempts to read from the file will fail.

Index